GRAY LADY DOWN

GRAY LADY DOWN

What the Decline and Fall of
THE NEW YORK TIMES
Means for America

William McGowan

Encounter Books ● New York ● London

First American edition published in 2010 by Encounter Books, an activity of Encounter for Culture and Education, Inc., a nonprofit, tax exempt corporation.
Encounter Books website address: www.encounterbooks.com

Manufactured in the United States and printed on acid-free paper. The paper used in this publication meets the minimum requirements of ANSI/NISO Z39.48 1992 (R 1997) (*Permanence of Paper*).

FIRST AMERICAN EDITION

LIBRARY OF CONGRESS CATALOGING-IN-PUBLICATION DATA
McGowan, William, 1956–
Gray lady down: what the decline and fall of the New York times means for America/by William McGowan.
p. cm.
Includes bibliographical references and index.
ISBN-13: 978-1-59403-486-2 (hardcover: alk. paper)
ISBN-10: 1-59403-486-9 (hardcover: alk. paper) 1. New York times.
2. Press and politics—United States—History—21st century.
3. Journalism—Objectivity—United States. I. Title.
PN4899.N42M35 2010
071'.471—dc22
2010019445

10 9 8 7 6 5 4 3 2 1

for Louise Salerno

Were the news standards of the *Times* more broadly emulated, the nation would be far better informed and more honorably served.

—"Is It True What They Say About the *New York Times*?" *National Review*, 1972

If you think The Times plays it down the middle on [divisive social issues], you've been reading the paper with your eyes closed.

—Daniel Okrent, *Times* Public Editor, "Is The New York Times a Liberal Newspaper?" 2004

Contents

Prologue

I am not one of those people "who love to hate the *Times*," as the paper's executive editor Bill Keller has phrased it. I've read the *New York Times* since I was a kid, and I am proud to have been published prominently in it very early in my career. (The first things I ever published appeared in the *Times Magazine* and on the op-ed page.) I still consider the *Times* an important national resource, albeit an endangered one, and I confess to being one of those New Yorkers who refer to it simply as "the paper." Pre-Internet, I would find myself wandering to the corner newsstand late at night and waiting like a junkie for a fix in the form of the next day's edition. If I was out of town and couldn't find it, I would jones.

But sadly, those days, that young man and that *New York Times* are long gone.

My aim is not to embarrass the *Times* or to feed a case for "going *Times*less," as some subscription cancellers and former readers have called it. Some may think the *Times* to be irrelevant in this age of media hyperchoice. I think it's actually more necessary than ever. But if "These Times Demand The Times," as the paper's advertising slogan goes, they also demand a better *Times* than the one we are getting, especially at this fraught point in our political, social and cultural history.

William McGowan
The Writers Room
New York City
September 2010

one

Abe Rosenthal
and the
Golden Age

Back in the seventies, during an alarming downturn in stock price, advertising sales, revenue and circulation at the *New York Times,* the famed executive editor A. M. (Abe) Rosenthal confessed to having a recurrent nightmare: It was an ordinary Wednesday morning and "there was no *New York Times.*" Rosenthal outlived his nightmare. Along with the publisher, Arthur Ochs Sulzberger, and a group of skillful news executives, he put the paper back into the black. In the process, this team revolutionized the way the paper reported the news and set an example that transformed newspaper journalism in the rest of the country.

Rosenthal retired from the executive editor position in 1986 and then wrote a twice-weekly column on the op-ed page until 1999. Along with James Reston and a handful of others, he is identified with the *New York Times'* golden age, a time when the paper spoke to—and for—the nation. In May 2006, Rosenthal died after a massive stroke at the age of eighty-four. He had worked fifty-three years for the *Times,* after coming aboard as a copyboy in 1946 in his early twenties.

Rosenthal's death prompted a week's worth of published tributes and flattering obituaries, describing how, as his *Times* obituary put it, "he climbed on rungs of talent, drive and ambition to the highest echelons of the *Times* and American journalism." The salutes culminated in the passionate eulogies delivered at his funeral, held at Central Synagogue in Manhattan. An estimated eight hundred people attended the service, representing a Who's Who of New York's business, media, political and cultural elite, including figures as diverse as Mike Wallace, Walter Cronkite, Beverly Sills, Charlie Rose, Midge Decter and Rudy Giuliani. The honorary pallbearers were led by the former mayor Ed Koch and William F. Buckley Jr. They were followed by a half-dozen men who had worked with Rosenthal at the *Times,* including his former boss, Arthur O. Sulzberger. That week, Buckley had hailed Rosenthal as the commanding figure in the evolution of serious daily journalism, which he had influenced as decisively, in Buckley's opinion, as William Randolph Hearst had the tabloids, and Henry Luce the weekly newsmagazines. Sulzberger, by then the former publisher, had told the *New York Sun* that "It was the golden age of journalism when Abe was at the Times."

Some of the tributes focused on Rosenthal's impoverished and tragic background. He was the son of a Byelorussian immigrant who became a Canadian fur trapper before coming to America to work as a housepainter. Abe's father died after falling off a ladder, four of his five sisters passed away before he was an adult, and Abe himself was afflicted with osteomyelitis, a rare bone disorder. The medical care he received was substandard. At one point an operation was performed on the wrong part of his leg, and as he was lying in a full body cast he was told that he would never walk again. It was only after being admitted to the Mayo Clinic as a charity case that he recovered, but he still experienced lifelong pain.

Other tributes focused on his remarkable career trajectory. Beginning as the *Times* stringer at New York's City College, he was formally hired as a copyboy without even graduating. He was a reporter for nineteen years, covering the fledgling United Nations before becoming a foreign correspondent in 1955, assigned to cover India, Japan and Poland. He was expelled from Poland for reporting that was "too probing" for the Communist government there, and won the Pulitzer Prize in 1960 for international reporting. In 1963 he returned to New York to assume a new title, "metropolitan editor." From there he climbed up the editorial hierarchy, becoming assistant managing editor, managing editor and finally executive editor of the entire paper in 1977.

Although a fierce protector of *Times* tradition, Rosenthal shook up the Metro staff, encouraging better, brighter writing from talented reporters like Gay Talese and rotating beat assignments that had previously been regarded as set in stone. He emphasized investigative reporting and broke precedent by assigning trend stories on controversial subjects like interracial marriage and homosexuality. Believing he had suffered some measure of career bias as a result of anti-Semitism, he upended the informal caste system at the *Times,* which had traditionally favored Ivy League WASPs over New York–bred Italians, Irish and Jews.

As executive editor, Rosenthal steered the *Times* through the coverage of the Vietnam War, the rise of the counterculture, the Watergate scandal and various Mideast crises. He played a central role in the decision to publish the Pentagon Papers in 1971, bucking up Sulzberger and other executives who feared that printing the government's own classified history of U.S. involvement in Vietnam would appear to the public as treasonous, expose the paper's executives to federal prosecution, and lead to financial ruin. Rosenthal himself was not a dove; at his funeral, his son recalled him putting on a cowboy hat at home and singing "I'm proud to be an Okie from Muskogee." But as a *Times* editorial after his death noted, he believed that "when something important is going on, silence is a lie."

Many of the tributes dwelled on Rosenthal's role in rescuing the paper from financial peril and journalistic irrelevance in an age when television was killing off newspapers right and left, which was just as important as the big-ticket news stories he shepherded. Facing declines in ad revenue and circulation, as well as charges that the paper's writing was dull, Rosenthal spearheaded efforts to broaden the paper's appeal and liven up its pages. The result was the "Sectional Revolution," expanding the daily paper from two sections to four, which encouraged a rebound in circulation along with ad sales and revenues.

At the same time, Rosenthal's legendary bad temper did not go unmentioned. The newsroom atmosphere was suffused with his "tempestuous personality," said the *Times* obituary writer Robert McFadden, "leading to stormy outbursts in which subordinates were berated for errors, reassigned for failing to meet the editor's expectations or sidetracked to lesser jobs for what he regarded as disloyalty to The Times." Some recalled Rosenthal as a vengeful man who kept a "shit-list in his head," as one writer put it, and as "a shouter and a curser" who would make or break careers on a whim.

The one theme that resounded through almost all the obituaries and tributes was Rosenthal's "tiger-ish" defense of high standards in reporting and editing, his call for "fairness, objectivity and good taste in news columns free of editorial comment, causes and political agendas, innuendo and unattributed, pejorative quotations," as McFadden phrased it. This sense of journalistic integrity perfectly embodied the *Times'* founding motto of delivering the news "impartially, without fear or favor, without concern for party interest or sect."

The reason why Rosenthal was obsessed with keeping editors and reporters from putting their "thumbs on the scale," wrote the *Times* columnist Thomas Friedman, was because he believed a "straight" *New York Times* was "essential to helping keep democracy healthy and our government honest." Rosenthal kept the *Times* "straight" by battling what he saw as the ingrained left-liberal tendencies of the newsroom, particularly the Washington bureau. He scolded reporters and editors he thought were romanticizing the sixties counterculture, which he viewed as a destructive force. While encouraging reporters to write with more flair, Rosenthal eschewed the subjectivity of the New Journalism, seeing this genre as substituting reportorial ego for a commitment to fact. He was vigilant about conflicts of interest, once firing a reporter who was found to have been sleeping with a Pennsylvania politician she covered while working for the *Philadelphia Inquirer.* "I don't care if my reporters are fucking elephants," Rosenthal was said to have declared, "as long as they aren't covering the circus."

A tribute of sorts to the ideological neutrality of *Times* news reporting under Rosenthal had come from a rather unusual source: William F. Buckley's *National Review,* the very bible of American conservatism. In 1972, as Spiro Agnew railed against the "elitist Eastern establishment press," and Richard Nixon was livid over the *Times'* publication of the Pentagon Papers and its looming endorsement of George McGovern, the *National Review* produced an article examining the charges of left-leaning bias. Conservatives had long dismissed the *Times* as "a hopeless hotbed of liberalism, biased beyond redemption and therefore not to be taken seriously," the magazine observed, asking, "But to what extent was this impression soundly based?" A subheadline telegraphed its findings: "Things on 43rd Street aren't as bad as they seem." The *National Review* audit examined five developing stories, which it said had a "distinct left-right line," and concluded: "The *Times* news administration was so evenhanded that it must have been deeply dismaying to the liberal opposition." It went on to state that conservatives and other Americans would be far more confident in other media—specifically newsmagazines and television networks—if those media "measured up to the same standard" of fairness. "Were the news standards of the *Times* more broadly emulated," *National Review* said, "the nation would be far better informed and more honorably served."

This was very much a validation for Rosenthal, and for Arthur O. "Punch" Sulzberger, who also upheld the tradition of politically agnostic news reporting despite the shrill liberalism of the editorial page and, increasingly, the journalistic activism of a new generation of reporters touched by the lengthening shadow of the counterculture. Indeed, Rosenthal would cite the *National Review* piece on other occasions when challenged by accusations of political bias at the *Times*. Even Joseph Lelyveld, who took over the top editor's job in 1994 and was undoubtedly to the left of Rosenthal, saw need for vigilance. "Abe would always say, with some justice, that you have to keep your hand on the tiller and steer to the right or it'll drift off to the left."

It was a priority of the postwar *Times* to become a national forum for opinion-free, straight news—as has been noted in numerous definitive books about the paper, such as *The Trust: The Private and Powerful Family Behind the New York Times*, by Susan Tifft and Alex Jones, and *Behind the Times: Inside the New York Times*, by Edwin Diamond. This goal was accomplished under a succession of larger-than-life editors who were granted great autonomy, as well as unparalleled financial resources, to produce what the Sulzberger family has always considered a quasi-public "trust." The paper held fast to several principles: ideological agnosticism, a sense of intellectual rigor, moral seriousness, and a respect for neutral recitation of the facts, free of political cant. It was a "theology" of gravitas and objectivity that allowed the *Times* to ask probing questions and to report often-uncomfortable answers without regard for consequences.

The need to be "straight," to report the news rather than drive it, was reflected in how the paper covered the Bay of Pigs. Like other news organizations, the *Times* had most of the details about the impending invasion; in fact, they had become one of the journalism world's biggest open secrets. But the *Times* hesitated to print the information since it could endanger the lives of the men landing on the beaches, it would effectively aid Castro, and it would interfere with national policy. In the end, the *Times* ran a one-column story instead of the four originally planned. No date for the invasion was mentioned—only a CBS News report that it was "imminent."

The lacerating political and journalistic self-assessment that followed the Bay of Pigs debacle was the backdrop for the *Times'* deliberations over whether to go into print with the infamous Pentagon Papers. "A tale of reckless military gambles and public deceptions" according to Max Frankel, executive editor from 1986 to 1994, the papers showed that "the government had hidden the true dimensions of its enterprise and its abundant doubts about the prospects for success" at every stage "along a twenty year arc." Yet far from being the journalistic no-brainer it might be considered today, the Pentagon Papers case provoked considerable agony and debate at the *Times*. For Punch Sulzberger, the idea of publishing live military secrets was anathema, and as the internal debate flared, he invoked the national interest to delay publication. Rosenthal, the managing editor, agreed with Sulzberger's qualms. According to Frankel, he asked "Were we on an ego trip?" before finally agreeing to publish the papers after it was found that no *current* military secrets would be disclosed.

The *New York Times* took a similarly cautious approach to the subject of civil rights in the late 1950s and well into the 1960s, maintaining careful neutrality in explaining the historic shifts that were afoot, as well as the resistance these shifts were provoking. The paper was solidly behind most of the major civil rights developments—*Brown v. Board of Education*, the March on Selma, the protests in Birmingham. But it also gave positive coverage to Daniel Patrick Moynihan's now-famous 1965 report, *The Negro Family: The Case for National Action*, while some media identified with the left excoriated it. The *Times* affirmed Moynihan's insight that, as with immigrants at the turn of the century, "Negro upliftment" would come through programs that asserted the primacy of the mainstream culture and promoted the values needed to enter it. Moynihan was not "blaming the victims," the *Times* took pains to explain, but was blaming three hundred years of white racism that had victimized them.

Another subject on which the *Times* showed far different leanings from today was cultural separatism, especially as associated with black militancy and the Black Power movement. An editorial in 1966 described Black Power as "racism in reverse" and said it "could only bring disaster to the cause of racial equality." When Malcolm X was assassinated in 1965, the editorial page called him "an extraordinary but twisted man, turning many gifts to evil purpose." The editorial concluded: "The world he saw through those horn-rimmed glasses of his was distorted and dark. But he made it darker still through his exaltation of fanaticism. Yesterday someone came out of the darkness he spawned and killed him."

The *Times* was hardly quick to embrace the emerging counterculture either, or its radical critique of American consumerism, family structure and political authority. Rosenthal himself was appalled at some of the destructive excesses of the antiwar movement, particularly the 1968 takeover of Columbia University and the sacking of President Grayson Kirk's office. He was dubious of the subjectivity and relativism inherent in the counterculture and its replacement of objectivity with political and cultural partisanship. "We live in a time of commitment and advocacy," he wrote somewhat sardonically in one staff memo. "'Tell it like it is' really means, 'tell it like I say it is, or tell it as I want it to be.' For precisely that reason it is more important than ever that the *Times* keep objectivity in its news columns as its number one, bedrock principle." A subsequent memo would tell the staff that the *Times* "shouldn't stick fingers in people's eyes just because we have the power to do so."

As Edwin Diamond notes, Rosenthal was especially on guard against the counterculture's reflexive anti-Americanism. In early November 1969, he wrote a memo about the "awry picture of America" that, he maintained, the *Times* was perpetuating. Drawing his examples from the November 7 issue, he cited a story on page 7 about a GI trial in Fort Dix, a report on an MIT sit-in on page 8, an account of the moratorium on page 9, a story on the Army memo of that antiwar protest on page 13, and a report on page 22 about the ongoing Chicago trial, flanked by two different stories about poverty and housing demonstrations. He ended his list with a story on page 27 about job discrimination, before declaring that "there were others." November 7 was not even a particularly outstanding day for that kind of thing, Rosenthal went on.

> But I get the impression, reading the Times, that the image
> we give of America is largely demonstrations, discrimina-

> *tion, anti-war movements, rallies, protests, etc. . . . . Obvi-*
> *ously all these things are an important part of the American*
> *scene. But I think that because of our own liberal interests*
> *and reporters' inclinations we overdo this. I am not sug-*
> *gesting eliminating any of these stories. I am suggesting that*
> *reporters and editors look a bit more around them to see what*
> *is going on in other fields and try to make an effort to repre-*
> *sent other shades of opinion than those held by the new left,*
> *the old left, the middle-aged left and anti-war people.*

Another time that Rosenthal's nose for radical chic got out of joint was over a story by Robert Reinhold in 1979, marking the tenth anniversary of Woodstock. Reinhold had called Woodstock a symbol of national, cultural and political awakening, extolling it as the culmination of a decade-long youth crusade for a freer style of life, for peace and for tolerance. Rosenthal did not see the story until the Saturday evening before it ran in the Sunday edition. Livid, he ordered it out of all subsequent editions.

A hallmark of Rosenthal's commitment to keeping the *Times* "as close to the center as possible" was his wariness of allowing culture critics to thread their political opinions into reviews of plays, books, movies and television shows. Political opinions don't belong in cultural reviews, Rosenthal believed. Otherwise the *Times* "would have ten extra commentators on the paper." The news columns would not be made "into a political broadsheet, period," he insisted; there would be no "editorial needles."

·~

Throughout his tenure, Rosenthal was backed up by Arthur O. "Punch" Sulzberger, who had become publisher in 1963 some-what accidentally after his predecessor, Orvil Dryfoos, a Sulz-berger in-law, died unexpectedly. Punch Sulzberger brought a special temperament to the job: content to stay "out of the way of the hired hands" was how someone once described his idea of his role. He tended to take an editorial interest in things that might appeal to or alienate advertisers, such as restaurants, movies and plays, and when he did choose to make his objections known, he did so within channels, complaining only to the top editor. Of course he would have general conversations with his editors, often at the end of the day, over a bottle of wine. Generally, though, he kept his power in reserve, like a "hidden hand." It was no wonder that many at the paper likened him to the Wizard of Oz.

In 1976, however, Punch Sulzberger became uncharacteristically involved in the paper's journalism. A World War II veteran with an abiding patriotism and a disdain for communism, he had long felt uncomfortable with the left-wing opinions on the editorial page, which was edited by his cousin John Oakes, a legacy appointment inherited from his predecessor. The editorial board had endorsed George McGovern for president in 1972. When Jimmy Carter ran in 1976, some on the editorial board were talking about backing Ramsey Clark. In addition, it appeared likely that the *Times* would lend its endorsement in New York's U.S. Senate race to the strident left-winger Bella Abzug over Daniel Patrick Moynihan, Sulzberger's preferred candidate.

Sulzberger's concern about the leftist slant of the editorial board coincided with a drastic drop in share value and profit. In 1968, the price of *Times* stock was $53 a share; by 1976, it was $14.50. A cover story in *Business Week,* headlined "Behind the Profit Squeeze at the Times," said, "Editorially and politically, the paper had also slid precipitously to the left and has become stridently anti-business in tone, ignoring the fact that the *Times* itself is a business." An internal analysis conducted by the marketing and advertising departments of the *Times* a few years earlier found that the editorial page had become the principal reason why some people questioned the paper's impartiality. Among those growing most impatient with the partisanship were members of "the Club," a group of Wall Street bankers upon whom the *Times* relied for financing.

Phase One of "Punch's Putsch," as the effort to bring the editorial page to heel and oust John Oakes became known, was Sulzberger's decision to overrule the endorsement of Bella Abzug and instead support Moynihan. This decision infuriated Oakes and some of his editorial writers, especially Roger Wilkins. Phase Two involved the hiring of William Safire, a former Nixon speechwriter, as a conservative columnist to temper the monolithic liberal tone of the editorial page. Within several months Oakes had stepped aside and all but a few of his editorial writers were reassigned or retired.

But Sulzberger's primary commitment was dealing with the alarming underperformance of the paper's stock, especially since it was matched by severe losses in circulation and advertising. In a one-month period in 1971, daily circulation dropped by 30,000, down to 814,000. This is when Rosenthal began to have his nightmare about waking up one Wednesday morning and there being no *New York Times*.

To help determine how to address this dire situation, the *Times* set up a network of in-house task forces and committees. Management also hired professional market analysts to survey readers and advertisers in order to gauge what was wanted—and what was wanting in the paper's coverage. The analysts returned shocking news: the *Times* had very little readership under the age of thirty-five. More distressing yet was what the polls and surveys suggested the *Times* should do. Interest in foreign and national news was practically nil, the market researchers reported, while arts and entertainment scored significantly higher. If the *Times* was to engage the under-thirty-five reader, it had to focus on the two questions that members of that demographic found most compelling: what to do with their time, and what to do with their money. In short, "lifestyle," embodied in special weekday sections devoted to leisure time, sports, home, fashion, popular entertainment and contemporary arts.

In a panic, the paper began looking around at publications that seemed to ring bells with younger, affluent urbanites. One was *New York* magazine, full of service features and celebrity profiles. The other was the *Village Voice,* with its radical-chic politics and hip take on the downtown scene. Still another was *People* magazine, which was demonstrating that a sensibility shaped in direct imitation of television could make for a winning format on the printed page as well.

For someone like Abe Rosenthal—an accomplished foreign correspondent, city editor and at this point the managing editor poised to take over the executive editorship in 1976—looking to these particular publications for guidance was distressing. In an interview, he had once described the *Voice* as "an urban ill, like dog shit in the street, to be stepped over." He admitted to one interviewer that *New York* magazine "used to drive me out of my mind." But eventually, Rosenthal's resistance was overcome by pragmatic acceptance of the demographic facts. Still, if the *Times* was going to do "soft" journalism, it would be superior soft journalism, he proclaimed. Instead of "thinning the soup" by watering down its serious coverage, the paper would be "adding more tomatoes" to create a richer broth, which would enhance its appeal in places it had not had appeal before.

The "Sectional Revolution," as this transformation came to be called, was managed by Rosenthal and Punch Sulzberger along with Walter Mattson, the senior financial manager. It basically saved the paper, restoring circulation and profits to the tune of $200 million in the late 1980s. But in terms of the paper's overall credibility and gravitas, and its tradition of neutral reporting without ideological taint, the lifestyle revolution was insidious, providing a back door to the countercultural values, liberationist ideologies and special interests that Rosenthal had tried so hard to keep at bay.

Even as this door opened, there was someone coming in the front door who changed the paper in far more fundamental ways. It was Punch's son, Arthur Sulzberger Jr., who sat somewhat distractedly in a front-row pew at Central Synagogue on the day that Rosenthal was being eulogized, along with the journalistic sensibility he both projected and protected at the *Times*. Just as Abe Rosenthal had epitomized the virtues of the paper's *ancien régime,* "Young Arthur" would symbolize the postmodernism that lay athwart its future.

two

The Rise of Arthur Jr.

Although he was a life-long rock climber, it was the golden ropes of nepotism that hoisted young Sulzberger aloft. In their 1999 book about the Sulzberger family, *The Trust: The Private and Powerful Family Behind the New York Times,* Susan Tifft and Alex Jones relate how Arthur Jr., a child of divorce at five, grew up with a great deal of insecurity over his inheritance and felt a nagging coldness from his own father, who seemed to favor his cousin Stephen Golden, son of Punch's sister. Sent away to boarding school after grammar school, young Sulzberger returned to New York pretty quickly and acted on a longstanding desire to go live with his father and stepmother, along with his half sister and stepsister. "I was

14 when I came to his [Punch's] house," Arthur Jr. told Tifft and Jones, indulging his penchant for off-tone phrasing. "So he had me for more than a year and a half before I became an asshole."

The tenuousness of his relationship with his father, combined with a certain measure of confusion over his mixed Jewish and Episcopalian heritage, has been said to have left young Arthur with the need "to prove himself to so many people," as his stepmother later put it. Very much a child of the sixties, he was suspended from Manhattan's Browning School for trying to organize a shutdown of classes in protest of the shootings at Kent State University. Following a number of his cousins to Tufts University in Boston, Arthur Jr. continued the antiwar activism and earned two arrests for civil disobedience.

Such attitudes did not endear him with his ex-Marine father. Walking across Boston Commons one day discussing the war, Punch asked Arthur Jr. which he would like to see get shot if an American soldier came across a North Vietnamese soldier in battle. Arthur Jr. defiantly answered that he would like the American to get shot because it was the other guy's country. For Punch, the remark bordered on treason, and the two began shouting. Sulzberger Jr. later said that his father's inquiry was the dumbest question he had ever heard in his life.

Despite the generational and ideological strains between them, Punch made sure that Arthur Jr. was well taken care of early in his career, set up with internships at the *Boston Globe* and the *Daily Telegraph* of London. There he soaked up the mod air and the sartorial styles, and returned home sporting an affected Carnaby Street look, complete with a wide-brimmed hat, wire-framed glasses, loud ties and a cane. His stepmother thought the affectation was a bid for attention. She once spoofed him by dressing up in the same garb for a family cocktail party.

In May 1975, Sulzberger Jr. married his girlfriend, Gail Gregg, whom he had met through his mother in Kansas City. (They separated in 2008.) As Edwin Diamond describes it in *Behind the Times*, the wedding was certainly "a scene from a modern marriage." Standing with Arthur were three fathers (his mother had remarried twice after leaving her marriage to Punch), two mothers, one stepsister, three sisters, a half brother and "an assortment of long haired cousins." For the rehearsal dinner the night before, according to Tifft and Jones, Arthur "had shown up in a long sleeved tee-shirt with a tuxedo design printed on it. In pictures from the wedding, the groom was wearing a headband, with white pants, white tuxedo shirt and a white belt, but with no tie. The bride, an avowed atheist and feminist, kept her maiden name."

His father arranged for Arthur Jr. to work at the *Raleigh Times.* Despite his prestigious internships, Arthur came off to his supervisors as "absolutely, totally green." Mike Yopp, the paper's managing editor, told Tifft and Jones that working with him was "very much like dealing with a college intern." His copy, mostly for light features, was riddled with basic spelling mistakes. In one unedited piece, Sulzberger had misspelled the word "hate" as "hait" not once, but several times. He was well liked, however, and though he drove a Porsche, he generally tried to be a man of the people, telling friends that the car actually had a Volkswagen engine.

Punch Sulzberger soon arranged a reporting job for Arthur at the AP in London, and another job for Gail at UPI. According to *The Trust,* Punch had originally written "we think she is smarter than he is" in his recommendation letter for Gail. His secretary drew Sulzberger Sr.'s attention to the slight, and it was excised from the final draft.

In 1978, Arthur Jr. went to work for the *Times* as a reporter in the Washington D.C. bureau. It was the staff there who gave him his unfortunate nickname, "Pinch," a play on his father's moniker. By all accounts, though, Arthur Jr. offset the connotations of the name and the baggage of his family influence through hard work and late-night socialization with other reporters, particularly the younger ones who carried themselves around town as a kind of Brat Pack. He often volunteered to work for other reporters if they needed time away and would work the phones as long as he could on a story, looking for yet one more source.

Undergoing another sartorial makeover, he adopted the Ben Bradlee "power look" of striped shirts with colorful suspenders and cigars. Some saw this as Arthur trying to look more serious and professional. Others saw it as a sign of immaturity, "like he was trying to be a man, to have weight or something," as a visiting friend from North Carolina described it.

During those D.C. years, Arthur Jr. did not generate a lot of story ideas and did not seem to have the managerial skills necessary to supervise other reporters. Nor did he have exceptional writing abilities. His political sympathies, however, seemed to leave a lasting impression. Michael Kramer recalled watching the presidential election returns in Houston with Sulzberger in 1980: "We sort of clung together in desperation as the Republicans won a major landslide and Reagan came in." Richard Burt, a former Pentagon official who was then the *Times'* defense expert, remembers getting into heated debates with Sulzberger over arms control in the early 1980s. Sulzberger, he said, liked to think of himself as an anti-establishment liberal. "But how can you be anti-establishment when you are a Sulzberger?" Burt asked rhetorically.

Sulzberger Jr. left the D.C. bureau in 1982 and moved back to New York as a *Times* Metro reporter. Eventually he was shifted over to a position as an assignment editor on the news desk. As Tifft and Jones explain, "Given his workmanlike prose and creative spelling, which made him unfit to blue-pencil copy, the duties of an assignment editor—coming up with story ideas and motivating people to produce them—were more in keeping with his talents."

It was fortunate for Sulzberger that he was arriving at the *Times* as the influence of Abe Rosenthal was beginning to ebb. Rosenthal was an up-by-the-bootstraps hardscrabbler who clawed his way to the top of the *Times*. Arthur Jr. was born with a silver spoon in his mouth and grew up as the presumed heir to one of the country's most important and richest media families. Rosenthal was deeply patriotic and temperamentally, culturally and socioeconomically allergic to the Woodstock Generation. Sulzberger was proud to the point of vanity to be part of the sixties and its emancipatory spirit. Nor had his efforts to submerge his sense of entitlement, successful on some people, worked with Rosenthal. According to some reports, Rosenthal had little regard for Sulzberger's talents and informal affectations. Once, barely containing his fury, Rosenthal grabbed a shoeless Sulzberger by the arm and told him never to come into an editorial meeting in his office that way. At another point, Rosenthal's secretary caught Arthur Jr. reading her boss's messages outside his office. "Who do you think you are?" she snapped. Sulzberger contritely apologized. "I'm a reporter. I've got all the instincts. I can't help it," he supposedly replied.

Years later, in 1999, when he had been firmly established as publisher since 1991, Sulzberger finally got his delayed revenge on Rosenthal when he called the older man into his office to tell him that he would no longer be writing his op-ed column. "It's time," Sulzberger said, giving little other explanation. After having given his life to the paper, Rosenthal felt betrayed and heartbroken. "I didn't expect it at all," he reportedly told his good friend William F. Buckley.

·--

Family control of the New York Times Company allowed the Sulzbergers to make news decisions free of the financial concerns and strictures that burden a publicly accountable company. The downside of family control is that it has not been able to guarantee that the best people rise to its topmost rungs. The all-pervasive climate of nepotism has also encouraged a kind of schizoid denial about the place that family members have in the hierarchy and how others—the several thousand employees—should treat them.

Punch Sulzberger, for instance, would say that family members would have to work harder than most people if they wanted to get to the top. Yet everyone knew this was not true. "The cousins," as Arthur Jr. and his immediate relatives working for the paper were called, were objects of a solicitude that would undermine frank, open relations based on workplace equality. No matter what nods to merit were made publicly, almost everyone at the *Times* knew that a member of the Sulzberger clan was going to run the paper. With the coming of the 1980s, that person looked increasingly to be Arthur Sulzberger Jr.

In managing the succession, Punch Sulzberger put the grooming of his son into the hands of Walter Mattson, a top executive who felt strongly that Arthur Jr. needed to be seen as having "earned his spurs" and that he would win respect for knowing what was going on at every level of the operation, from boiler room to bridge. Mattson structured the apprenticeship, of sorts, that would circulate Sulzberger Jr. through the production, advertising, finance and other key departments. This would expose him to almost every job in the organization and every kind of employee—pressmen, truckers, ad salespeople, night production workers. It was a democratizing experience. If he had felt serious self-consciousness over the nepotism that would propel him into one of the most important positions in American journalism, Arthur Jr. nevertheless grew comfortable with second- and third-generation pressmen who got their jobs from their fathers and grandfathers. "I never knew you could use fuck as an adjective, verb and noun, all in the same sentence," he once quipped about what he had learned from his contact with the paper's blue-collar workers.

During Sulzberger Jr.'s apprenticeship, Mattson and Sulzberger Sr. coined a new corporate title just for him, that of "assistant publisher," although it was said that Mattson himself somewhat teasingly referred to Arthur Jr. as "Deputy Dawg." In 1988, Arthur Jr. was named "deputy publisher," at which point he began acting as a kind of "publisher-in-waiting," sharing in major decisions. In fact, he made the final call on many of those decisions, except for those involved with the editorial page, although he is said to have sat frequently in on meetings there. He was still young, just thirty-five, and even younger looking. His own secretary referred to him as "the Kid."

Almost from day one, Arthur Jr. demonstrated a management style drastically different from his father's. While Punch had embraced the "hidden hand" approach and went to considerable lengths to avoid direct confrontation, young Arthur very visibly got involved in almost every facet of the paper and relished being in the middle of battle. His father had allowed strong news executives like Rosenthal virtually as much autonomy as they wanted. By contrast, Arthur Jr., a former reporter—although of mediocre accomplishment—was set on running both sides of the paper, business and editorial, in every respect, no matter how far down the management ladder the decisions had been made in the past. A micromanager, he injected himself into decisions about budgets and finances and also got deeply involved in various labor disputes, which Punch had always let others handle. His friend Anna Quindlen, a former *Times* columnist, chalked it up to self-doubt: "Arthur is going through his whole life with something to prove," she told Tifft and Jones. "Every day he wakes up and thinks, 'How can I show them today that I am the man I want to be?'"

By all accounts, those working around Sulzberger Jr. found the experience an exasperating one. He tended to view the world in black-and-white terms, unaware of, or at least unbothered by, shades of gray. People at the *Times* talked about a lack of *sachel*— Yiddish for common sense, tact and diplomacy. Max Frankel, who was made editor when Rosenthal retired in 1986, tried to play mentor and run interference for Arthur, often imperceptibly grimacing inside when Arthur Jr. made glib, inappropriate comments or went off in a mistaken direction. He played behind the scenes to rectify the damage and soothe ruffled feathers. ("I'll say this about Arthur," Frankel was said to have quipped privately. "He never makes the same mistake three times.")

Despite the extensive grooming, as the time drew near for "Punch" Sulzberger to hand over the reins, questions about Arthur Jr.'s management style and personality were mounting. According to Tifft and Jones, at the board of directors meeting after Punch announced his intention to step aside and have Arthur Jr. step into his shoes, the hesitation in the boardroom was "palpable." The single presentation that Arthur had made to the board left them unimpressed. Many of them didn't know him at all except for his reputation; his lack of maturity and his questionable leadership skills had left them worried. "We heard a lot of stories," one board member told Tifft and Jones. "People would say: I was talking to so and so and he tells me that Arthur Sulzberger Jr. is the most impossible SOB."

The board responded by delaying the succession proposal. They were not rejecting Arthur Jr., board members wanted to ensure Punch; they just wanted to get to know him better. The board also wanted reassurance that naming Arthur Jr. publisher would not automatically mean that he would become chairman and CEO, out of concern for Wall Street's dim view of "irresponsible nepotism." Punch Sulzberger could have overruled the board. Instead, he chose to lobby them for a few months to set a better stage for Arthur's debut. When the board assembled again in January, they ratified Punch's choice.

According to Tifft and Jones, a pair of eerie omens cast shadows on the occasion. The day that Arthur was made publisher, the bulbs blew out on the large clock hanging outside the *Times* building on 43rd Street, with its Gothic letters spelling TIMES. Upstairs in the mahogany-paneled boardroom, just as Punch Sulzberger introduced Arthur as the man who was going to be named publisher, one of the heavy bottom windows in the august room flew up and a cold rush of wind caused a framed photograph of the Shah of Iran to crash onto the floor. One board member joked that it was the spirit of Adolph Ochs. Another jested, "No, it's the winds of change." Mike Ryan, the *Times'* attorney, told Tifft and Jones that the experience was "frightening." In thirty-five years he had never seen anything like it in the boardroom.

·⤳

Insiders were right to worry about the transition. Sulzberger Jr. was about to face a financial and journalistic crisis even worse than the one his father and Abe Rosenthal calmed in the 1970s. As Edwin Diamond observed in *Behind the Times,* among these challenges was the need to create new news products for an emerging multimedia world while still maintaining the most important aspect of the organization's franchise: the role of defining the nation's news agenda and reporting news with fairness, accuracy and context. The paper also had to find a way to balance the interests of its older, elite audience with those of a younger readership—a readership increasingly foreign born. "The *Times* could once at a minimum count on an intellectual audience that not only wanted to read the *Times* but felt that it had to. The paper's authority was unchallenged," wrote Diamond, but "These certitudes no longer exist[ed]."

At the time of his ascension, Arthur Sulzberger Jr. had been running the paper on a day-to-day basis since 1988, casting critical votes in various company decisions, if not having explicit veto power. But with the new title, he began to act with more force, revamping both the management culture of the paper and its news product to fit his vision for the needs of the future. It was a vision reflecting his own values, beliefs, temperament and experience, defined by a combination of New Age management theory, aging liberal pieties, sixties-style countercultural advocacy and affectations, as well as the identity politics of the 1980s and early 1990s. It was a vision preoccupied with the pursuit of youth demographics, one that encouraged the *Times* to be self-consciously hip and its reporters to write with flair, or at least make the attempt. And it was a vision that promoted opportunities for "opinion" to an unprecedented degree.

A New Age management theory that Sulzberger found intriguing was William Edward Deming's notion of "management by obligation." Demingism asked managers to embrace three virtues: "self-esteem, intrinsic motivation and the curiosity to learn." Sulzberger Jr. had been much impressed by his teenage experience in Outward Bound; and Demingism, with its emphasis on self-discovery, bonding and team play, has been likened to "Outward Bound in a business suit." Deming's ideas also provided Sulzberger with a way of adding gravitas to his leadership abilities.

But the management revolution that Sulzberger wanted to encourage stumbled badly from the outset, further damaging morale as egos were bruised and tempers flared in seminars that were supposed to help close fissures. Sulzberger was undeterred, however. When the *New Yorker*'s Ken Auletta told him some of the old-timers at the paper were complaining that he was trying to establish his legacy too quickly, Sulzberger quipped: "I'll outlive the bastards."

Meanwhile, Sulzberger took the concern over trends and age cohorts to a level beyond what drove the Sectional Revolution of the 1970s. The old thinking about the *Times* was that it "should not be too popular and should not try to be," as Edwin Diamond phrased it. But as Diamond also explained, market research and focus groups indicated a disturbing trend toward "aliteracy," with otherwise educated young professionals saying "they had no interest in picking up a copy of the *Times*." And it wasn't just a local problem. In 1967, roughly two-thirds of those between the ages of eighteen and twenty-nine read a newspaper; in 1988 the figure was 29 percent.

The research commissioned by the *Times* showed that the paper was defining itself too narrowly to appeal to an elite that no longer existed in its traditional form. It needed to adjust its journalistic offerings, and its pool of talent, to appeal to an evolving elite that included the educated classes from the city's booming immigrant populations.

One manifestation of demographic anxiety was the crusade for "diversity" that Arthur Jr. mounted in his newsroom and led in the newspaper industry at large. Diversity, he argued, was not just a moral issue, a vehicle for taking the civil rights movement to another level; it was also an economic necessity if newspapers were to survive in an America whose demographic reality was rapidly changing. Enthusiastically mouthing the slogan "diversity makes good business sense; makes moral sense too," Sulzberger blithely ignored warnings that the ideological and political dimension of diversity risked fragmenting newsrooms along racial, ethnic and gender lines, and could make the *Times* more partisan as he forged ahead to make it "look like America," in Bill Clinton's words.

Arthur Jr. had clearly telegraphed his fixation on diversity before he assumed the throne at the *Times*. Shortly after he was named deputy publisher in 1988, he started assembling certain middle and senior managers and giving what came to be dubbed "The Speech." At its intellectual center was one demographic fact that he believed had more resonance for the future of the *Times* than any other: by the end of the 1990s, 80 percent of all new American employees would be women, minorities or first-generation immigrants. This rapidly shifting demographic mix of future employees—and future readers—did not give the *Times* very long "to get its white male house in order," Sulzberger told a management seminar in 1989, again stressing that diversity was "the single most important issue" the *Times* faced. At the 1991 convention of the National Association of Black Journalists in Kansas City, Sulzberger spoke of the difficult climate for racial change and the roadblocks standing in the way of "our cause." To considerable applause, he told the audience: "Keep pushing. Keep pushing to turn your vision of Diversity into our reality."

Once he became publisher in 1991, he banged the drum even harder, amplifying, refining and implementing "The Speech." As one of the principal figures in the American Newspaper Publishers Association, Sulzberger pushed diversity as an industry obligation. At the *Times* itself, he encouraged a variety of corporate and newsroom initiatives to get the paper into the Promised Land. He aimed to replace the *Times'* pledge to "give the news impartially, without fear or favor," with the more amorphous promise to "enhance society by creating, collecting and distributing high-quality news, information and entertainment." The new motto never got any traction in or out of the newsroom.

On a more practical level, Sulzberger put all managers, especially newsroom managers, on notice that they must reject what he called the "comfort factor" of hiring and promoting only white men. He set up committees to examine diversity in all its permutations at the *Times,* on both the editorial and the business side, scrutinizing everything from salaries to career paths. Training was key, he believed. In a strong endorsement of cultural relativism, Sulzberger declared, "We are all going to have to understand [differences]. Be aware of them, know what they mean, understand that we don't all see the world or a moment in time in the same way."

This fixation translated into a number of high-profile hiring, promotion and assignment decisions that reverberated across every news desk in the newsroom. To enhance minority hiring at lower levels, Max Frankel, functioning as Sulzberger's de facto diversity officer, instituted what he would refer to as his "own little quota plan," based on "one-for-one" hiring—one minority for one white male—"until the numbers get better," as Frankel put it in 1991.

In short order, blacks and Latinos were appointed bureau chiefs, national reporters and foreign correspondents; the number of racial-minority desk editors increased as well. Eventually the *Times* would institute a minorities-only internship program. Sulzberger cleared the way for Gerald Boyd to be named the paper's first Metro editor, and later for him to become one of the paper's assistant managing editors, which made him the first black ever on the *Times* masthead and put him on track to be considered for the paper's executive editorship.

Under Sulzberger's leadership, the *Times* developed new beats to reflect multicultural change and boosted the importance of certain beats already in existence, allowing some to become vehicles for ethnic and racial advocacy. Sulzberger was adroit at telegraphing his diversity priority through his monthly "Publisher's Award." The recipients of the cash award were well balanced by race, ethnicity, gender and sexual orientation, while the subject matter of the stories was in keeping with the new multicultural orthodoxy.

Arthur Jr.'s vision of diversity encompassed a more expanded role for women. In some early speeches he made the highly symbolic gesture of using "she" as a general pronoun. He also made no secret of his close association with Anna Quindlen, the op-ed columnist who became an unofficial part of his brain trust and was, many thought, on track to become a top editor.

Sulzberger also encouraged more open attitudes toward gays, a sharp break from what were increasingly portrayed in newsroom culture as the bad old days of Abe Rosenthal, who felt it best for gays to stay in the closet. In a videotaped speech he sent to the 1992 National Lesbian and Gay Journalists Convention, Sulzberger affirmed newsroom identity politics when he said, "We can no longer offer our readers a white, straight male vision of events and say we are doing our job." In that same speech, he declared he wanted the *Times* to extend company benefits to same-sex couples. Afterward, he let it be known that those who discriminated against gays would risk losing their jobs. Even before he became publisher, Sulzberger, in league with Max Frankel, also got his father to drop his opposition to the use of the term "gay" in news reports. Sulzberger Jr. met with openly gay staff members and assured them times had changed. He committed considerable company resources to underwrite panel discussions and job fairs sponsored by the National Lesbian and Gay Journalists Association, and made sure the *Times* sent sizable delegations to NLGJA conventions and other events.

Accelerated minority hiring and promotions rankled some of the old guard, who complained that some of the blacks, Latinos and women were being moved into senior leadership positions years before they were ready. Others bristled at a generally antagonistic atmosphere, which Peter Boyer, a former Timesman, described in a 1991 *Esquire* article as "moderate white men should die." Boyer left the *Times* to become a staff writer at the *New Yorker*. Other accomplished midcareer Timesmen left too, taking with them vital experience, institutional memory and a special old-fashioned *Times* sensibility and culture. Rubbing salt into some of the old guard's wounds, Frankel, backed by Sulzberger, virtually admitted that the commitment to diversity made double standards acceptable. At a forum at Columbia University, Frankel conceded that it would be difficult to fire a black woman, even if she were less good than another candidate.

The 1991 piece on the *Times* by Robert Sam Anson in *Esquire* described a newspaper increasingly dominated by ideology. N. R. Kleinfield, a veteran business and Metro reporter, told Anson that Frankel wanted "a subtle point of view" in stories—code for a more politicized take. Anonymously, one "senior Metro reporter" said "The *Times* is basically guided by the principles of political correctness. It is terrified to offend any of the victimized groups." Anson described reporters complaining of being told they couldn't work on certain stories because they were white, and others admitting that they tailored some articles to liberal political tastes. "Don't make it too nice" is what one reporter told Anson he was instructed when assigned a profile about a conservative. Anson also cited veteran media insiders, like Richard Cohen of the *Washington Post,* who said the *Times* now was "not as trusted. . . . People are saying it's got a line."

Yet unlike his father, who was bothered by complaints of ideological bias and relayed that annoyance to his top editors, Sulzberger Jr. had little patience with what he regarded as quibblers and naysayers. As legitimate questions were raised about diversity as a force in news coverage, he would hear none of it. Instead, he displayed a righteous, even sanctimonious insistence that he was "setting a moral standard."

Not surprisingly, the diversity dissidents in the newsroom—and there were quite a few—became skittish. As John Leo of *U.S. News and World Report* put it, the paper's "hardening line on racial issues, built around affirmative action, group representation and government intervention," was difficult for staffers to buck. "Reporters do not thrive by resisting the deeply held views of their publisher. . . . When opinionated publishers are heavily committed to any cause, the staff usually responds by avoiding coverage that casts that cause in a bad light." Or as one veteran Timesman told me when I was writing *Coloring the News,* no one was going to tell Arthur "We've gone too far. We're losing our credibility." William Stockton, a former senior editor, described the chilling effect of Sulzberger's agenda: "With Arthur Jr. saying all those things about diversity in public speeches, clearly it was not good for your career to ask tough questions," he told me.

In his bid to boost readership among a less news-literate generation, Sulzberger Jr. increased the amount of attention given to soft news and lifestyle. "Junior's paper," as the *Times* was now being sarcastically called by some on the staff, also encouraged some reporters to write with more "voice," which further loosened the definition of news. Soon, features in *People* magazine style were making their way to the front page, sometimes little different from tabloid gossip aside from quality of writing.

In 1991, the *Times* hired Adam Moss, a former editor at *Esquire,* as a consultant to help revamp its coverage of lifestyle and popular culture. The result was Styles of the Times, a bid to appeal to the ad-rich world of downtown chic. Styles of the Times was Arthur Jr.'s first visible move as publisher, and he seemed to sense that it was a high-profile gamble. "Younger readers had better like it," he joked to some reporters in the Washington bureau, "because all the older ones will drop dead when they see it." Moss ran edgy, "transgressive" stories on gay rodeos, dominatrix wear, cyberpunk novels and *outré* celebrities.

The rest of the media took notice. *Time* magazine wrote of "Tarting Up the Gray Lady of 43rd St." and likened the *Times'* hip affections to "a grandmother squeezing into neon biking shorts after everyone else has moved on to black skirts." Sulzberger Jr. struck a pose, expressing pleasure at the reaction. At a dinner, a fellow guest who lamented the passing of hard news was informed by Sulzberger that he was an anachronistic "child of the fifties." At another public function, Arthur Jr. told a crowd of people that alienating older white male readers meant "we're doing something right," and if they were *not* complaining, "it would be an indication that we were not succeeding."

Styles of the Times eventually tanked, at least in its first incarnation. So many of the original advertisers defected that the *Times* had to give away ad space. Moss was reassigned to the Sunday magazine, importing a similar sensibility to a long-sturdy feature section that had once been a central forum for debate of the most important domestic and international issues. Soon the magazine featured photo shoots of grown women dressed as little girls, evocative of "kiddie porn," along with stories about the market in Nazi memorabilia, including items made from human skin, and a Fourth of July photo-illustration of a man with his pants down sitting on an outdoor latrine, waving an American flag in one hand and flashing a peace sign with the other. Sulzberger Jr. backed Moss. But as Tifft and Jones relate it in *The Trust,* when the magazine ran a photograph of a naked Japanese actress bound with ropes for a film to be made for "Prisoner Productions," Sulzberger Jr. reached his limit. He sent an angry memo to the magazine's top editor, Jack Rosenthal, ordered Frankel to publish an editor's note apologizing for the picture, and "conspicuously" copied his father, even though he was retired.

Besides diluting the paper's overall gravitas, the push for softer, hipper journalism required an influx of journalists with far less hard-news experience; it called for grad-school-educated "specialists" in popular culture, consumerism and trendy esoterica. Fluff-ball features on junk culture and other trivia like "the return of tight jeans" and "micro plastic surgery," amid a crush of television-obsessed reports and analysis, caused serious readers of the *Times* to roll their eyes and cancel their subscriptions. The paper, according to the *New York Observer*'s Michael Thomas, kept "plumbing the depths of trivialization."

The fact that the soft news was restricted to the back sections of the paper at first provided a defense. But as editors tried to make the front news section more hip, the paper's decline in seriousness came increasingly under attack. The barbs were particularly fierce after the *Times* published a front-page report echoing salacious, uncorroborated details from a Kitty Kelly biography of Nancy Reagan alleging that she had had an affair with Frank Sinatra. Controversy about slipping standards erupted again a short while later when the *Times* ran another dubious front-page story about rape allegations against a Kennedy cousin, William Smith, which named Smith's alleged victim, Patricia Bowman, and offered up insinuations about her personal life and sexual past. Many critics read the lurid piece as a classic example of blaming the victim that sprang from a pre-feminist era. Women staffers at the *Times* circulated a petition and secured a meeting with Frankel in the *Times* auditorium, where three hundred staff members put him up against the wall. "How could you say that woman was a whore?" one staffer wanted to know.

·—

Sulzberger Jr. regarded such unpleasant experiences as road bumps on the way to putting his personal mark on the editorial voice of *his* paper and bringing it into the new age. One of the first moves he made was to hire Howell Raines as editorial page editor. Unlike his father, who had tried to mute the editorial page's stridency, Arthur Jr. wanted to make it more outspoken, edited by someone who reflected his own taste for confrontation and countercultural values.

Born in Birmingham, Alabama, Raines had sat on the sidelines during the mid-sixties civil rights demonstrations there, leaving him with a lifelong sense of Southern guilt and a determination never again to shrink from declaring his beliefs and opinions. Embracing a simplistic, perhaps even Manichean political vision, he once declared that "Every Southerner must choose between two psychic roads, the road of racism or the road of brotherhood." According to Tifft and Jones, Arthur Jr. saw in the passionate Raines "a kindred spirit, a contrarian whose values had taken shape during the sixties, who viewed the world as a moral battleground, who relished intellectual combat, and who wasn't shy about expressing his convictions in muscular unequivocal language."

Under Raines, the editorial page assumed a caustic, take-no-prisoners tone reminiscent of the days of the ultra-liberal John Oakes. The page also became a platform for the new publisher's preoccupations, focusing, sometimes obsessively, on diversity, gay rights, feminism, the history of racial guilt and other fixations of the cultural left.

Some of the editorial writers whom Raines inherited were not happy with the change, contending that there was more "shrill braying" than "sound argumentation" on the page. Now in retirement, even Max Frankel wrote that "mere invective is no substitute for vigor and verve." Timothy Noah of *Slate* said that Raines' editorial page "routinely attempts to hide simpleminded logic behind lapidary prose and promiscuous contempt." Michael Tomasky, then at *New York* magazine, accused him of "using the country's most important newspaper as his personal soapbox."

Sulzberger also made Raines part of an informal "brain-trust," composed of the executive editor and selected senior corporate managers, to plan the paper's future. This gave Raines power and influence over other parts of the *Times* that no other editorial page editor ever had. It also had the effect of weakening the firewall between news and opinion, particularly on the publisher's pet issues, especially that of diversity.

Sulzberger Jr.'s effort to reinvigorate the editorial page also involved a substantial change among op-ed columnists. Packing the roster with his personal and political favorites, he added Maureen Dowd, Frank Rich and Bob Herbert to Anna Quindlen, who had secured her place several years earlier when Arthur Jr. was deputy publisher and had become an important ally. According to a growing cadre of *Times* critics, the problem was not that Sulzberger Jr. hired liberal op-ed columnists, but that he hired them in a vastly disproportionate ratio to conservative voices. At one point after Sulzberger abruptly relieved Abe Rosenthal of his column in 1999, William Safire was the only conservative on the op-ed page. Sulzberger's choices were also markedly narrow in journalistic experience. Of the four aforementioned, none had spent any time as a foreign correspondent, and the national-level reporting experience of the group as a whole was limited. It seemed that Arthur Jr. chose most of his columnists on the basis of how much they agreed with his own sixties-era values and with the P.C. agenda he embraced.

Had Sulzberger merely allowed Raines to sharpen the combative edge of the editorial page, and turned the op-ed page into a mirror of his liberal politics and self-consciously iconoclastic values, his innovations might have been defensible. But he also initiated changes that encouraged the infiltration of opinion into the news pages. He did so chiefly by increasing the number of columnists on the inside pages; by relaxing or ignoring rules that had barred television, film, theater and literary critics from injecting their politics into reviews; by increasing the amount of space devoted to news analysis and other forms of explanatory journalism; and by expanding the importance of popular culture in the news mix.

Up until well into the 1960s the *Times* had had very few columnists; by the early 2000s there were four dozen, scattered throughout the paper. In late 2009, there were eighteen "cultural critics" alone, courtesy of the expanded coverage of popular culture. Had someone like Abe Rosenthal been there to keep a weather eye out for critics using their perch to introduce political or social commentary into what were supposed to be "straight" reviews, the boost in the number of critics and "inside" columnists would not have been such a problem. But the new Timesmen and Timeswomen were encouraged to write with "voice." Given the ideological proclivities of the people hired by Sulzberger, that meant a liberal voice as well as political posturing.

And so, writing about *Goodnight and Good Luck* in his 2006 Oscar predictions column, David Carr called the film "A well crafted look at a time in American history when anything less than complete fealty to the republic was seen as treason, which sounds familiar to some movie goers." In a review of *Sophie Stoll* (2006), a World War II German period film about the fate of civil liberties under the Nazis, Stephen Holden said, "It raises an unspoken question: could it happen here?" Holden also hailed Oliver Stone's documentary about Hugo Chavez (2010) for depicting the anti-American Venezuelan dictator as "a rough-hewn but good-hearted man of the people whose bullheaded determination is softened by a sense of humor." The television critic Anita Gates lauded a British show called *Cracker* for providing "the punch of confirmation that much of the rest of the world may indeed despise the United States for what the Bush administration calls the war on terror." The choreographer Bill T. Jones' performance piece *Blind Date* (2005) was praised by Ginia Bellafante for questioning "the expediency of war," for reflecting on "limited opportunities for the urban poor," and for remarking on "the centrality of sexual moralism to the Republican agenda."

The biggest erosion of the wall between news and opinion, however, came in the elevation of Howell Raines to the position of executive editor in 2001. The *Times* now practically dropped the pretense of objective reporting altogether, opting for crusading zeal and advocacy on a level heretofore unseen in the paper. Besides bringing dogmatic political opinions to the job, Raines blurred the line between news and opinion by putting editorial department staff into key newsroom positions. For example, he made the columnist Frank Rich an associate editor, with responsibilities for cultural coverage. Rich had been moved from the op-ed page to the Sunday Arts section, then back to the op-ed page on Sundays with a much bigger platform—usually at least half a page. What the new position meant was that Rich was not only opining on various subjects linking culture and politics, but also determining how the *Times* was covering arts and culture.

Robert Samuelson of *Newsweek* commented on the changes that came to the *Times* with Howell Raines' promotion:

> *Every editor and reporter holds private views. The difference is that Raines' opinions are now highly public. His [editorial page] was pro choice, pro gun control, and pro campaign finance reform. . . . Does anyone believe that, in his new job, Raines will instantly purge himself of these and other views? And because they are so public, Raines' positions compromise the Times' ability to act and appear fair-minded. Many critics already believe that the news columns of the Times are animated—and distorted—by the same values as its editorials. Making the chief of the editorial page the chief of the news columns will not quiet those suspicions.*

Sulzberger tried to dismiss such concerns. "A great journalist knows the difference between those two roles. Howell is certainly a great journalist," he insisted. But as Raines' tenure proceeded, it would become abundantly clear that Samuelson's prediction was right.

three

Bullets over Arthur Jr.

A be Rosenthal's funeral in 2006 became an occasion for nostalgia over the death of the *Times'* golden days, a recessional for the paper's transition from the voice of America to an increasingly self-righteous, and politically correct, left-liberal publication. It also became a moment for pause when the effects of young Arthur's fifteen-year reign could be evaluated.

It was not a pretty picture. In a relatively few years, a paper that had been known as the gold standard of American journalism had been tarnished by a string of embarrassing incidents, casting it in the harshest of spotlights, putting its credibility and even its patriotism on the line. Its newsroom had been accused of hypocrisy, corruption, ineptitude, ethical misconduct, fraud, plagiarism, credulousness and, most seriously, ideological bias. The business side was equally under siege, and its board—stacked with Sulzbergers—had presided over a plummeting of stock value to half what it had been in 2002, with advertising revenues in free fall. This steady parade of embarrassing lowlights, where the *Times* had become the focus of the news instead of merely the bearer of it, had revealed cracks in its foundations and made it a target for public anger and derision—as well as a possible candidate for a corporate takeover.

Every time one of these incidents occurred, the *Times* and its partisan defenders—led by Arthur Jr. himself—had tried to depict it as an isolated case, refusing to acknowledge any pattern. But in aggregate these regularly occurring scandals and other expressions of journalistic dysfunction paint a damning portrait of an institution stumbling through chaos of its own making. As *Vanity Fair*'s Michael Wolff would write in May 2008, "The ever growing list of its own journalistic missteps, blunders, and offenses threatens to become one of the things the *Times* most stands for: putting its foot in it. And the expectation, both within the *Times* and among those who obsessively watch it, is that there is always some further black eye, calumny, screw-up, or remarkable instance of tone-deafness on the horizon."

The list of major stumbles on the *Times*' downward path reads like a bill of particulars against the Sulzberger Jr. years, a chronicle of decline unparalleled in modern American media history.

The Blair Affair.   It began in the spring of 2003 with revelations that one of the paper's rising African American reporters, Jayson Blair, had plagiarized and fabricated material in scores of articles over a four-year period, including such high-profile stories as the Washington D.C. sniper case in 2002, and U.S. casualties from the first months of the Iraq War in 2003. It ended when Arthur Sulzberger Jr., who had pledged in the pages of his own paper that there would be no newsroom scapegoats, fired his close friend and handpicked executive editor, Howell Raines, as well as the managing editor, Gerald Boyd, the highest-ranking black ever in the newsroom. Facing a staff rebellion, public humiliation and a charge of bureaucratic disarray, Sulzberger admitted that the plagiarism scandal was "the low point in the paper's 150 year history."

The depressing story was told in the *Times'* own 14,000-word reconstruction of the Blair fiasco, headlined "Times Reporter Who Resigned Leaves Long Trail of Deception." This inquiry declared that Blair had "violated the cardinal tenet of journalism, which is simply truth." It said that 36 of 73 articles Blair had written since he started to get national reporting assignments in October of the previous year had serious problems.

Blair, who had been at the *Times* for almost five years and had racked up an inordinate record of "corrections," had used his cell phone, his laptop and access to databases, particularly photo databases, to "blur his true whereabouts" as he "fabricated comments," "concocted scenes," "lifted details from other newspapers and wire services" and "selected details from photographs to create the impression he had been somewhere or seen something" in order to write falsely about some of the most "emotionally charged moments in recent history." While Blair created the impression that he was emailing his editors from the field, on key stories he was sending these transmissions from his Brooklyn apartment or from another floor in the *Times* building. The report admitted that one of Blair's biggest "scoops" on the D.C. sniper case, which involved a local police station confession by John Allen Muhammad that was allegedly cut short by turf-conscious U.S. attorneys, had five anonymous sources—all fake. Law-enforcement beat reporters in the Washington bureau had complained, but were ignored.

Touching on the combustible issue of racial preferences as a factor in Blair's rise, the report explained that he had joined the *Times* through a minority-only internship and then was promoted to full-time reporter in January 2001, and that his immediate supervisor, Jonathan Landman, the Metro editor, objected but ultimately deferred to the paper's "commitment to diversity." Landman did warn his higher-ups that editors had to "stop Jayson from writing for the Times," but that memo had little effect. Although the *Times* denied any connection between Blair and the broader issue of affirmative action, such a conclusion was hard to get around. The recently retired *Times* columnist William Safire said, "Apparently, this 27-year-old was given too many second chances by editors eager for this ambitious black journalist to succeed."

As part of its lacerating self-inquiry, the paper held a special off-site "town meeting" of newsroom employees to address the worsening staff morale and many still-unanswered questions. Hundreds of *Times* newsroom personnel filed down the sidewalk into a rented Broadway movie theater in what one tabloid reporter standing next to me on-scene called "the world's longest perp walk." Nearby, a prankster costumed as "Baghdad Bob," the infamously prevaricating former spokesman for the Iraqi Ministry of Information, held up a sign that said "New York Times Reporter: Will Lie for Food."

The meeting, which Raines would later call "a disaster," began with an odd statement from Arthur Jr.: "If we had done this [handling the Blair fiasco] right, we would not be here today. We didn't do this right. We regret that deeply. It sucks." From here, the meeting quickly degenerated into tense, angry, profanity-laced accusations. Raines and his deputies, one editor charged, had lost "the confidence of much of the newsroom."

To the surprise of many, Raines admitted that Blair had been a beneficiary of racial favoritism. "Where I come from, when it comes to principles on race, you have to pick a ditch to die in," Raines intoned in his best Southern drawl. "And let it come rough or smooth, you'll find me in the trenches for justice. Does that mean I personally favored Jayson? Not consciously," he continued. "But you have a right to ask if I, as a white man from Alabama with those convictions, gave him one chance too many by not stopping his appointment to the sniper team. When I look into my heart for the truth of that, the answer is yes." Raines also said he had no intention of stepping down voluntarily. To which Sulzberger chimed, "If he were to offer his resignation, I would not accept it."

Sulzberger's tone-deafness and the vote of confidence in Raines left many staffers deflated. One *Times* reporter told *New York* magazine that the meeting "only served to make the scandal—and the mockery—to build." Even late-night comedians like Letterman and Leno got into the act. The old slogan at the *Times*, "All the news that's fit to print," had just been replaced by a new one, Letterman declared: "We make it up."

As it unfolded, the scandal sorely tested the friendship and ideological affinity between Raines and Sulzberger, as well as Sulzberger's public pledge that there would be no newsroom scapegoats. The day after members of the influential Washington bureau convinced him that the paper would never recover until the two top editors left, Sulzberger stood in the newsroom and announced that Raines and Boyd would step down. He implied that the departures were voluntary, saying he wanted to "applaud Howell and Gerald for putting the interest of this newspaper, a newspaper we all love, above their own." In an interview afterward, Sulzberger emphasized that he had not been pressured to fire them, either by the board or by family shareholders. (Within months, Raines would go on television flatly contradicting Sulzberger; according to Raines, after returning from D.C. that day Sulzberger had told him "there was too much blood on the floor" for him to remain.) The headline on the page-one *Times* story said only: "Times's 2 Top Editors Resign After Furor on Writer's Fraud." Like much of what Jayson Blair wrote, the headline that closed the scandalous circle was a lie.

Sulzberger's Ill-Considered Public Utterances. The counter-cultural values that Sulzberger likes to flaunt generated notable controversy when he gave a commencement speech at the State University of New York at New Paltz in May 2006. Coming so shortly after Rosenthal's death and the weeklong celebration of his journalistic values—especially his dedication to keeping the paper "straight"—Sulzberger's speech attracted wide attention, and was featured on talk radio and cable news across the nation.

The core of the speech was a generational expression of guilt over the horrible condition of the world that the graduates would be entering. When he was a student, Sulzberger said, only slightly tongue in cheek, young people had helped end the war and forced Nixon's resignation. "We entered the real world committed to making it a better, safer, cleaner, more equal place. We were determined not to repeat the mistakes of our predecessors. We had seen the horrors and futility of war and smelled the stench of corruption in government. Our children, we vowed, would never know that," Sulzberger said. "So, well, sorry. It wasn't supposed to be this way."

Critics found the speech a risible compendium of 1960s romanticism, generational vanity and self-conferred moral superiority. It reflected a misunderstood conflation of interest-group politics—illegal aliens, gays, abortion—with "fundamental rights." Citing the speech's defeatism and gloom, the conservative radio host Laura Ingraham summarized much of the media reaction when she declared Sulzberger "the most negative media figure" in the country, "the Grim Reaper of American Journalism." In Sulzberger's worldview, she said, "it's not 'Morning in America,' it's evening and there's no end in sight."

Weapons of Mass Destruction. Judith Miller's erroneous reporting on Saddam Hussein's alleged weapons of mass destruction led many, especially on the left, to charge that the *Times* had become a propaganda conduit for the Bush administration. Miller was close to the administration both professionally and personally. She was also close to the Iraqi exile Ahmad Chalabi, who turned out to be unreliable on many fronts. According to columnist/blogger Arianna Huffington, Miller and others in the media who followed her lead were guilty of "selling a war to the American public based on lies." Some of Miller's reporting, even some of her wording, was used by administration officials as they made the prewar rounds on the Sunday talk shows to warn about "mushroom clouds" appearing on the horizon. When no WMDs were found in Iraq, the *Times* conducted a postmortem, combing through Miller's reporting; this resulted in mortifying *mea culpas* in both a special "editor's note" and an editorial admitting that the paper had been "taken in."

Plamegate. The *Times* got its fingers broken again in another fiasco involving Judith Miller. In this instance, the issue was the leaking of a covert CIA operative's name, Valerie Plame, to the media. Allegedly this was done by high-ranking officials in the Bush White House in retaliation against Plame's husband, Joseph Wilson, the former ambassador who had disparaged the administration's claim that Saddam Hussein tried to buy yellow-cake uranium in Niger. The *Times* initially editorialized fiercely for a special prosecutor, but quickly changed its tune when that prosecutor, Patrick Fitzgerald, sent a subpoena to Miller. Invoking journalistic confidentiality, Miller refused to name the source who had "outed" Plame to her, and she defied Fitzgerald's grand jury subpoena, a jailable offense, even though she had written nothing about the case.

Miller's case became a *cause célèbre* throughout journalism. To Sulzberger, it was a moral crusade, as he took to the airwaves and had "Free Judy" buttons printed up. After losing in protracted court proceedings, Miller finally went to jail, but after eighty-eight days there she decided to testify. When she named Lewis "Scooter" Libby as her source, many believed that she might have been invoking journalistic privilege to protect someone in the White House who had committed a crime or had been engaged in a vengeance-driven smear campaign against Joe Wilson.

Its credibility once again under attack, *Times* editors commissioned yet another internal inquiry, and produced a long take-out in late October 2005, which unfortunately for the *Times* had the same effect as their infamous postmortem on Jayson Blair. It painted an unflattering picture of its own reporter, who had agreed to identify Libby as a "former Hill staffer" to hide his fingerprints on the leak, had "forgotten" a meeting with Libby as well as the notes she took during that meeting, and had written Plame's name in her notebook as "Valerie Flame." As the *New York Observer* characterized the accounts, they told "a tale of a dysfunctional staffer running loose at a dysfunctional institution, with historic consequences."

Within a week of her release, Miller went from being a *Times* hero to a pariah. The editor, Bill Keller, the public editor, Byron

Calame, and columnist Maureen Dowd all took aim, making it clear that Miller would never return to the *Times* newsroom. Miller soon engineered a graceful, lucrative exit and announced her "retirement" from the paper, saying, "Arthur was there for me—until he wasn't." As Gay Talese, a former *Times* reporter, said to the *New Yorker* in reference to Sulzberger Jr.'s handling of Plamegate, "You get a bad king every once in a while."

NSA Wiretapping.   The paper was thrust into a defensive position once again by a December 2005 story about the National Security Agency's warrantless and possibly illegal wiretapping of international communications between people on U.S. soil and people abroad who were suspected of ties to terrorism. The sources for the story, by the Washington bureau reporters James Risen and Eric Lichtblau, were "nearly a dozen current and former officials, who were granted anonymity because of the classified nature of the program." They had talked to the *Times* "because of their concerns about the operation's legality and oversight."

But the NSA story raised the issue of exposing national secrets during wartime. President Bush called the front-page report a "shameful act." Others accused the *Times* of treason. The story got Washington so steamed it almost scuttled the reauthorization of the USA Patriot Act.

The SWIFT Program.   According to the same reporters who broke the NSA story, Risen and Lichtblau, the Bush administration's Treasury Department had been conducting a top-secret program to monitor financial transactions of known and possible international terrorists. There was nothing illegal about the program, known by the acronym SWIFT, and it was highly effective, resulting in arrests of terrorists and the disrupting of terror plots.

The *Times*' exposé on SWIFT in June 2006—coming on the heels of the NSA story and a controversial report about secret "renditions" of terror suspects to third-country locations for interrogation—ignited wide condemnation. While some of the fury was partisan, much of it reflected a broad public exasperation with the paper's repeated efforts to divulge classified national security secrets and hobble counterterrorism efforts.

Radcliffe Rant.   In June 2006, less than a month after Sulzberger's generational apologia at New Paltz, the *Times'* Supreme Court correspondent, Linda Greenhouse, vented her own ideological preoccupations when she received an award from her alma mater, Harvard's Radcliffe College. During her remarks in front of eight hundred people, Greenhouse described weeping uncontrollably at a recent Simon and Garfield concert, overwhelmed by the realization that the grand promise of the 1960s generation had been unfulfilled, yielding to the corruption and oppression of the current political moment. She then charged that "our government had turned its energy and attention away from upholding the rule of law and toward creating law-free zones at Guantanamo Bay, Abu Ghraib, Haditha, and other places around the world, the U.S. Congress, whatever." She also attacked "the sustained assault on women's reproductive freedom and the hijacking of public policy by religious fundamentalism," adding, "To say that these last years have been dispiriting is an understatement." Greenhouse also took a potshot at immigration enforcement, saying that she felt "a growing obligation to reach out across the ridiculous" fence about to be built on the Mexican border.

Greenhouse took heat from all over, including *Times* public editors. Byron Calame cited the paper's ethical guidelines stipulating that reporters and editors who appear on television or radio "should avoid expressing views that go beyond what they would be allowed to say in the paper." He continued: "Keeping personal opinions out of the public realm is simply one of the obligations for those who remain committed to the importance of impartial news coverage. . . . The merest perception of bias in a reporter's personal views can plant seeds of doubt that may grow in a reader's mind to become a major concern about the credibility of the paper." Daniel Okrent, the former public editor, said he was amazed by Greenhouse's remarks: "It's been a basic tenet of journalism . . . that the reporter's ideology [has] to be suppressed and submerged, so the reader has absolute confidence that what he or she is reading is not colored by previous views."

Frauds and Hoaxes. In numerous instances, the *Times* has allowed itself to be conned or otherwise used as a vehicle by people who wanted to manipulate or defraud its readers. Some of these mortifying hoaxes reflect the volume and velocity of news in the information age, such that inexperienced editors cannot or do not properly analyze it all for authenticity. But veterans have been conned too, largely because they are submerged in a tide of political correctness: in soft-headed idealism, righteous naiveté, and unconscious double standards resulting from the paper's preoccupation with diversity. The nature of the hoaxes is varied, but most have involved some designated "victim" group— blacks, illegal immigrants, Muslims, the transgendered, military women—as the object of a journalistic sensitivity that often becomes solicitude.

In a March 2006 news feature, Nicholas Confessore described the plight of a Hurricane Katrina victim from Biloxi, Mississippi, who had been stranded by bureaucratic ineptitude in a New York City welfare hotel with four of her children and her oldest son's fiancée. Although she called FEMA, the Red Cross and the city welfare office, no assistance was forthcoming. Her health had deteriorated, requiring numerous hospital stays. But in reality, the woman was a con artist. She had never lived in Biloxi, did not have custody of her children, was on probation for a check-forging charge, and was under investigation by the Brooklyn district attorney's office. She was arrested shortly after Confessore's report ran in the paper.

The *Times* has fallen prey to several literary con jobs as well. A 2004 profile of the cult novelist JT LeRoy said the author had been a cross-dressing hooker who was rescued by a bohemian couple in San Francisco and a prominent psychiatrist. In 2006 it was revealed that JT LeRoy was a publicity invention, and the actual novelist was not a man. Then in 2008 there was the case of Margaret B. Jones and a memoir about a life submerged in the world of guns, crack, gang violence and police brutality in South Central Los Angeles, followed by a scholarship and graduation from the University of Oregon. In fact, Margaret B. Jones was really Margaret Seltzer, who had grown up in a Los Angeles suburb and graduated from a top private school, and got her "experience" of the gang and drug culture from conversations with people in coffee shops.

In a report from Iraq, the *Times* got snookered by an Iraqi human rights activist who claimed to be the Abu Ghraib detainee infamously photographed standing on a box with wires attached to his body. In fact, he was not that man, but was using the photo on his business card to whip up anger on a publicity tour of the Arab world. Another hoax related to the Iraq War came in a *Times Magazine* cover story about American servicewomen in Iraq. One of the subjects, a Navy construction worker, claimed to have been raped in Guam while awaiting deployment to Iraq, saying it was the second time she had been raped in the service. She also claimed to be suffering brain damage from an IED in Iraq. In fact, the Navy confirmed that she had never been to Iraq.

Ghosts of Frauds Past.   In addition to contemporary hoaxes, there were phantoms of frauds from earlier days, when they were still a rarity, that returned to haunt the *Times*. One of the most egregious involved Walter Duranty, the paper's Moscow correspondent for twelve years who won the 1931 Pulitzer Prize for his reporting on Stalin's Russia. At the time, the Pulitzer Prize Board said that Duranty's work showed "a profound and intimate comprehension of conditions in Russia" and was consistent with "the best type of foreign correspondence." His contemporaries in Russia saw differently. According to Malcolm Muggeridge, a British reporter, Duranty was "the greatest liar of any journalist I have met in 50 years of journalism." In exchange for access to Stalin and material privileges, his critics said, Duranty wrote favorably about Soviet policies of forced collectivization that later resulted in the deaths of millions due to famine in 1932 and 1933. To many, he became known as "Stalin's Apologist."

Duranty's Pulitzer had long posed a dilemma for the *Times,* although a portrait of Duranty still hung on the eleventh floor of the 43rd Street building, near the executive dining room. In 1990, an editorial on Duranty's apologetics chastised him for "indifference to the catastrophic famine . . . when millions perished in the Ukraine." There was discussion about giving the Pulitzer Prize back, but the *Times* stonewalled.

In 2003, pressure from Ukrainian American groups, who liken their famine to the Holocaust, prompted the Pulitzer Prize Board to open an investigation on rescinding Duranty's prize. Arthur Sulzberger hired Mark von Hagen, a Columbia historian, to perform an independent assessment of Duranty's work, expecting validation. Instead, von Hagen said that Duranty's reporting showed a "lack of balance and uncritical acceptance of the Soviet self-justification for its cruel and wasteful regime" that was a "disservice to the American readers of The New York Times." Sulzberger raised hackles when, without explanation, he cautioned that revoking the award was somewhat akin to the Stalinist urge "to airbrush purged figures out of official records and histories." Von Hagen was furious. Such "airbrushing" had been intended to suppress the truth about what was happening under Stalin, he shot back. "The aim of revoking Walter Duranty's prize is the opposite: to bring greater awareness of the potential long-term damage that his reporting did for our understanding of the Soviet Union." In the end, the Pulitzer Board voted not to rescind the award. Duranty's portrait continued to hang on the wall near the executive dining room until the *Times* moved to its new building in 2008.

Sulzberger's Financial Missteps.   The price of *Times* stock, which traded at about $53 a share during the Blair scandal, has dropped through the floor, as have quarterly operating profits and ad revenue, while circulation continues to decline. The paper's bond rating is practically "junk," and a cash flow crisis in 2009 led it to borrow from a Mexican investor at rates considered almost usurious. Wall Street has smelled blood, resulting in an unprecedented shareholder challenge through which one firm, Harbinger Capital, gained two seats on the board of directors.

Meanwhile, there have been company-wide layoffs and, for the first time, newsroom downsizing. Employee stock options and contributions to the Newspaper Guild's health fund have been adversely affected. The size of the paper itself has shrunk, with a 5 percent reduction in the space devoted to news.

The dark financial picture—a product of general newspaper industry dynamics as well as bad business decisions—has certainly not helped Sulzberger's eroded position. According to a *New Yorker* piece by Ken Auletta in 2006, the publisher had become "a particular source of concern," and in late 2005 a family friend asked, "Is Arthur going to get fired?" A *Times* staffer told *New York* magazine that no one at the paper felt in good hands "because people believe [Sulzberger] is an incredible boob."

·–

The bottom line? Instead of functioning as an impartial referee in the national conversation about controversial issues, the *New York Times* has become a cheerleader, an advocate, even a combatant, some critics have argued. Rather than maintain professional detachment and objectivity, the paper has embraced activism. Rather than foster true intellectual and ideological diversity, the paper has become the victim of an insular group-think, turning into a tattered symbol of liberal orthodoxy that is increasingly out of touch. And rather than let the chips fall where they may no matter who is embarrassed or shamed by their reporting, the paper's news sections have been shaded by a fear of offending certain groups and favoritism toward certain causes. Stories that should be done in a timely and responsible manner are often not done at all, or they are done years after news pegs for them have come and gone. Although the paper can be scrupulous about factual corrections, it has shown limited inclination or ability to come to terms with larger mistakes of meaning and interpretation, especially when doing so might transgress a liberal party line or expose its biases.

How precipitously this once-mighty institution has fallen and how deeply compromised its principles have become are questions inextricably entwined with what must now be regarded as the *Times'* ideological commitments: race and "diversity," immigration, homosexuality and gender, the "culture wars," and perhaps most crucially, its dismissive attitude toward the War on Terror, including U.S. military actions in Iraq and Afghanistan. In the sixties, Arthur Sulzberger Jr.'s favorite era, it was common to hear that "the personal is political." In the case of the *Times,* it is the personnel that have made for the politicization.

four
Race

In 1964, on assignment in Mississippi attending church services for three slain civil rights workers, Joseph Lelyveld, a *New York Times* reporter who would eventually become the paper's editor in chief, witnessed a scene so striking he included it in his 2005 memoir, *Omaha Blues:* "The network reporters, the wire service reporters, the *Time* magazine correspondent, and other newspaper reporters were all holding hands and singing. Having the idea that reporters weren't supposed to show their feelings or take sides, I was one of the abstainers. It was an uncomfortable moment."

That sense of professional detachment, very much a product of institutional tradition that was drilled into every reporter, especially during the Rosenthal years, has not endured. Today, when it comes to the issue of race, the *Times* is sitting front and center in the choir, singing with a moral fervor and gusto that would have been considered journalistically unseemly in the past. An orthodoxy of racial engagement and "diversity" now governs the personnel policies of its newsroom, but even more so the political sensibility behind much of its news coverage.

To some degree, the *Times* may be trying to use diversity to assuage a guilty conscience. In the 1940s the paper's first black reporter, George Streetor, had to be terminated after he was caught fabricating quotations and had amassed a considerable corrections file. After that was a long drought. A confidential company memo in 1961 revealed that the news department had only one black copy editor and only two black reporters; some departments had no blacks at all. There was also a marked shortage of news about the black community. Indeed, up until 1950, the NAACP considered the paper "anti-Negro." The racial unrest of the 1960s, particularly in Harlem, spurred management to open the paper's doors to a number of high-profile recruits. Yet the few who managed to take hold at the paper had little effect on what remained an overwhelmingly white newsroom.

In the early 1980s, as publisher-in-waiting Arthur Sulzberger Jr. began to preach the Gospel of Diversity more forcefully, Abe Rosenthal stepped up efforts to diversify the staff. In 1984 he actually gave a speech to the National Association of Black Journalists announcing a commitment to diversity, which would have been unthinkable for him ten years before.

One of the senior newsroom managers put in charge of this initiative was William Stockton, who had come to the *Times* in 1982 from the Associated Press, eventually rising to business news editor and sitting in on front-page meetings. Stockton's brief involved traveling to journalism schools and meeting qualified minority candidates whom the *Times* could either hire directly or tag as hopefuls to be watched while they developed their talent at "minor league" papers. As Stockton recalls, "There was fierce competition for essentially a very small group of people, to hire

someone who could make it. The struggle to hire people mini-
mally qualified—people who could do the job—was intense."

In his memoir, *The Times of My Life,* Max Frankel, who succeeded Rosenthal as executive editor in 1986, wrote that his exer-
tions for racial integration at the *Times* "were not just affirmative
but prodigious." Yet Frankel was wary of placing moral and legal
concerns over professionalism, having seen "the cause betrayed
by too many merely sentimental decisions." For him, it was
a pragmatic matter of avoiding situations where "Too often we
found ourselves discussing articles about racial strife without a
single black face in the room." Although great reporters "learn to
transcend their own experience and to deal with alien peoples and
strange surroundings," the need to gain the confidence of "contending factions" in newsworthy situations demanded the presence of reporters who could immediately cut through the cultural
baggage, Frankel believed.

Once Arthur Jr. took over the publisher's position in 1991,
the *Times* created more diversity-related managerial incentives
and requirements. According to Bill Stockton, the bonus program was changed to reflect how well managers did in minority
recruitment, training and retention, with 25 percent of the compensation based on how many journalists of color officially took
jobs. Stockton remembered senior-level editorial meetings where
Frankel and his second in command, Joe Lelyveld, put the squeeze
on their subordinates because of the pressure they felt from Sulzberger. Editors were asking, "Who can we send abroad? Put on
the national desk? Make bureau chief?" Stockton recalled, adding,
"They were pushing, really pushing. There was pressure all the
time."

But like the effort to hire minorities in the 1960s, the 1980s
initiative was hampered by an inability to hold on to minority
talent. "The truth," Frankel wrote, "was that we did have a problem
keeping people of color: the most successful blacks were repeatedly tempted by opportunities elsewhere and the least successful
were often left wondering whether they were victims of prejudice
or cultural alienation." Meanwhile, dissension was growing on the

white side of the newsroom. According to Frankel, the "diversity training" seminars that the *Times* sponsored were often "delivered by shameless charlatans," by "peddlers of pop psychology" who were indulged so the paper could "avoid being branded as racist." These sessions were an occasion for some black employees to demand that racial identifications be abandoned in news reports, even in the case of criminals at large. One editor even wanted a ban on all idiomatic negative uses of "black," such as "black magic" and "Black Monday," or even "film noir." Frankel's number two, Joe Lelyveld, thought the sessions a questionable expenditure, and withheld money that he thought was better spent in the news budget.

The most controversial and ultimately the most tragic beneficiary of the diversity campaign was the former managing editor Gerald Boyd. Although Boyd was not the Ivy League type historically favored by the *Times,* he "represented a terrifically hard-nosed black reporter that senior management could relate to," Bill Stockton maintained. "Someone who could be black but still fit in." The paper saw tremendous potential in Boyd. According to Stockton, "As Gerry Boyd moved up it became apparent to very senior management that he was their one best hope—their last best hope—to springboard a minority to the top." The plan, says Stockton, was to bring Boyd to New York and rotate him through various senior managerial positions. "If he did not fall flat on his face, he would be promoted to some top destination."

Boyd guided the paper's exceptional coverage of the 1993 World Trade Center bombing, and edited the year 2000 Pulitzer-winning fifteen-part series on race in America. But many blamed him for egregious and embarrassing miscoverage of a string of race-related incidents in New York in the early 1990s, including the infamous anti-Jewish riot in Brooklyn's Crown Heights in 1991. While Jews were clearly victims of the overwhelmingly black rioting, Boyd injected a tone of moral equivalence into the coverage he supervised, angering many New Yorkers.

Boyd's missteps, however, did not affect his upward mobility. In late 1990, Frankel had called the correspondent to New York and told him, in so many words, that he would be the *Times'* Jackie

Robinson. Adapting a page from the Branch Rickey handbook, he warned Boyd about "the tough time" ahead, "because a lot of people are going to be saying we're doing this because of your race—and to a degree we are, and I think you can handle that." Although he was passed over for managing editor when Joe Lelyveld became editor in chief in 1997, Boyd got the job when Howell Raines replaced Lelyveld in 2001. Boyd was now one step away from the very top, in a position of imminent historic significance, as Bill Stockton recalls: "The first black editor of the NYT!!! What a statement that would be for the Sulzbergers to make! To their peers. To the nation! See how far we have come—A black man as the editor of the NYT!"

But the Jayson Blair scandal—in which Boyd's documented racial favoritism toward a liar and plagiarist wound up destroying not only his career but that of Howell Raines as well—brought the chickens home to roost in terms of diversity's inherent double standards. "If this hadn't eventually blown up, and Gerry did get the top job, you would have had an African American shaping the news coverage of the nation's most important newspaper for more than a decade," Stockton said, adding that "Arthur just took it too far too fast."

Gerald Boyd died in November 2006, but left a memoir that was published in 2010, called *My Times in Black and White: Race and Power at The New York Times.* "Second only to my family, The Times defined me; I was addicted to the paper and all it represented, cloaking myself in its power and prestige," he wrote. In his *Times* review of Boyd's book, headlined "A Blessing and a Burden," Robert Boyton wrote: "Much of the book is devoted to the racial slights Boyd suffered during his 20 years at the paper. White subordinates bridled at taking orders from him; white superiors alternately patronized and betrayed him. 'The Times was a place where blacks felt they had to convince their white peers that they were good enough to be there,' he writes." Indeed, as elevated as the *Times* made him feel, Boyd also often felt "sandbagged, cornered and disrespected," and was especially bitter about taking the fall for the Blair scandal. He singled out Jonathan Landman, the Metro editor and generally regarded as a hero in the Blair case, as a man of "no decency and integrity" who had backstabbed him. A *Washington Post* reviewer wrote, "A skeptic—or just a good reporter—might find it hard to accept that a man who climbed so high at the politically driven Times could be as guileless as Boyd portrays himself."

·⤻

The *Times'* racial script, which has come to resemble the journalistic equivalent of reparations, is particularly evident in stories about instances of historical racism. Some of these stories are newsworthy and do a service in reminding readers of forgotten injustices that lie behind economic inequities, educational disparities, high incarceration rates and enduring prejudice against African Americans. But many others seem to have been assigned in the spirit of racial hectoring, which feeds what John McWhorter calls "therapeutic alienation in blacks" and creates an "exaggerated sense of victimization."

Stories on the retrial of those involved with the 1955 Emmett Till killing in 2005, for instance, were surely newsworthy, especially one that unearthed the only surviving transcript from an earlier acquittal. So were the stories about the sentencing of the yet-unpunished perpetrators of the 1963 Birmingham church bombing. Likewise Brent Staples' "editorial notebook" piece on the organized bloody pogrom that drove blacks from Wilmington, North Carolina, in 1898, an event that became a blueprint for other racist actions throughout parts of the South.

Yet the bulk of the *Times'* reporting and commentary on the racial past is distinguished by a sense of grievance and cynicism. The fiftieth anniversary of the landmark *Brown v. Board of Education* case, for instance, was not an occasion to celebrate for Adam Cohen, an editorial writer who instead wondered if the civil rights situation in America had become even worse. A 2005 report on the number of African immigrants coming to America—more than in the days of slavery, according to the reporter, Sam Roberts—allowed Howard Dodson, a radical activist at Harlem's Schomburg Center for Research in Black Culture, to assert that

"Basically, people are coming to reclaim the wealth that's been taken from their countries."

To a large degree, the *Times'* reporting and commentary on contemporary racial developments seems based on William Faulkner's famous comment that the past is never dead, it isn't even past. For example, voter identification laws in states like Georgia, Missouri and Indiana have been referred to editorially as the functional equivalent of an "illegal poll tax." According to the editorial writer Brent Staples, disqualification of convicted felons from voting "recalls the early U.S. under slavery" and is no different from tools used to limit the political power of emancipated slaves in the Jim Crow era.

Some of the stories on hate crimes against blacks that have appeared in the *Times* are deserving of the coverage, like the death of James Byrd, a Texas black man who was dragged behind a truck by racist whites in 1998, and a similar case in 2008. Yet in many other cases, the paper has been suckered by people who are perpetrating a scam or indulging in propaganda.

In October 2007, the *Times* got caught up in a racial hoax—as it had several times in the 1990s—because it was eager to break news of rampant white racism. The story involved the discovery of a four-foot-long hangman's noose on the doorknob of a black professor's office at Columbia University's Teachers College. The victim was Madonna G. Constantine, a professor of psychology and education, whose specialty is race, racial identity, multiculturalism and racial justice. The noose was particularly upsetting for Teachers College, which prides itself as "a bastion of liberalism and multiculturalism." The local police said that their hate-crimes unit had mounted a full investigation, including testing the rope for DNA. The Department of Justice opened an investigation.

Professor Constantine called the episode "an unbelievably blatant act of racism," telling about two hundred supporters who had gathered outside Teachers College that she would not be intimidated. "I want to let the perpetrator know that I will not be silenced." The *Times* gave ample space to accusations of racism. "This incident really gives you a new perspective on the state of race relations in this country," said Michael J. Feyen, a doctoral student at Teachers College. Another student insisted to the *Times* that "It's the latest and maybe most visible and extreme case of a climate of racism that we face in our entire society but of course is manifested at Columbia as well."

Yet the more street-smart *New York Post* and *Daily News,* citing unnamed sources, said the noose might have been the result of an academic dispute with a rival professor, who was white, which had led Constantine to file a lawsuit in May 2007 charging her with defamation. The investigation mounted by the Hate Crime Task Force of the New York Police Department yielded few leads or clues. But in June 2008, more than a year after the incident, the *Times* was forced to reveal that the university had fired Constantine after what was reported to have been an eighteen-month investigation found that charges of plagiarism against her were accurate. According to the school, Constantine had lifted material from two former students and a former colleague prior to the noose incident. In fact, Columbia had sanctioned the professor in February, but allowed her to stay in her job to appeal the ruling. Columbia, however, had never released that information, and the *Times,* which has close contacts and good sources at the school, either never found out about it or chose not to report it. To date, the *Times* has still never performed a postmortem, acknowledged its role in yet another racial hoax, or followed up in any way to determine who exactly was behind the noose, or whether Constantine should have been charged criminally.

Meanwhile, as responsive as the paper is to allegations of hate crimes against blacks, it has not demonstrated the same responsiveness in cases where the races are reversed and whites are the victims. In December 2000, for instance, Jonathan and Reginald Carr went on a heinous rape and killing spree in Wichita, Kansas. The two brothers were black; their victims were all white. After breaking into the residence of three young men, the Carr brothers forced the two women who were their guests to perform sexual acts on each other, and then forced the men to participate. The Carrs raped the women, and then drove the five victims to an ATM machine for money. Next they headed to a soccer field, where the victims were made to kneel in the snow and beg for their lives. All five were shot in the head, before the Carrs ran over them with their truck. One of the women survived and walked more than a mile in the snow for help; her fiancé was among those killed.

Two years later, the Carr brothers were found guilty of four counts of capital murder, along with rape, aggravated robbery, burglary and theft. As Michelle Malkin wrote in her account of the case, "The horrific James Byrd dragging case in Texas and the Matthew Shepard murder in Wyoming, for example, garnered front-page headlines and continuous coverage," yet there was little national coverage of the Wichita murders, and none at all from the *New York Times*. Malkin quoted one Wichita resident in a letter to the local paper: "If this had been two white males accused of killing four black individuals, the media would be on a feeding frenzy and every satellite news organization would be in Wichita doing live reports." Malkin concluded: "If you read The New York Times or The Washington Post or watched the evening news this week, the Wichita Massacre never happened."

In October 2004, in New York's East Village, a black man from Brooklyn shot three people and terrorized patrons in a bar, threatening to burn the place with kerosene and a lighter. At one point he held fifteen people hostage. At trial, prosecutors charged that the man was "on a mission of hate" to kill white people, and explained that the police had found tapes of anti-white rap music interspersed with the man's own anti-white rants. "Get ready to pull your guns out on these crackers, son. All they do is party and have a good time off of our expense, son," one tape said. "Blast the first couple you see having a good time. Let them visit your side of the tracks." If the racial roles were reversed, the *Times* would have given the case far more attention and used it for a springboard— as it has often done—for pieces that searched for Larger Racial Meanings. Instead, the case was buried in the Metro pages.

In April 2006, a New York University student emerged from the subway for a visit with an old friend who lived in a Harlem neighborhood. A gang of black teens attacked him. Fleeing into traffic, the student was struck by a car and died a few days later. The story was newsworthy: in a gentrifying neighborhood, gangs of black teens ("wolf packs," as the *New York Post* called them) were on the loose, systematically preying on people who appeared well-to-do, overwhelmingly white. Indeed, a similar case involving a black man chased into traffic by a white gang in the Howard Beach neighborhood of Queens in the late 1980s was given wall-to-wall coverage by the *Times* and eventually brought down Mayor Ed Koch. The death of the NYU student was covered by other New York papers. "Harlem Thugs Yuppie Hunting," read the *New York Post* headline. The *Times* mentioned the case in a one-paragraph "Metro Briefing."

Black crime in general causes skittishness at the *Times*, leading to classic liberal avoidance and denial. The perpetrators of these crimes are often portrayed as society's victims, with the high rates of black crime and incarceration blamed on institutional racism and "racial profiling" in the criminal justice system. This representation is actually a disservice to the very minority group that the *Times* would like to think it is protecting. Although blacks attack whites at a much higher rate than the reverse, the vast majority of victims in black crime are also black.

In January 2007, a young black man named Ronnell Wilson was convicted of killing two undercover police officers on Staten Island several years before. Both of the undercovers were black. Wilson faced a federal death penalty and, as Trymaine Lee put it in a *Times* report set in Wilson's neighborhood, "much of the [defense] testimony this week focused on Mr. Wilson's upbringing, on his struggling existence from an early age that his defense lawyers contend played a role at the moment he pulled the trigger." Lee's piece largely echoed the mitigating arguments of the defense attorneys. "While prosecutors paint Mr. Wilson as a cold-blooded killer, bully and gang member who depicted his violent lifestyle in rap lyrics," Lee wrote, "neighbors who knew him said he was just a young man lost."

After quoting other residents of the projects on the justice of the death penalty, Lee closed with the perspective of twenty-two-year-old Fred Tuller, who made Wilson seem like a mere victim of his environment. Tuller had told Lee that "it was a rough neighborhood to live in, that violence and poverty are seared into who they are and how they see themselves. He saw his first dead body at age 5 or 6. The victim had been shot and left for dead in the stairwell of his building." Lee described Tuller looking into the hills where the big houses seemed to be leering down on the neighborhood: "Look at us, in the middle of the projects, down here like lab rats," he said. "They're laughing at us."

Wilson's death sentence was reversed on appeal in July 2010, a decision the *Times* seemed to endorse in two news reports. The first one ended with Wilson's defense attorney saying she was "thrilled."

Another story that showed a little too much victimology involved the suspended season of Brooklyn's Paul Robeson High School basketball team in February 2007. Written by another young black reporter, Timothy Williams, the story was headlined "A Team Feared by Rivals Now Sits Idle, and Angry." Williams explained that a violent brawl during the final minutes of a game had led city athletic officials to bench the team for the rest of the season. The Paul Robeson team was perennially ranked among the best in the city, Williams reported, and had a chance to win the city title that year. It attracted scouts and coaches from basketball powerhouses, and players regularly received scholarships, some to NCAA Division One schools. But there was something "toxic" about the school's basketball program, Wilson noted. "Its popular former coach, Lawrence Major, committed suicide in 2005 at age 45 after being charged with statutory rape, accused of carrying on a three-year relationship with a student that started when she was 14." In past seasons, "several rival coaches have agreed to play games in Robeson's gym only if they bring their own security guards, saying they are fearful of being assaulted by Robeson fans. At least one coach has vowed never to take his basketball teams to Robeson again."

The incident that led to the suspension came after a hard foul on a rebound with thirty seconds remaining in a game against Thomas Jefferson High. A Robeson player then shoved the ball into the chest of the Jefferson player who had fouled. Benches of both teams cleared and the crowd surged out of the stands.

The Jefferson team was trapped in a corner as a violent confrontation ensued. The Jefferson team coach said it was a "Brooklyn mauling" and that "we had to fight for our lives."

Despite the obvious pathology of the Robeson team, Williams chose to focus on the dashed hopes of the players and their anger over being suspended, reporting that one player started to cry. Williams also endorsed the school principal's complaints that the punishment was too rough for the crime: "They wanted to send a real strong message, but it is not proportionate to the offense. The question we should be asking is, what lesson are these kids learning about fairness and justice?"

A hallmark of the *Times'* coverage of black crime is a fixation on racial profiling, which it sees as an expression of institutional racism in the criminal justice system. One example involved a study of speeding on the New Jersey Turnpike, conducted by the state in 2002, which concluded that blacks and Hispanics are more likely to speed than other drivers. The Metro editor, Jonathan Landman, proposed a story on it, which would have been an exclusive. But the study's conclusion rankled the sensitivities of Howell Raines, who had not read the report but nevertheless said that the methodology was flawed and that the *Times* was being "spun."

The story was held for a week. When it did run, it acknowledged a sizable gap between minorities and whites in speeding behavior, and noted that the issue was a political hot potato between civil libertarians and state troopers, but finished with liberal conventional wisdom: "Whatever the reasons for the speeding rates found in the study, civil rights advocates and lawyers said they cannot obscure the state's acknowledgment that racial profiling was an accepted tactic in the department for years."

The fixation on racial profiling appeared also in a 2007 report by Trymaine Lee, under the headline "As Officers Stop and Frisk, Residents Raise Their Guard." Its pull quote said, "In Brooklyn, some neighbors see searches as police harassment." Set in one of the most violent housing projects in the city, Brooklyn's Red Hook Houses, the piece was about the aggressive "stop and frisk" tactic taken up by the NYPD under Commissioner Raymond Kelly. It had taken many guns off the street and played an important role in dramatically reducing New York's murder rate.

Lee's story emphasized that more than half of those stopped and frisked by the police citywide were black. One of the Red Hook residents he interviewed, Mikel Jamison, said that in Brooklyn it was "hard being an African-American, hard to live and walk down the street without the police harassing us." After having a police officer jam a gun in his chest a few years ago, "in an incident he said he would rather not discuss," Lee wrote, "Mr. Jamison said he converted to Islam and is now more conscious of the way the community is affected by such police actions." (Why Lee allowed Jamison to dismiss the incident as something he "would rather not discuss" is journalistically dubious.)

Lee included fifteen paragraphs where residents disparaged the "stop and frisk" policy and just four where residents supported it. The closing paragraph described a press conference outside police headquarters the previous day, where representatives of black and Hispanic officers' groups called for Police Commissioner Kelly to step down. "These numbers substantiate what we've been saying for years," Lee quoted Noel Leader, a cofounder of 100 Blacks in Law Enforcement Who Care. "The New York Police Department under Raymond Kelly is actively committing some of the grossest forms of racial profiling in the history of the New York Police Department."

The commentary on the unfortunate encounter that Professor Henry Louis Gates of Harvard had with the Cambridge police in July 2009 provided the *Times* with another soapbox to denounce racial profiling. "The clash in Cambridge about ID and racial profiling, about identity and expectation and respect was just a snippet of our culture's ongoing meta-narrative about race," according to Judith Warner, a *Times* Web columnist. Bob Herbert devoted two columns to the case. In the first, headlined "Anger Has Its Place," he wrote: "Black people are constantly being stopped, searched, harassed, publicly humiliated, assaulted, arrested and sometimes killed by police officers in this country for no good reason." In the second column, headlined "Innocence Is No Defense," Herbert complained: "Young, old, innocent as the day is long—it doesn't matter. Your skin color can leave you perpetually vulnerable to a sudden and devastating injustice."

⸱⸱

In the past, a faith in integration had guided the *Times'* coverage of race, as revealed in the paper's response to the rise of the Black Power movement and its radical notions of cultural separatism. On the confrontation between the Student Nonviolent Coordinating Committee and Dr. Martin Luther King in 1966 over the issue of white involvement in the civil rights struggle, the *Times* ran an editorial under the headline "Black Power Is Black Death." It applauded the activist Roger Wilkins for telling the NAACP that "the way out of America's racial dilemma" was "the inclusion of the Negro American in the nation's life, not their exclusion." A year earlier, after Malcolm X was assassinated, a *Times* editorial decried his "ruthless and fanatical belief in violence."

By contrast, a *Times* news report about a Harlem exhibition in 2004 referred to Malcolm X as a "Civil Rights Giant" and extolled the exhibition for its description of a "driving intellectual quest for truth." When John Carlos and Tommie Smith had given the Black Power salute at the 1968 Olympic Games in Mexico City, the *Times* condemned the action; forty years later, the reporter Katie Thomas called it a "heroic gesture."

The *Times* has endorsed a separatist black identity by reporting favorably on Afrocentric education, which its supporters see as a way to overcome alienation and boost self-esteem in underperforming inner-city black schoolchildren, by teaching them that they are descendants of a scientifically and artistically rich African culture. The fans of Afrocentrism claim that Africa, not Europe, was the cradle of Western civilization, and that racist "Eurocentric" scholarship has systemically denied it. Afrocentric education also emphasizes a "distinctly black learning style."

To its critics, however, Afrocentrism is "a heavy dose of fantasy mixed with racism," and an "ethnic religion" based on shoddy scholarship, with a dangerous potential to encourage racial insularity and intolerance. Claims that black children learn differently from whites are largely seen by professional educators as nonsense, an effort to teach history as group therapy. The notion of introducing a separate black curriculum would undermine the function of the public school as an instrument to instill a common culture and a shared sense of the past.

The debate over Afrocentric education was one that the *Times* should have monitored closely. At the very least, the paper should have provided a complete and candid description of what Afrocentric educators were teaching, as well as an inventory of the pedagogical and scholarly assumptions these teaching materials embodied. Instead, the *Times* shrank from the challenge, and treated the competing claims about Afrocentrism as equally valid "perspectives" whose multiplicity should be celebrated. The *Times* ignored some of the more patently ridiculous claims and airbrushed uncomfortable realities about Afrocentrism as well as the controversy around it. For example, there was no research to support a link between self-esteem and educational achievement. Yet news analysis in the *Times* routinely quoted supporters of Afrocentrism making that linkage. The paper made no attempt to evaluate the strength of Afrocentric scholarship, including claims that Cleopatra (along with the rest of ancient Egypt) was black, and that Africans discovered mathematics, built the first airplanes and were the first to sail to America.

As far back as 1990, the education reporter Suzanne Daley produced a fairly critical report on Afrocentric education, quoting experts who questioned whether history should become an exercise in self-esteem, emphasizing what many experts called the pedagogical "slipperiness" of Afrocentrism, and explaining that much of its curriculum accented white scholarly conspiracies against African achievement. Daley's report set off protests by black staffers, who ensured that subsequent treatments of the subject were much more flattering and made supporters sound more convincing than critics. In one of those later treatments, Calvin Sims, a black reporter, claimed that the "scholarly underpinnings" of Afrocentric theories and curricula were "firm" and based on "the work of scholars who are trained in the ancient classics of northern Europe and Africa."

The *Times* also affirms separatist values in its coverage of the black family and the problem of illegitimacy. As already noted, back in the 1960s the paper had no problem with making value judgments about black illegitimacy. It gave sympathetic treatment to Daniel Patrick Moynihan's famous report on the cultural disarray of "the negro family," which was attacked by civil rights leaders and leftist publications. The *Times* reporter John Herbers explained that Moynihan's work was not intended to fuel contempt for black Americans by drawing attention to the problem of illegitimacy; rather, its purpose was to show that "white America by means of slavery, humiliation and unemployment has so degraded the Negro male that most lower class Negro families are headed by females." This, Herbers quoted Moynihan approvingly, had made it impossible for "Negroes as a group to compete on even terms in the US."

Today the general public has no trouble seeing the prophetic nature of Moynihan's argument. In 1965, when he first tried to draw attention to the problem, the rate of black illegitimacy was 25 percent; by 2009 it was 70 percent. A consensus has emerged on solutions, emphasizing welfare reform, which it is hoped will make young, out-of-wedlock motherhood an undesirable experience for teenage girls. But for most of the last two decades, when the debate has been sharpest, the *Times* has been reluctant to admit that the issue is serious and has disparaged proposals floated to address it.

The *Times* has been remiss, too, in reporting on social policy for dysfunctional black families and their relationship to the foster care system in New York City. In the early 1990s, the city began an experiment aimed at better protecting the black and Latino children whose parents have lost custody to the foster care system. The experiment was the work of Robert Little, the brother of Malcolm X and himself a former foster child, who believed that black children placed in white foster homes would lose their "black identity." This racist assumption was shared most ardently by a child welfare advocate named Luis Medina, who believed, as the *Times* would write in late 2007, "that foster care in New York had become an evil and racist system that was engaged in little more than rounding up poor minority children." At another point, Medina said the foster care system felt like "some version of apartheid."

Medina took over a venerable child care agency called St. Christopher's, based up the Hudson River in Dobbs Ferry, New York. As the *Times* retroactively explained,

> *He hired additional black and Latino caseworkers, and made a priority of appointing minorities to the agency's board of directors. He promised to recruit local foster parents from the same neighborhoods as the children coming into their care. He argued that black and Latino families had a "sacred right" to stay together, and pledged that his agency would do everything it could to keep intact the families torn by poverty, illness and drugs.*

As a symbolic touch, Medina ordered that the pictures of white children at the agency's administrative office be replaced with pictures of black and Latino children.

Eventually, St. Christopher's would expand, opening offices in the Bronx and in Harlem. But Medina's ideology began to divide the staff, and some felt there was too much operational chaos. "Mr. Medina's main Bronx office became overrun by parents, some of whom were dangerous and some of whom came simply to hang out," the *Times* wrote in 2007. "The presence of the parents—often confused or furious—and a chronic shortage of staff created disorder, particularly during visiting hours with their children. Telephones could go unanswered, dirty diapers often collected in the corners, toilets went unfixed, fights broke out, children were snatched."

According to Starr Lozada, a caseworker based in Medina's River Avenue office in the Bronx in 2004, "The birth parents would come and hang out all day. Maybe they would come for the breakfast. Talk with each other. Stay until we closed." The parents would bring in people from the neighborhood, and there would be screaming and carrying on. "We felt unsafe," Lozada said.

As this chaos was brewing, the *Times* ran a front-page piece on St. Christopher's in 1995, extolling Medina and his approach in an account that relied on unverifiable claims by parents who either had been involved with or were still involved with drugs or alcohol, or domestic violence. A father claimed that after his son was taken from them, he and his wife walked into St. Christopher's–Jennie Clarkson prepared to fight a hostile bureaucracy. Instead, they found case supervisors who promised to do everything they could to help the parents regain custody. "You have to give people something to shoot for," one senior supervisor was quoted as saying, "not just hold something over their heads." The 1995 article quoted Jeremy Kohomban, director of family services: "Most important was a shift of power from agency workers to parents."

A dozen years later, in the 2007 article, the *Times* did finally get around to acknowledging the problems at St. Christopher's—problems in its racial philosophy and also in its operational administration. But by then the damage had been done. "Children with St. Christopher's, city records show, were abused or neglected at disturbing rates," the article reported. "Family Court judges and lawyers cited the agency for years for ineptitude in handling children's cases. In 2002, St. Christopher's got so few children adopted that the city gave it a grade of zero in its performance scoring system. And from 1999 to 2005, seven children whose families had been involved with St. Christopher's wound up dead."

To be sure, the *Times'* approach to the black family has undergone welcome change, as its retrospective on St. Christopher's shows. In a mid-2005 column headlined "Dad's Empty Chair," Bob Herbert wrote: "I don't have the statistics to prove it, but black kids would be tremendously better off if the cultural winds changed and more fathers felt the need to come home." For Herbert it was an easy call: "Moms are crucial. Dads too." Yet if we—and the *Times*—are at what the sociologist Kay Hymowitz calls a cultural inflection point that portends change, "the lost generations of ghetto men, women, and children" could be forgiven if they found "cold comfort" in this much-overdue shift.

A double standard has been manifest in how the *Times* treats black political figures, going easy on black demagogues such as Louis Farrakhan and machine politicians such as New York City's first black mayor, David Dinkins. And it has practically given a gold-plated free pass to New York's premier racial agitator, Al Sharpton.

No matter what his sins against the civic fabric—Tawana Brawley, Crown Heights, the Harlem Massacre at Freddy's Department Store—Sharpton has been rehabilitated on a regular basis. When he ran for the U.S. Senate in 1993, the *Times Magazine* ran a cover story called "The Reformation of a Street Preacher." Omitting his more incendiary remarks during the 1991 Crown Heights riots and his controversial actions at other racially fraught moments, the magazine said that Sharpton was now "softer, more focused, more intellectually polished." His comments about "white interlopers" had certainly raised the rabble in the 1995 Harlem Massacre, which culminated when a black militant set fire to a Jewish-owned department store next to a black-owned record business that was losing its lease, after which he shot a number of the department store's employees, resulting in seven deaths in addition to that of the gunman, who took his own life. But the *Times* threw another life preserver to Sharpton, who was "Buoyant in a Storm" according to a report by Charisse Jones. Ignoring the damning evidence of his role in the massacre, Jones said that Sharpton was playing the role of "consoler, conciliator and political jouster." She even let Sharpton claim the victim's mantle: "In my life I've had to walk alone sometimes. . . . I've been lied on, I've been talked about, mistreated, stabbed and indicted. But through it all, I've learned to trust in Jesus. I've learned to trust in God. It's only a test."

More recently, in 2008, Sharpton attached the loaded term "greedy" to Anthony Weiner, a New York City councilman (now a U.S. congressman) who is Jewish. The slur elicited no response from any *Times* columnists or its editorial board. As the urban historian Fred Siegel observed in the wake of the Harlem Massacre, "After each major outrage, Mr. Sharpton draws in the press and some selected rubes, and assures them that this time he's really reformed." And the *Times*—along with other media—effaces the facts of Sharpton's role from the public record "Stalinist-style," stuffing them down a "memory hole."

It's one thing for the *Times'* double standards to throw a lifeline to a race hustler like Al Sharpton, allowing him to secure respectability as a national civil rights leader despite an ongoing record of racial arson. Yet it was something else when the *Times* became a pep squad for the 2008 presidential campaign of Barack Obama. When John McCain's campaign manager, Steve Schmidt, said during the campaign that the *Times* was "completely, totally, 150% in the tank" for Obama, he was dismissed as a biased observer. But the charge itself sticks. Mark Halperin, a straight shooter from *Time* magazine, uses the *New York Times'* reporting as Exhibit A in making a case that coverage of the 2008 campaign was "the most disgusting failure of people in our business since the Iraq war."

Halperin did not analyze the underlying reasons for that bias, but looking through the *Times'* coverage it is absolutely clear that the favoritism is racial. The first and foremost example of favoritism toward Obama in the *New York Times* was the protective coverage it offered regarding his relationship with the Reverend Jeremiah Wright, pastor of Chicago's Trinity United Church of Christ. Obama had belonged to Trinity United for nearly two decades, and credited Wright's sermons as a major factor in bringing him to Christianity. Obama was married there and his two daughters were baptized there too. Wright blessed Obama's house, and Obama says that one of Wright's sermons furnished the title of his second book, *The Audacity of Hope*.

In a sermon delivered on the Sunday after September 11, 2001, Wright notoriously told his congregation that the United States had brought on al-Qaeda's attacks because of its own terrorism:

We bombed Hiroshima, we bombed Nagasaki, and we nuked far more than the thousands in New York and the Pentagon,

and we never batted an eye. We have supported state ter-
rorism against the Palestinians and black South Africans,
and now we are indignant because the stuff we have done
overseas is now brought right back to our own front yards.
America's chickens are coming home to roost.

Other sermons included charges that the U.S. government invented AIDS to kill black people, and that Israel and South Africa invented an ethnic bomb that would kill Arabs and blacks but spare whites and Jews. Wright endorsed Louis Farrakhan— anti-Semitism and all—and traveled with him to visit Muammar Gaddafi in Libya. He called the United States "the U.S. of KKK A," and recommended that the slogan "God bless America" be changed to "God damn America."

Yet even with all this material so readily available, when Obama disinvited Wright from making the invocation at the official launch of his presidential campaign in March 2007, the *Times* reported on Wright's radical comments in a way that blandly euphemized them, and characterized Trinity United as a "mainstream" church, scrubbing the more extreme aspects of its Afrocentric theological bearings. A follow-up article by Jodi Kantor at the end of April referred to Wright as "a dynamic pastor who preached Afrocentric theology, dabbled in radical politics and delivered music-and-pro-fanity-spiked sermons." Kantor referred to Wright's "assertions of widespread white racism and his scorching remarks about American government," but left out the "God damn America," and instead of reporting that Wright believed and preached that the U.S. government invented AIDS as a tool of racial euthanasia, she merely said that "Like conservative Christians, he speaks of AIDS as a moral crisis." Of the controversial 9/11 remarks, she simply wrote that "On the Sunday after the terrorist attacks of 9/11, Mr. Wright said the attacks were a consequence of violent American policies."

Kantor also gave Obama a wide berth to contextualize Wright's remarks and explain how he was probably "trying to be provoca-tive." Reverend Wright was "a child of the 60s," Obama noted, "and he often expresses himself in that language of concern with institutional racism and the struggles the African-American community has gone through. . . . He analyzes public events in the context of race. I tend to look at them through the context of social justice and inequality."

In March 2008, almost a year after Kantor's airbrushed pieces, ABC News broadcast the most incendiary of the clips from Wright's sermons it had secured, including "No, no, no, not God bless America; God damn America!" This triggered a media frenzy, putting Obama in the harshest spotlight he would face in his campaign.

The *Times* duly reported on the controversy, and finally reported Wright's inflammatory remarks about 9/11, although it didn't directly quote "God damn America" in any news story and didn't address Obama's blatant lies about not knowing of Wright's offensive statements. Even some Obama backers, such as Gerald Posner, were dubious: "If the parishioners of Trinity United Church were not buzzing about Reverend Wright's post 9/11 comments, then it could only seem to be because those comments were not out of character with what he preached from the pulpit many times before."

The "no-go" zone that the *Times* erected around Obama also encompassed "black liberation theology," to which Reverend Wright was committed. On the Trinity United website, Wright cited James Cone, a professor at New York's Union Theological Seminary, as the one who "systematized" this strain of Christianity. Cone had written, "If God is not for us and against white people, then he is a murderer, and we had better kill him." In the *Times*, however, black liberation theology came off merely as something "different" from what whites were used to hearing.

According to Jodi Kantor's first article in 2007, black liberation theology "interprets the Bible as the story of the struggles of black people, who by virtue of their oppression are better able to understand Scripture than those who have suffered less." A longer analysis by Michael Powell in May 2008, headlined "Race and the Race: A Fiery Theology under Fire," called Reverend Wright a "man of capacious learning and ego," and "one of the foremost adherents of this [black liberation] theology." Powell quoted James Cone in a jocular mood, chuckling as he remarked, "You might say we took our Christianity from Martin and our emphasis on blackness from Malcolm."

For his part, Obama would not give up Wright. But as pressure mounted, he and his campaign decided that Obama should make a major speech on race in America, a speech which some later saw as one of American political history's great orations, while others dismissed it as a "subject-changing speech." There was some criticism of the speech at the *New York Times*. Maureen Dowd saw through the lofty rhetoric and charged that it was pitched to superdelegates queasy about Obama's spiritual guide, the virulent racial pride, the separatism, the deep suspicion of America and the white man—the very things that Obama's "postracial" identity was supposed to transcend. Dowd, almost alone, underscored the fact that Obama had now reversed his previous statement that he had never heard any of Wright's controversial remarks while he sat in the pews. But she also lent a note of tough-love support: "Leaders don't need to be messiahs."

Yet almost everything else the *Times* ran on the speech was celebratory, with the editorial, op-ed and news pages so harmonically converged that it was hard to tell the difference. There was no notice, let alone evaluation, of Obama's equating his grandmother's private prejudices with the systemized racial hatred that underlay Wright's comments and worldview. Nor did anyone at the *Times* note the speech's central contradiction, as Rich Lowry did, that "In the end, Obama made the case for the respectability of a man who is a hater—and did it, amazingly enough, in a speech devoted to ending divisiveness."

Janny Scott's starry-eyed "news analysis" called it "a speech whose frankness about race many historians said could be likened only to speeches by Presidents Lyndon B. Johnson, John F. Kennedy and Abraham Lincoln." While it acknowledged the country's troubled racial past, she wrote, "the speech was also hopeful, patriotic, quintessentially American—delivered against a blue backdrop and a phalanx of stars and stripes." Scott also quoted Obama supporters and longtime activist-intellectuals like John Hope Franklin and a tearful Julian Bond, but her analysis featured no one with a less triumphalist point of view.

Under unremitting pressure, although not from the *Times,* Obama eventually gave up on Wright and cut his ties to Trinity United Church of Christ. Wright made a series of appearances where his fury was noticeable and bizarrely expressed. In late April 2008, for instance, he gave a televised sit-down interview with Bill Moyers, a speech to the NAACP, and a press conference at the National Press Club in Washington. In his publicity trifecta, he claimed that attacks on him and Obama were really attacks on the black church. He refused to apologize for his "God damn America" remark and also refused to retract his claim that AIDS was an invention of the U.S. government, citing the Tuskegee experiment to argue that the government was "capable of anything." Along the way, he also compared U.S. troops to the Roman legions who murdered Christ.

The *Times* barely covered the Moyers interview and the NAACP event, but finally, after the Press Club appearance, did a front-pager on the publicity spree. Yet the effect of the piece, written by the television reporter Alessandra Stanley and headlined "Not Speaking for Obama, Pastor Speaks for Himself, at Length," was to trivialize the issues raised by the whole controversy. "Mr. Wright, Senator Barack Obama's former pastor, was cocky, defiant, declamatory, inflammatory and mischievous, but most of all, he was all over the place, performing a television triathlon of interview, lecture and live news conference that pushed Mr. Obama aside and placed himself front and center in the presidential election campaign," Stanley wrote. "And he went deep into context—a rich, stem-winding brew of black history, Scripture, hallelujahs and hermeneutics."

Meanwhile, the *Times'* coverage of the McCain campaign was riddled with unfair political characterizations and cheap shots, delving into the personal lives of the candidate and his wife, Cindy, with journalistic ethics worthy of the *National Enquirer.* Part of the problem was the depth of coverage, as well as the tone. A careful analysis by the TimesWatch website of the coverage from June

5 to July 5 found that of the 90 stories the *Times* did on Obama, 40 (44 percent) could be classified as positive portrayals, while only 13 (14 percent) were negative, for a positive-negative ratio of 3:1. The remaining 37 were described as neutral. During the same month, the *Times* published 57 stories on McCain, of which only 9 were positive (16 percent), compared with 24 negative (42 percent) and 24 neutral. This made for a positive-negative ratio of nearly 1:3, the opposite of Obama's positive ink.

The Obamamania of the *Times* also surfaced in stories about political rallies along the campaign trail. Obama's were portrayed as something like transcendental be-ins, with huge crowds, exhibiting political intelligence as well as diversity. By contrast, McCain's rallies were depicted as being filled with "Weimar-like rage," as Frank Rich described it, alluding to pre-Nazi Germany.

The *Times* went disproportionately hard on McCain's campaign advertising as well. Ads that questioned Obama's honesty were dismissed as either misleading or a breach of the civility that McCain had originally pledged. Ads that questioned the politically explosive subject of Obama's association with the former Weather Underground terrorist William Ayers were criticized as the hack work of right-wing zealots and an echo of the Swiftboat crew from 2004.

One particularly egregious case of double standards involved a McCain op-ed piece backing "the surge" in Iraq that the *Times* rejected shortly after it had run one against the surge by Obama. The *Columbia Journalism Review,* hardly a right-wing publication, said that the *Times*' "tenuous arguments about [the] newsworthiness" of McCain's op-ed fed "the paper's reputation as a vehicle for thinly veiled liberal bias." In a cable segment on the issue, the former Clinton press aide DeeDee Meyers said it was a "legitimate question" to ask how "balanced" between the two candidates the coverage was. Even some Timesmen were scratching their heads. On the cable show *Hardball,* the paper's political writer John Harwood said: "The question is how different is the standard when you are talking about a nominee of a major party to be president of the United States. . . . I was surprised that they did not take it, especially having just run Barack Obama."

But it was the *Times'* disparate treatment of the candidates' personal lives that most clearly underlined a pro-Obama bias. Exhibit A was the front-page investigative report that was intended to be a window into McCain's reputation as a reformer, a reputation he made after an early fall from grace involving the "Keating Five" banking scandal. But the story quickly became notorious for insinuating that McCain had had an affair with a lobbyist more than thirty years his junior—without ever citing anything resembling journalistic proof, except the accusation made by one admittedly "disgruntled" former staffer. At least 20 out of the article's 61 paragraphs concerned the alleged romantic relationship. The McCain campaign denounced the "gutter politics" of the *Times* and its "hit and run smear campaign." The article also drew criticism from the paper's public editor, Clark Hoyt, who scorned editor Bill Keller's explanation that the story was about McCain's reckless behavior and potential conflicts of interest, not about an affair.

A late-campaign profile of McCain's wife, Cindy, reflected the same hostility. Written by Jodi Kantor, whose reporting on Jeremiah Wright had been understanding to an extreme, the story was a hatchet job of the first order and catty to boot. Kantor claimed that Cindy McCain was not liked by other congressional wives and was so neglected by her husband that her parents occasionally bought her presents on his behalf. In an effort to impeach her truthfulness, Kantor criticized Cindy's assertion that she had gone to Rwanda during the genocide for relief work when she had "only" gone to the Rwanda-Zaire border. It was later learned that Kantor, in trying to get a take on what kind of mother Cindy McCain was, had actually gone on Facebook to contact some of her daughter's friends.

"Vicious" was the word Mark Halperin of *Time* used to describe the story. "It looked for every negative thing they could find about her and it cast her in an extraordinarily negative light. It didn't talk about her work, for instance, as a mother for her children, and they cherry-picked every negative thing that's ever been written about her." It was the Cindy McCain profile, along with the story of an extramarital affair, that Halperin cited when he castigated the press for its "extreme bias, extreme pro-Obama coverage" in the 2008 election campaigns.

In addition to criticizing his opponent, the *Times* helped Obama with image management, particularly about his racial background. The fact that Obama had a black Kenyan father and a white American mother who took him to Indonesia for several years when he was a child prompted anxiety about his roots—and his religion. The *Times* took several different tacks in trying to keep the candidate from appearing as "the Other." One strategy, typified by the columnist Roger Cohen, was to extol Obama's multicultural roots. In a column about some of his far-flung relatives, Cohen wrote that "If elected, Obama would be the first genuinely 21st-century leader. The China-Indonesia-Kenya-Britain-Hawaii web mirrors a world in flux. . . . Obama's bridge-building instincts come from somewhere. They are rooted and proven. For an expectant and often alienated world, they are of central significance."

Another strategy was to emphasize Obama's alleged connections to the heartland. For instance, Alessandra Stanley wrote about "Obama's hardscrabble Kansas roots." But Obama had never lived in Kansas. He was born in Hawaii and returned there from Indonesia to live with his grandparents, who had moved there from Kansas to help Obama's single mother. In fact, Obama had never even been to his grandfather's hometown in Kansas until 2008.

The *Times* showed the same kind of reluctance to examine Obama's relationship to Bill Ayers as it had in the case of Jeremiah Wright. Ayers had been a founder of the Weather Underground, the antiwar terrorist group of the Vietnam War era, and had participated in bombings in New York and Washington D.C. After emerging from years underground, he had become an educational activist in Chicago and published a memoir called *Fugitive Days,* about which the *Times* wrote a feature article that appeared on September 11. In the ill-timed story, Ayers bragged about his days as a domestic terrorist and stated he "did not do enough."

Since Obama and Ayers ran in the same circle in Chicago, and since Ayers and his wife, Bernardine Dohrn (also a former Weatherman), hosted Obama's first fundraiser when he ran for his first political office as Illinois state senator in 1996, the association was red meat for those suspicious of Obama. Even centrist organizations like ABC News and *Politico* said it was a legitimate issue to explore, cutting to questions of Obama's character and his political and ideological bearings. Yet for some at the *Times,* the mere asking of the question was "a disgusting spectacle," as the media reporter David Carr phrased it.

Less than a month before the election, as the McCain campaign itself began to raise the question, Scott Shane reported in the *Times* that Ayers and Obama "do not appear to be close." He soft-pedaled the fact that both had served for almost ten years on the boards of the Woods Foundation and the Chicago Annenberg Challenge, two blue-ribbon charities; instead, he bought Obama's claim that their contact over the years was only "sporadic." And rather than acknowledge that Obama lied about his connection to Ayers, Shane merely said that he had "played down" the relationship. Conservative media critics called Shane's report less an investigation than "an inoculation."

The *New York Times* that appeared the day after Obama's electoral victory was the journalistic equivalent of a ticker-tape parade celebrating victory in a hard-fought war. The *Times* broke out a 32-page special section, "President Obama," that was hard to distinguish from a fanzine. "In a country long divided," Rachel Swarns wrote, "Mr. Obama had a singular appeal: he is biracial and Ivy League educated; a stirring speaker who shoots hoops and quotes the theologian Reinhold Niebuhr; a politician who grooves to the rapper Jay-Z and loves the lyricism of the cellist Yo-Yo Ma; a man of remarkable control and startling boldness . . . ."

Writing from Washington on Inauguration Day, Francis X. Clines of the editorial board rhapsodized that Obama's very name was a "healing mantra." Dennis Overbye, a science reporter, soon wrote of weeping in relief that the incoming administration would lift the "dark cloud" hanging over "the scientific community in this country." When Obama vowed to harness wind and solar energy and to "wield technology's wonders," Overbye said he "felt the glow of a spring sunrise washing my cheeks, and I could almost imagine I heard the music of swords being hammered into plowshares." The Obama administration had a long honeymoon at the *Times,* which cheered on the new president's most important foreign policy and domestic initiatives and often appeared to cover for his blunders.

The paper was especially keen on Obama's efforts at rapprochement with the Islamic world, giving generous accolades to the speech he delivered in Cairo in June 2009—a speech shaped by political correctness and cultural relativism. Not once did Obama say the words "Islamic extremism" or "jihadism." Instead, he referred generically to "violent extremists." His account of the achievements of Islamic civilization was flattering and fallacious, as Victor Davis Hanson pointed out:

> *In the Cairo speech, nearly every historical allusion was nonfactual or inexact: the fraudulent claims that Muslims were responsible for European, Chinese, and Hindu discoveries; the notion that a Christian Córdoba was an example of Islamic tolerance during the Inquisition; the politically correct canard that the Renaissance and Enlightenment were fueled by Arab learning; the idea that abolition and civil rights in the United States were accomplished without violence—as if 600,000 did not die in the Civil War, or entire swaths of Detroit, Gary, Newark, and Los Angeles did not go up in flames in the 1960s.*

Fouad Ajami of Johns Hopkins remarked that the speech highlighted the need for Obama to recognize "the foreignness of foreign lands." Ajami also took the air out of those who asserted that the speech was a big hit on the Arab street, reporting in the *Wall Street Journal* that some there remarked that Obama "talks too much."

Yet the speech was music to the *Times'* ears. An editorial headlined "The Cairo Speech" maintained that eight years of George Bush's "arrogance and bullying" had made the country unrecognizable. "His vision was of a country racked with fear and bent on vengeance, one that imposed invidious choices on the world and on itself. When we listened to President Obama speak in Cairo on Thursday, we recognized the United States."

The *Times'* infatuation with Obama continued in its support for his health care agenda, popularly known as "Obamacare." To be sure, the *Times* had its truck with the effort. But its criticism did not focus on the shadowy horse-trading behind the bill, nor on how it would affect the deficit, nor on the constitutional issue of the federal government forcing citizens to buy insurance or face a penalty. Its major criticism came from Obama's left, especially when he backed away from the so-called "public option," and seemed to be dragging his feet in using his bully pulpit to lobby lawmakers, particularly Democratic representatives who might lose their seats in the midterm elections. When the final bill passed, the *Times* hailed it in practically messianic terms. Carl Hulse's front-page story on March 21, "Another Long March in the Name of Change," likened the passing of the bill to "society-shifting" milestones in the civil rights movement. A report filed by Robert Pear and David Herszenhorn was headlined "Obama Hails Vote on Health Care as Answering 'the Call of History.'" The editorial page was effusive too. "Barack Obama put his presidency on the line for an accomplishment of historic proportions," read "Health Care Reform, at Last."

Obama's initial steps toward immigration reform in June 2010 also stirred the *Times,* which opined that "President Obama's first major speech on immigration had the eloquence and clarity we have come to expect when he engages a wrenching national debate." In a dig at the majority of Americans who want border enforcement before any legalization of the undocumented, the editorial pronounced Obama correct in maintaining that "sealing off that vast space [the border] with troops and fences alone is a fantasy."

Even the Obamas' domestic life in the White House elicited a swoon. In October 2009, the *Times Magazine* ran a 7,500-word cover story titled "The Obamas' Marriage," by Jodi Kantor, who said "the Obamas mix politics and romance in a way that no first couple quite have before." Then, in November, Kantor was reported to have received a seven-figure deal from Little, Brown for a book on Obama.

The *Times'* cheerleading for Obama was heavily underscored by its unstinting criticism of his chief opposition during his first year—the Tea Party. Although they almost always came across as angry and strident in the *Times,* the Tea Partiers raised many issues that were perfectly legitimate, such as taxation and immigration policy, and what role the federal government should play in the lives of individual citizens.

One particularly unfair aspect of the *Times'* disparagement of the Tea Party concerned the extent to which race and racism animated the movement. Yes, there were a few ugly moments of churlishness where race may have played a role. But to say that the ranks of the Tea Party were "foul, mean-spirited and bigoted" and that the movement "genuflects at the altar of right-wing talk radio, with its insane, nauseating nonstop commitment to hatred and bigotry," as Bob Herbert did in his March 22 column, was to outstrip the facts. Echoing Herbert a few days later was the columnist Charles Blow, who charged the Tea Partiers with "rabid bigotry" and an underlying white fear over changing demographics. "President Obama and what he represents has jolted extremists into the present and forced them to confront that future. And it scares them."

The *Times'* obsession with the alleged racism of the Tea Party was summed up well by the *Wall Street Journal's* James Taranto: "When the only tool you have is a hammer, every problem looks like a nail."

·ﻭ

Like race in politics, another subject whose coverage is laced with double standards is affirmative action and "diversity" as it pertains to the civil services and government contracting, and especially higher education. As John Leo has written, diversity has become a kind of "civic religion" at the *Times,* and it isn't surprising. "Having made diversity such an obsession in its own newsroom, it is hard for reporters and editors to maintain professional detachment about racial preferences elsewhere in society."

The *Times* has shown predictable bias in its coverage of pivotal Supreme Court rulings involving diversity, especially the ambiguous justification the idea received in the 2003 *Gratz v. Bollinger* decision regarding university admissions. But its bias may be even sharper toward diversity in the composition of the Court itself. This was especially so during the confirmation hearings for Sonia Sotomayor, who was nominated from her seat on the U.S. Court of Appeals for the Second Circuit in the spring of 2009.

As a lower court judge, Sotomayor, a Puerto Rican New Yorker, had pushed for quotas for Latino and black policemen. In *Ricci v. DeStephano,* she wrote a key decision as part of the appellate court that ruled against white firefighters in Connecticut who claimed they had been discriminated against when the City of New Haven threw out a promotion exam because blacks scored disproportionately low. She also had a long string of remarks in her record reflecting a commitment to identity politics that bordered on racial and ethnic chauvinism. In one 2001 speech she said, "I would hope that a wise Latina woman with the richness of her experiences would more often than not reach a better conclusion [as a judge] than a white male who hasn't lived that life." She referenced her "Latina soul" and argued that diversity on the bench was necessary because "inherent physiological or cultural differences make a difference in our judging."

These were signs of a judicial philosophy that put race and ethnicity ahead of legal reasoning, and conservatives rightly went after her. But the *Times* stood as one of her staunchest defenders. When the White House announced her nomination, the headline of a report by Sheryl Gay Stolberg referred to Sotomayor as "A Trailblazer and a Dreamer." As Sotomayor moved through the Senate confirmation process, Manny Fernandez produced a string of valentines to the judge as "a daughter of the Bronx." His story about the reaction of students in Sotomayor's old parochial school at least had a solid peg, but two others following it were built on air. One focused on a lawyer in private practice who served mostly lower-income clients and felt pride in Sotomayor's life story. The other was a slice of life at the Bronx courthouse, where Sotomayor had never served.

A glowing biographical take-out of more than 2,000 words, written by three reporters, was headlined "To Get to Sotomayor's Core, Start in New York—Milestones in Work and Life, Set to a City's Rhythms." The piece described the judge's common touch: the Christmas parties "where judges and janitors spill into the hallway"; her status as "godmother to the children of lawyers and secretaries alike." The media critic Mary Katherine Ham noted that all this might indicate character, "Unless, of course, Sotomayor approaches her relationships in the same way the *New York Times* writes about them—collecting blue collar chits and counting friends of color as karmic cool points."

In response to complaints about Sotomayor's racialism, the *Times* editorial page charged that such grumbling was racism in disguise. Conservative groups and Republican elected officials saw the nomination "as a way to score points off wedge issues that excite their base," read one editorial. "It diminishes everyone when a nomination process deteriorates into character assassination and ethnic intolerance." In his column, Bob Herbert wrote, "One can only hope that the hysterical howling of right-wingers against the nomination of Sonia Sotomayor to the Supreme Court is something approaching a death rattle for this profoundly destructive force in American life." Maureen Dowd followed up with a column headlined "White Man's Last Stand." Sotomayor would "bring a fresh perspective to the court," Dowd wrote. "It was a disgrace that W. [George Bush Jr.] appointed two white men to a court stocked with white men."

Sotomayor ultimately passed muster. But the case involving the New Haven firefighters, or at least the side on which she had ruled, did not. In the middle of her confirmation battle, the Supreme Court ruled 5-4 that New Haven had acted illegally when it threw out the promotional exam on which minority firefighters had done poorly. In response, the *Times* editorial page warned darkly that the decision "dealt a blow to diversity in the American workplace."

⌐

Given its commitment to the notion that America's racial past still weighs on the present, it is no surprise that the *Times'* reporting on big national stories is heavy on white oppression and black victimization. During the Hurricane Katrina catastrophe, the *Times* performed some great reporting in a chaotic and hysterical environment that had qualities of a Mad Max movie. But it also exaggerated the chaos and violence, used the event as an opportunity to bash President Bush, often gratuitously, and legitimized rumor-based accusations of "institutional" racism. In the process, the *Times* spared local officials from responsibility, provided a ready platform for racial demagogues, and allowed itself to be duped by a reflexive commitment to black victimology. Paul Krugman maintained that in a larger sense, the president's "lethally inept" response to Katrina had a lot to do with race, which he called "the biggest reason the U.S., uniquely among advanced countries, is ruled by a political movement that is hostile to the idea of helping cities in need."

A March 2006 profile detailing the fate of an alleged victim of Hurricane Katrina said to be languishing in a New York City welfare hotel, in a purgatory induced by bureaucratic unresponsiveness, underscored the paper's eagerness to embrace a script based on racial victimization. According to the reporter Nicholas Confessore, the victim, a 37-year-old African American mother of five named Donna Fenton, had been a restaurant manager in Biloxi, Mississippi, a city hit hard by Katrina. Fleeing Biloxi, she and her family, including her oldest son's fiancée, ended up in New York City "with a change of clothes and a tapped out bank account." The Red Cross placed Fenton with her husband and four of her children in a Queens hotel and gave them a $1,500 debit card. Fenton also got several thousand dollars from the Federal Emergency Management Agency (FEMA), but that was soon used up on clothes, food and transportation as the family sought to put down roots in a new place.

The focus of the piece was on Fenton's efforts to secure more aid, including a new place to live. According to Confessore, she had memorized the phone numbers for the Red Cross and FEMA, as well as the city welfare offices: "I call them every day. That's my job." Because of bureaucratic ineptitude, filing paperwork was a constant headache; faxes to and from agencies seemed to disappear regularly. "Everything they asked for, I sent in," Fenton said. "I sent it in the second time, and then I sent it in a third time." Confessore wrote, "With all the time she spends on the phone, she said, she cannot start the job waiting for her at a Brooklyn check-cashing business." Twice, Fenton had found apartments "but was afraid to sign leases because she was not sure FEMA's promised rental assistance would arrive."

Donna Fenton's woes went far beyond bureaucratic frustration, Confessore reported. She had lupus, and had collapsed at a Manhattan welcome center after filling out paperwork from half a dozen agencies and charities. The stress on fleeing Katrina had "worsened her condition, producing an enlarged heart and an irregular heartbeat," and resulting in "four days in the hospital." Later, a hotel maid found her unconscious, Confessore said. "More hospital stays followed, six in all, as she battled to control her lupus. Then, in February, her appendix burst, resulting in a two-week hospital stay."

Fenton may have been "polite, organized and determined," as Confessore depicted her, but she was also a veteran con artist. Even as Confessore was filing his heart-tugging reports, the Brooklyn district attorney's office had had Fenton under investigation for a month, tipped off by welfare caseworkers who had become suspicious months earlier. In fact, Fenton was not a Katrina victim from Biloxi, had never lived in Biloxi, had a long record of fraud and other criminal activity, and was on five years' probation for a recent check-forging charge. Much to the paper's embarrassment, very little of what Confessore had reported was true, making this article one of the most egregious instances of journalistic gullibility to afflict the *Times* since the Jayson Blair scandal.

The result was yet another editor's note, which ran on March 23 and admitted, "For its profile, The Times did not conduct adequate interviews or public record checks to verify Ms. Fenton's account, including her claim that she had lived in Biloxi." An accompanying article, also written by Confessore, admitted that "The Times did not verify many aspects of Ms. Fenton's claims, never interviewed her children, and did not confirm the identity of the man she described as her husband." Her children were not even in her custody; they had either been placed in foster care or adopted.

·⤳

The shoddy, sometimes yellow journalism in New Orleans after Hurricane Katrina was just a warm-up for the unseemly haste in declaring lacrosse players at Duke University guilty of a heinous rape, which in the *Times'* script reflected a pattern of white supremacy deeply embedded in American culture. In reality, it was another fraud. The reporting on the case stands as the most unjust example of an obsession with race and an insistence on spotlighting racism as the quintessential American evil.

The case began in late March 2006 when one of two local black exotic dancers hired to perform at a lacrosse team party claimed she was raped, hit, kicked, strangled and sodomized by at least three players that evening, in a brutal assault that took place over a thirty-minute period. The Duke campus was convulsed with racial rage, egged on by the media as it played out a narrative of overprivileged white men abusing a poor single mother who was compelled to strip in order to support her child. Wanted posters went up on campus with pictures of the accused and calls for their castration. Eighty-eight members of the faculty sponsored an ad in the college paper effectively supporting the protesters. The university's president suspended two of the accused upon their indictment (the third had already graduated), cancelled the rest of the season for the lacrosse team, and forced the coach to resign. Racial unrest flared throughout the town of Durham, with black activists and militants creating so threatening an environment that some students left campus.

Within a few weeks, however, the case was exposed as a malicious fiction. The stripper's accusations were dismissed as utterly false, and the indictment itself was shown to have been the result of investigative irregularities and prosecutorial lies. Durham's district attorney, Michael Nifong, was forced to step down and ultimately disbarred for ethics violations; he also served a symbolic one-day jail sentence. Meanwhile, Duke University settled with the students for an undisclosed sum.

KC Johnson, a historian who ran a blog documenting the case, "Durham-in-Wonderland," called the Duke rape saga "the highest-profile case of prosecutorial misconduct in modern American history." Shortly after the case imploded, Peter Applebome, a *New York Times* columnist and Duke alumnus whose son was attending the school, asked: "How did college kids with no shortage of character witnesses become such a free-fire zone for the correct thinkers in academia, the news media and the socially conscious left? . . . Why did denouncing them remain fair game long after it was clear that the charges against them could not be true, and that even most of the misbehavior originally alleged about the team party was distorted or false?"

The question was a good one, but the answer was readily at hand: Applebome's own newspaper. The *Times* had plenty of opportunities to save itself as the story developed and the discrepancies in the accuser's version became clear, as did irregularities in the investigation. But the *Times* was committed to the lacrosse players' guilt from the beginning and refused to budge as the evidence accumulated. Even after North Carolina's attorney general declared, in an unprecedented press conference, that the suspects "were innocent of these charges" and that "we have no credible evidence that an attack occurred in that house on that night," the *Times*—its editors, ombudsman and some columnists—continued to defend its own coverage. The *Times* also failed to do the follow-up reporting it should have done, exempting the politically correct Duke faculty, the university's cowardly president and the corrupt Durham police department from the sort of inquiry that would have made them account-able for their actions. According to Stuart Taylor, a legal jour-nalist and the author of a book on the case, the *New York Times* along with other media "seemed to have a powerful emotional need to believe. . . . A need to believe that those they classify as victims must be virtuous and those they classify as oppressors must be villains." The *Times* treated the story as "a fable of evil, rich white men running amok and abusing poor black women." As the former *Times* public editor Daniel Okrent told a reporter, "It was too delicious a story. It conformed too well to too many preconceived notions of too many in the press: white over black, rich over poor, athletes over non-athletes, men over women, edu-cated over non-educated."

The *Times'* coverage of the Duke case began with a front-page story on March 29 headlined "Rape Allegation Against Athletes Is Roiling Duke." In the following two weeks, the paper ran sev-enteen different news articles, five columns and four letters on the case, according to an account that Okrent gave to Harvard's Neiman Foundation. This fast-and-furious coverage was marked by serious mistakes made on the wing, which the Duke adminis-tration tried to get the *Times* to address. Regarding op-eds, "There was one two-week period where we asked for about 10 corrections in the Times and probably got about five," recalled John Burness, a Duke spokesman.

One major mistake in the coverage was to set the "incident" in a context of racial victimization, using loaded rhetoric where the facts as then determined made it journalistically reckless. In a March column headlined "Bonded in Barbarity," the sports col-umnist Selena Roberts almost choked with hatred for "a group of privileged players of fine pedigree entangled in a night that threatens to belie their social standing as human beings." Roberts also parroted false prosecution claims that all team members had observed a "code of silence," likening them to "drug dealers and gang members engaged in an anti-snitch campaign." (A correction ran six days later.)

Harvey Araton, another sports columnist, took the Duke girls' lacrosse team to task for wearing sweatbands declaring their male counterparts "INNOCENT." Araton asked, "Does cross-team friendship and university pride negate common sense at a college as difficult to gain admission to as Duke? Has anyone—from the women's lacrosse coach, Kerstin Kimel, to the Duke president, Richard H. Brodhead—reminded the players of the kind of behavior they are staking their own reputations on?"

Another journalistic sin was to give credence to the Durham DA's claim that the lacrosse players were stonewalling. Nifong said, "There are three people who went into the bathroom with the young lady, and whether the other people there knew what was going on at the time, they do now and have not come forward." In fact, the players had all given their DNA, and the team captains had met with the police for several hours, voluntarily, without legal counsel, and had cooperated with the police as they searched the house. The players volunteered to take a polygraph, though none was administered.

The *Times* also emphasized the lacrosse team's reputation for poor character. In "A Team's Troubles Shock Few at Duke," reporters Warren St. John and Joe Drape claimed that "students, professors and members of the Duke community said they were not surprised to hear that trouble had found the lacrosse team, a clubby, hard-partying outfit with roots in the elite prep schools of the Northeast." A similar piece, "New Strain on Duke's Ties with Durham" by Rick Lyman, described neighbors complaining about the lacrosse players "screaming at the top of their lungs at 2 in the morning, urinating on lawns, throwing beer cans around, driving fast, that sort of stuff."

At the same time, the paper gave undeniable short shrift to the lynch-mob mentality that pervaded the campus in the weeks following the party incident. Protesters on campus and in the city waved "castrate" banners, put up Wanted posters with pictures of the forty-six players on the lacrosse team, and threatened the physical safety of the players. Houston Baker, a radical professor of English, called the lacrosse players "white, violent, drunken men veritably given license to rape," men who could "claim innocence . . . safe under the cover of silent whiteness."

A letter signed by eighty-eight faculty members and published in *The Chronicle,* the Duke student newspaper, rejected President Brodhead's calls for patience in determining guilt. The letter spoke of "the anger and fear of many students who know themselves to be objects of racism and sexism, who see illuminated in this moment's extraordinary spotlight what they live with every day." The faculty letter added, "We're turning up the volume in a moment when some of the most vulnerable among us are being asked to quiet down while we wait."

As race relations grew tense in the town of Durham, the *Times* saw confirmation of a deeply embedded racism that was spreading violence into the community like a bloodstain. In a piece headlined "With City on Edge, Duke Students Retreat," Juliet Macur reported on rumors of planned drive-by shootings of the lacrosse house. Neighbors had been yelled at by people driving past, and some had left the city or relocated at nighttime. Macur attended a vigil for the accuser at North Carolina Central College, a historically black school nearby, where she was said to study. (In fact, she had taken only one course.) In a piece headlined "3 Miles and World Away, Vigil for the Accuser," Macur quoted a student government leader who spoke before a crowd, saying, "We want the woman to know that we're not going to let this issue just slide by. We're not going to let Duke keep sweeping this under the rug just because they want to save their lacrosse team's season." Macur closed her piece with a statement by Jami Hyman, a freshman from Winston-Salem: "There's a lot of potential violence once Central students really grab hold of this. I wouldn't be surprised if someone got shot or something."

The *Times* made hay out of an outside report charging that Duke University officials had failed to see the gravity of the initial rape report. In his independent report, William Bowen, a former president of Princeton and a crusader for affirmative action, concluded that Duke's senior leadership—five white men, an Asian American man and a white woman—had been "handicapped by its own limited diversity."

A telling sign of the extent of the *Times'* institutional investment in DA Nifong's irrational persecution of the Duke athletes, as it would come to seem, was what happened to Joe Drape, a reporter who in late March filed a somewhat mitigating report headlined "Lawyers for Lacrosse Players Dispute Allegations." Drape gave space for the players' defense attorneys to attack the accuser's story and to predict that the DNA evidence would exonerate their clients. The piece closed with a sympathetic comment by one of the attorneys: "We're trying to prove a negative here that they didn't do it. That's not supposed to be the way our system works. The state is supposed to make a case. If all 46 are exonerated, they've still been branded as racists and rapists."

Soon after filing this piece, Drape was taken off the story. According to Stuart Taylor, Drape had told friends and his editors that the case looked like another Tawana Brawley hoax, and later claimed that the editors wanted a more pro-prosecution line and also wanted to stress the race-sex-class angle without dwelling on evidence of innocence.

The perception of a sinking prosecutorial case was an obvious concern in the *Times* newsroom, especially after it had invested so much of its authority in laying down the story line that Nifong was right and the lacrosse players were a bunch of coddled, depraved racist misogynists at best. According to *New York* magazine's Kurt Andersen, who had inside newsroom sources, editors wanted their reporter Duff Wilson, who replaced Joe Drape, "to get back into the game" and restore the story line's credibility.

The result was a 5,600-word front-page reassessment of the case, which appeared on August 25. Written by Wilson and Jonathan Glater, the article's central point was that "By disclosing pieces of evidence favorable to the defendants, the defense has created an image of a case heading for the rocks. But an examination of the entire 1,850 pages of evidence gathered by the prosecution in the four months after the accusation yields a more ambiguous picture. It shows that while there are big weaknesses in Mr. Nifong's case, there is also a body of evidence to support his decision to take the matter to a jury."

The piece did note that the internal investigator's 33-page memo of his findings, along with three pages of notes just made available to journalists, could be interpreted as a "make-up document," and that one of the defense lawyers said the sergeant's report was "transparently written to try to make up for holes in the prosecution's case" and "smacks of almost desperation." It also reported that the second dancer had called the accusation of rape "a crock." And it did recite the problems with physical evidence, including the lack of DNA, and problems with the photo identification of the players. Still, it bolstered Nifong's contention that there was enough evidence to bring a trial before a jury, giving new life to what many legal experts and close observers said was a dead case. The *Times* editor, Bill Keller, later said that the August story "wasn't a perfect piece, but it was a detailed and subtle piece that left you with no illusions about the strength of Nifong's case." But on MSNBC, Dan Abrams called it "shameful . . . an editorial on the front page of what's supposed to be a news division of the newspaper."

Stuart Taylor's attack was probably the most stinging. Citing all the nonexistent and contradictory evidence in the article—including the huge amount of alibi evidence, the accuser's shifting stories and the lack of confirmational DNA—Taylor wrote:

> *Imagine you are the world's most powerful newspaper and you have invested your credibility in yet another story line that is falling apart, crumbling as inexorably as Jayson Blair's fabrications and the flawed reporting on Saddam Hussein's supposed WMD. What to do? If you're the New York Times and the story is the alleged gang rape of a black woman by three white Duke lacrosse players—a claim shown by mounting evidence to be almost certainly fraudulent—you tone down your rhetoric while doing your utmost to prop up a case that's been almost wholly driven by prosecutorial and police misconduct.*

Taylor later said that the August 25 piece was "the worst single piece of journalism I've ever seen in long form in a newspaper."

Other citadels of the media had no trouble treating the case more objectively. The *New Yorker* ran a long narrative during the first week in September that confirmed all the claims of the defense and refuted almost all the claims of the prosecution, setting the case in context of a nervous university president new to his job, a politically juvenile faculty, and a politically ambitious district attorney. The lacrosse players came across as a "cohesive, hard working, disciplined, and respectful athletic team" who had cooperated with police from the get-go. By contrast, the accuser appeared to be highly unreliable, said to have offered as many as ten accounts of what happened that night.

More high-profile investigative journalism came from *60 Minutes*. Right at the top, Ed Bradley's report gave a devastating indictment of the prosecution. "Over the past six months, *60 Minutes* has examined nearly the entire case file," Bradley said. "The evidence we've seen reveals disturbing facts about the conduct of the police and the district attorney and raises serious concerns about whether or not a rape even occurred."

In his column for *New York* magazine, Kurt Andersen took both the handling of the Duke case and the *Times'* coverage of it seriously to task. One reporter at the paper had told him, "I've never felt so ill over *Times* coverage." Andersen commented that this was saying a lot for a paper "that published Jayson Blair's fabrications and Judy Miller on WMD." "It's institutional," said one editor. "You see it again and again, the way the *Times* lumbers into trouble." The former public editor Daniel Okrent told Andersen, "The only thing we can look forward to now is what the *Times* will say to the accused once the charges are dropped, or once acquittals are delivered."

The *Times* dutifully reported the revelations of the *60 Minutes* exposé. There was also a story on how the lacrosse players said the rape accusation had ruined their lives, and a story on how the accuser had returned to dancing at her strip club within two weeks, although this story appeared almost three weeks after *60*

Minutes reported the same, with video. But the *Times* would still not do what it should have done weeks earlier: acknowledge the absence of physical evidence behind the case, expose the accuser as a liar, and reveal Nifong to be a deceitful opportunist.

In a courtroom motion hearing in December, the case finally fell apart with a sickening thud. The director of the forensic laboratory who did the DNA testing admitted on the stand that there was no DNA from any of the lacrosse players, but there was DNA from "several" other men. Worse, he admitted that he and Nifong had conspired not to report this information to the defense as law demands.

Yet even here, on the biggest bombshell of the case, the *Times* allowed two weeks to elapse before reporting this testimony. In fact, the *Times* did not even have a reporter in the courtroom when the revelations were made; its account was cobbled together from reports by spectators and other witnesses. When its own reporter, a heavy-hitting investigative reporter named David Barstow—brought in to compensate for the less-than-rigorous Duff Wilson—finally wrote about the dropping of the rape charges, he did so using Nifong as an anonymous source at one point, and granting Nifong room to rationalize why he had basically told the forensic scientist not to include the exculpatory DNA in his report, and to maintain that the case for assault and kidnapping was actually stronger without the rape charge.

Soon, Nifong was taken off the case. The attorney general of North Carolina, Roy Cooper, took over and released a scathing report at the end of April 2007, thirteen months after the ordeal began. Of the accuser, the report charged:

> *In meetings with the special prosecutors, the accusing witness, when recounting the events of that night, changed her story on so many important issues as to give the impression she was improvising as the interviews progressed, even when she was faced with irrefutable evidence that what she was saying was not credible. . . . The accusing witness attempted to avoid the contradictions by changing her story, contra-*

*dicting previous stories or alleging the evidence was fabri-
cated.*

KC Johnson, author of the Durham-in-Wonderland blog,
quoted Cooper's statement that "a lot of people owe a lot of apologies to, to other people. I think that those people ought to consider
doing that." Johnson went on to specify who should start apologizing: the *Times* columnists Selena Roberts and Harvey Araton,
the reporter Duff Wilson, and the paper's senior editors.

As one Duke student asked, if the *Times* had restrained its
coverage a little bit, or perhaps been more skeptical, "would the
entire story, the entire case, the entire 'perfect storm' have been
the same? Would it still have been a story of such national promi-
nence if The Times had run something else on its front page?" As
the case collapsed, Daniel Okrent added: "If and when The Times
does a big story on what went wrong in the Duke case, unless
they're a part of the story, unless they report on themselves, it will
be an incomplete story." Okrent liked to imagine an apology that
would candidly say, "We blew it. We're sorry. We accept responsibility for having blown it."

But that mea culpa never came. Editorials denouncing Nifong
ran in other papers, including the *Los Angeles Times,* the *Washington Post,* the *Wall Street Journal* and *USA Today.* But not in the
New York Times. Stuart Taylor and KC Johnson's book on the case,
*Until Proven Innocent: Political Correctness and the Shameful Injus-
tices of the Duke Lacrosse Rape Case,* came out in 2007. The *Times
Book Review* devoted only two sentences to the scores of passages
that eviscerated the paper's coverage of the case.

five
Immigration

The narrative about "a nation of immigrants" is a powerful American ideal, and so there's always been a certain measure of romanticism in reporting on immigrants. But the *New York Times'* willingness to recast the narrative as "a nation of victims" is so striking that it seems a calculated act of journalistic aggression. The paper has either ignored, miscovered or muted the less appealing realities of immigration—especially those involving the illegal immigration that has threatened to swamp the southwestern part of the country in recent decades.

First there are the blatant sins of omission: fully newsworthy stories that are salient to various facets of the immigration debate, but don't get reported at all. They are airbrushed out of the record, *Pravda*-like.

- In Denver in 2007, a Mexican illegal alien dragged a woman to death after beating her. The man had been arrested before, but was released after one night even though he had a crudely forged ID card, which was returned to him. The story got no coverage by the *Times*.

- In Tennessee in 2007, an illegal alien committed vehicular manslaughter, killing a husband and wife, Sean and Donna Wilson. It was found that the perpetrator had fourteen prior arrests but had done no jail time. Local commentators, such as the syndicated radio talk show host Phil Valentine, voiced the possibility that politicians, judges and prosecutors—all Democrats—were going easy on such offenders to court the Latino vote. Again, no coverage in the *Times*.

- In New York, as around the country, illegals are overrepresented in hit-and-run accidents—as perpetrators, not victims. But instead of exploring this trend, the *Times* chooses to emphasize the more multiculturally correct side of the coin: stories where illegal immigrants are *victims* of vehicular accidents. In 2009, Lawrence Downes wrote an editorial about immigrants leading "quiet but precarious" lives who have been killed while traveling the streets of Long Island suburbs on foot or bicycle, because they could not afford a car.

- In New Haven, Connecticut, in March 2009, an illegal Mexican busboy asked a 25-year-old waitress, with whom he had worked for a year, for a ride home. The man punched the woman in the face, knocking her out of the car. He proceeded to smash her cell phone, beat her and rape her. Then he drove to a more secluded location, where he raped and beat her again, this time trying to kill her by hitting her with tree branches and trying to gouge out her eyes. The victim played dead, and later crawled to a nearby house for help. Despite the heinousness of the crime, the *Times* chose not to cover it, even though it routinely covers other developments in New Haven, including the controversies over granting identity cards to illegal immigrants, and the immigrant community's fears over federal raids on illegal immigrants with outstanding arrest warrants.

■ The *Times* did a piece on how happy immigrant parents were with ethnically themed public charter schools, dismissing concerns about assimilation by quoting ethnic studies professors saying that these parents were being "as American as apple pie." Meanwhile, the paper has ignored the workings of a Muslim charter school outside Minneapolis where public monies are being spent to advance an Islamist agenda. Although the ACLU was looking into the school to determine whether it violated the Constitution's establishment clause, and anti-jihadi watchdog groups were calling for the school's deaccreditation, the *Times* didn't go near it.

■ In 2009, responding to an online discussion among Muslim students at MIT about the Islamic position on death for apostasy, Harvard's Muslim chaplain Taha Abdul-Basser told the students that "there is great wisdom (*hikma*) associated with the established and preserved position (capital punishment) and so, even if it makes some uncomfortable in the face of the hegemonic modern human rights discourse, one should not dismiss it out of hand." Concerned Harvard alumni, both Muslim and non-Muslim, wrote the school to complain, some calling for Abdul-Basser's removal. This is exactly the sort of story the *Times* would have jumped at if ethnic sensitivities were not involved. But the *Times* ignored it.

■ In mid 2010, a 21-year-old Indian girl filed suit for "slavery and peonage" against an Indian government official posted to the United Nations who, ironically, was known as a champion of women's rights. Brought into the United States illegally as a minor in 2007 by the diplomat and her husband, who had lied to immigration authorities, the girl charged that she was forced to work sixteen hours a day, seven days a week; that she slept on the floor of the Indian mission to the U.N. and was often starved; that she received little of the pittance she was promised, and was told that if she attempted to leave, "the police would beat and arrest her" and send her back to India as "cargo." MSNBC, the *Boston Globe,* the *Philadelphia Inquirer,* the *Fresno Bee,* the *Wall Street Journal* and the *New York Post* all ran the story. But despite the obvious news angle of a supposed women's rights crusader being sued for "slavery and peonage," as well as a foreign diplomat lying to U.S. authorities, the *Times* did not do the story.

■ In early November 2009, a member of the ruthless Salvadoran gang MS-13, who was a legal immigrant from El Salvador, confessed to authorities that he had been hired by a gang leader in his home country to arrange the assassination of a ranking Immigration and Customs Enforcement (ICE) agent who had led a crackdown on the gang's New York operations. The plot's revelation led to a "blitz" of arrests, as the *New York Daily News* put it, involving hundreds of federal agents. The attempt to murder the ICE agent came as Central American criminal violence, particularly the intimidation of law enforcement and criminal justice officials, had begun seeping into the United States, which certainly made the assassination plot newsworthy, as did the cross-border nature of the attempted hit, the forceful federal response to it, and the local New York angle. Yet the *Times* did not report on it, prompting Mark Krikorian of the Center for Immigration Studies to say, "What's it gonna take for the *Times* to report something like this? The beheading of a federal judge?"

In addition to such conspicuous silences, the paper's immigration reporting is marked by sins of commission too—by underreported and ideologically one-sided stories where significant information and salient facts have been avoided, deflected or euphemized to the point where the information lacuna causes the reader to lose the essence of what the story is really about and what has really taken place.

■ In what many considered a Muslim "honor killing" in Buffalo, New York, a prominent Pakistani-born Muslim executive of a television network—which he established to fight stereotypes about Islam—stabbed and beheaded his wife in 2009 after she had served him with divorce papers and obtained a restraining order to keep him away from their house and children, following a long pattern of abuse and violence. Despite the heinous details and the culturally inflammatory nature of the crime, which cut to the issue of Muslim compatibility with American norms, it took a week for the *Times* to get on the story. When it did, the Web report described the decapitation euphemistically. *Times* reports also carried copious denials that the murder was an "honor killing" from Muslim advocacy groups.

■ The *Times* gave incomplete information on a 2006 story from Maywood, California, where an American flag was stomped on by illegal aliens demanding amnesty, and a Mexican flag was hoisted in its place. In addition to minimizing the number of Mexican and Central American flags at the protest, the *Times* scrubbed some of the rhetoric at this demonstration and others, such as comments by groups like La Raza that Mexicans are involved in the *Reconquista* of lands stolen by gringos long ago.

■ The *Times* has given short shrift to the way towns and cities with high densities of illegal immigrants have undermined immigration laws. Many have enacted so-called "sanctuary laws" making it illegal for local officials, including police, to report illegal aliens to federal authorities unless they have committed major crimes. Maywood, where the U.S. flag was stomped, has gone even further. As Heather Mac Donald explained in *City Journal*, it "abolished its drunk-driving checkpoints, because they were nabbing too many illegal aliens. Next, this 96 percent Latino city, almost half of whose adult population lacks a ninth-grade education, disbanded its police traffic division entirely, so that illegals wouldn't need to worry about having their cars towed for being unlicensed. . . . At a March 2006 city council meeting in Maywood, a resident suggested that a councilmember was using English as a sign of disrespect." The *Times* ignored these developments.

■ The *Times* did report on a caste-based killing in Chicago, where in 2008 an Indian immigrant set fire to his pregnant daughter's apartment over a "cultural slight." The fire killed four people—the daughter, her husband, and their three-year-old child. The *Times* noted that the father was angry that his daughter married without permission and that the husband was of a lower caste. But it gave no sense of the presence of caste-related violence and resentment in the United States, as represented by the many high-caste wealthy Indian couples who bring over lower-caste girls as servants but wind up sexually exploiting and physically abusing them. Most of these cases have gone unreported. When the *Times* has reported on caste, it says—against considerable evidence to the contrary—that the tradition is "withering."

■ In January 2008, when a Mexican American U.S. Marine was shot by cops in the largely Mexican immigrant town of Ceres, California, after shooting one policeman and wounding another, the *Times* reported that he was under stress because of an order to return to Iraq for another tour and was not in one of the gangs that dominate the town. The account was threaded with quotes from friends saying that the Marine was "a good Mexican boy" and that he "died like a real Mexican, standing up." Soon after-word, Michelle Malkin reported that in fact he did have gang associations, showing pictures of him with gang paraphernalia, and that he was high on coke. Malkin also reported that he was not being redeployed to Iraq and had never served there—confabulated assertions in the *Times* report.

■ In December 2007, a woman was savagely raped in a Queens park by four Mexican illegals. Once arrested, they were found to have long rap sheets and a long record of missed court appearances, which made them deportable. The *Times* did not report their illegal status, referring to them merely as "homeless men." Nor did it connect the dots back to New York City's sanctuary policies, which protected three of the four from deportation for offenses such as assault, attempted robbery, criminal trespass, illegal gun possession and drug offenses. Around this time, however, the *Times* hailed Mayor Michael Bloomberg's reversal of a proposal that city workers check identities of illegals, declaring that doing so would "deny privacy rights for immigrants" and that "at the end of the day mandatory status disclosure would hurt everyone's public safety" by "chilling illegals from coming forward to report crime and abuse."

■ The *Times* has given protective coverage to intolerant acts by immigrant Muslims. A case in point was the threats by fellow Muslims against an imam in Brooklyn because of the relatively liberal views he expressed to Andrea Elliott for her three-part series "An Imam in America." Elliott did not report these threats—which encouraged the imam to relocate to New Jersey—until nearly a year after he started receiving them. While her stories acknowledged many negative things about the imam, the series as a whole was largely positive, sparking controversy.

·‑

The *Times'* journalistic lapses, failures and blunders on the immigration issue do not stem from deadline pressure, a lack of newsroom resources and personnel, or carelessness. Rather, they stem from a slavish devotion to the ideology of diversity, along with wishful thinking, naiveté, double standards, social distance, elite guilt, intellectual dishonesty, historical shallowness and old-fashioned partisanship.

The paper's reluctance to face the realities of illegal immigration squarely is reflected in its queasy coverage of alien criminality, as well as the different attitudes, values and customs that some immigrant groups bring as baggage, and the implications these differences carry for the American tradition of assimilation. The relativism that the *Times* brings to its reporting on these subjects, as well as the issue of dual citizenship and divided loyalty, suggests an attempt to undermine the ideal of assimilation as a "dated, even racist concept."

Two things appear to be driving immigration reporting. The first is a failure of confidence in America and its history—a "punitive liberalism," as James Piereson has called it, or "penitential narcissism" in Oriana Fallaci's phrase. The second driver is an intellectual and journalistic framework that romanticizes "the

Other" and shrugs off the question of a Latinization or Islamization of American culture as if it were meaningless. Like other liberal institutions, the *Times* puts the "human rights" of illegal immigrants ahead of the collective right of ordinary American citizens to decide who should be allowed to immigrate and who should not—thereby essentially voiding one of the most fundamental aspects of any country's sovereignty.

At the *Times,* pressure has steadily increased to erase the distinction between "legal" and "illegal" immigration. As Randal Archibold wrote in April 2006, there is "the awkward question of who is legal and how much it should matter." Officially, the paper's style guide says a distinction should be made, but the newsroom reflects a calculated confusion. Sometimes headlines will use the word "migrant"; the text of reports may use "undocumented worker," "undocumented migrant," or "immigrants who are undocumented." The *Times* rarely uses the term "illegal alien." A 2004 story headlined "160 Migrants Seized at Upscale Arizona Home" was obviously about illegal immigrants being smuggled into the country, but the headline refused to say so.

One editorial writer, Lawrence Downes, gave an explanation for the evasive vocabulary when he wrote that "America has a big problem with illegal immigration, but a big part of it stems from the word 'illegal.' It pollutes the debate. It blocks solutions. Used dispassionately and technically, there is nothing wrong with it. Used as an irreducible modifier for a large and largely decent group of people, it is badly damaging. And as a code word for racial and ethnic hatred, it is detestable." Many readers thought this was moral preening on Downes' part—and offensive to boot. Wrote one:

> *I am repeatedly frustrated by the implication by Lawrence Downes and others that by default those who oppose illegal immigration are promoting (or at the very least laying the ground for) a racist agenda. The word "illegal" is not a dirty word. It is to the point and honest, as it spells out the obvious difference in this case between those who are here lawfully and those who are not. To suggest that it is a "code word for*

racial and ethnic hatred" is disingenuous at best and only adds fuel to the fire. It has been used over and over in an attempt to stifle honest discussion on this topic as well as on a range of others.

The *Times* also shows its bias in the numbers it chooses to report. In a mid-2009 panel discussion, Jeffrey Passel of the Pew Research Center estimated that nearly one million illegal immigrants enter America annually, but the *Times* has used the figure of 400,000 and doesn't acknowledge the discrepancy, much less explain it.

While minimizing the numbers of illegal immigrants, the *Times* plays down the social costs they impose as well. According to William Bratton, former police chief of Los Angeles, gang violence is "the emerging monster of crime in America." At least 90 percent of all the outstanding homicide warrants in Los Angeles are for illegal immigrant criminals, most of them gangbangers. Because of their social marginality, immigrant children are particularly likely to be seduced by the gang culture. But the *New York Times* has often reported on gangs as if they were created by the United States itself, and as if deporting alleged gang members were a human rights abuse. Pieces such as Ginger Thompson's September 2004 report called "Tattooed Warriors: Shuttling Between Nations, Latino Gangs Confound the Law" rarely involve interviews with victims of immigrant gang crime, and seldom reveal that expelling gang members helps reduce crime in Los Angeles and other cities.

Illegal Mexican immigrants are heavily involved in the production and distribution of methamphetamine. But in a February 2002 Web report by Timothy Egan, headlined "Meth Building Its Hell's Kitchen in Rural America," the role of illegals is not mentioned. A report on California's "Emerald Triangle," consisting of Humboldt, Trinity and Mendocino counties, mentioned only "Mexican nationals."

One of the strangest treatments of the illegal immigrant gang/drug nexus came from Tim Golden in a 2002 piece headlined "Mexican Drug Dealers Turning US Towns into Major Depots," which focused on small towns in Georgia where thousands of "Mexican immigrants" have flocked to the mills. "The same pipeline of immigration and trade has been exploited by Mexican drug dealers," Golden reported, adding that they have emerged as major wholesalers throughout the country. He noted that the number of Mexicans in federal prison on drug charges doubled from 1994 to 2000, but did not say what percentage of them were illegal.

There are many other types of crime where the perpetrators' status goes unreported. In 2003, for example, a Long Island commuter was stabbed in front of his house after walking home from the railroad station. When five illegal immigrants were arraigned five months later, Patrick Healy made no mention of their status in the *Times*, though he did report that police believed "some of the defendants were gang members." In fact, they were MS-13. Healy quoted a sister of one of the men giving the oldest cliché in criminal justice, "He must have been with the wrong people at the wrong time," but failed to note something that the *New York Post* reported: the defendants were laughing while being booked.

The *Times* showed its protective instincts toward illegals in its coverage of a 2005 murder case in New City, a Rockland County suburb of New York. Douglas Herrera, a 39-year-old Guatemalan who had overstayed a six-month visa issued in 2001, was left to clean up after a landscaping job. He beat, raped and strangled the woman of the house, then stole her husband's clothes and her cell phone, using it to call her friends and relatives to taunt them and boast about the rape. The story was certainly newsworthy. The perpetrator was using a fake name with fake documents, at a time when New York's governor, Eliot Spitzer, had proposed giving driver's licenses to illegals, and when identity theft was very much on the media's radar screen. The case also put a spotlight on the sanctuary policies that had prevented the police from detaining the man in previous traffic violations and had allowed him to remain free after being charged in 2002 with misdemeanor assault on his girlfriend and never showing up for court—a deportable offense given his status.

The *Times*, however, shunted the story into the Metro section and omitted the perpetrator's illegal status, even though it was in the AP "brief" that the paper used on one day. (When I called the *Times* to ask about this, I could not get a straight answer.) And instead of using the case as a peg for a wider examination of illegal alien crime in suburbs, or answering the question of how someone using a fake name can get released from jail, it produced a smarmy report focused on how other Latino landscapers feared a backlash that would make it harder for them to get work. Critics charged that if the races were reversed and some "nativist" had done this to an immigrant, the *Times* would have been all over the story. Their criticism gained some traction from the fact that the story of an African immigrant teenage girl who was wrongly detained on suspicion of terrorism and then released was featured on the front page at the same time the gardener's misdeeds were buried inside.

In 2005, an actress in Greenwich Village was killed by an illegal construction worker after complaining about the noise coming from the apartment below hers. The worker strangled her, then hung her on a shower curtain rod to make it look like a suicide, which investigators saw through quickly. The status of the suspect was reported from day one by the New York tabloids, but the *Times* took a few days to get around to it.

So-called "sanctuary laws," which essentially bar local law enforcement officials from inquiring into immigration status, have caused legal and judicial chaos in cities like New York, New Haven, Los Angeles and San Francisco. Yet a database search turns up only one piece by the *Times* that candidly discussed how these laws obstruct the fight against crime. An April 2005 report by Charlie LeDuff, "Police Say Immigrant Policy Is Hindrance," gave a good account of frustration among Los Angeles police over not being able to pick up known illegal criminals who had snuck back into the country until they were caught for a felony. But LeDuff also gave a lot of space to those wringing their hands about ethnic profiling. He missed or ignored the substantial penalties that police officers face if they do inquire into a criminal suspect's immigration status. He also did not mention the history of the sanctuary law, known in Los Angeles as Special Order 40, and how in the late 1990s there was an effort to roll it back, but the ethnic lobby put such intense pressure on politicians that it became even more sacrosanct.

Sanctuary policies were a heated issue during the 2008 Republican presidential primaries, but according to the *Times* columnist Gail Collins, "sanctuary city" was just "a right-wing buzzword aimed at freaking out red state voters." With remarkable glibness, Collins joked:

> *By the way, doesn't the term "sanctuary city" sound sort of nice, actually? Remember all those sci-fi movies where the heroes were stuck in a terrible world where everybody but them was a mutant or a pod person or a hologram and their only hope was to reach a legendary and possibly mythical refuge? Next time you hear a politician ranting about a "sanctuary city," say: "Wasn't that where Keanu Reeves was trying to get in 'The Matrix'?"*

The *Times* has low-balled other issues involved in illegal immigration, such as the diseases that are brought across the border, like tuberculosis. The housing that illegals live in is often overcrowded and dangerous, which is partly the fault of unscrupulous landlords, often immigrants themselves. In early 2009, overcrowding led to the deaths of four New York City firemen, trapped in a burning apartment that had been illegally subdivided. "Partitioned Apartments Are Risky but Common in New York," read the anodyne February 2002 headline over a blasé report by Manny Fernandez. Even on the issue of illegal sidewalk sales of counterfeit goods, the paper is in denial. One 2006 piece on counterfeiting in the garment district by Nicholas Confessore, a cub reporter, said the vendors were African Americans, though almost any New Yorker could tell you that the majority of vendors selling knock-offs are African illegals.

⤳

Births to foreign-born women in the United States are at their highest rate ever, nearly one in four. As the *Christian Science*

Monitor has written, some experts worry that the traditional rapid assimilation of immigrants may be breaking down, with potentially troublesome consequences. Muslim immigration has brought its own set of concerns for assimilation to American norms. Based on a study of immigrants from the Middle East, Steven Camarota, from the Center for Immigration Studies in Washington, told the *Monitor* he estimates that there are some 600,000 children of Muslim immigrants in the United States. "These facts, set in the context of new twists in Islamic terrorism, are raising questions about how well the children of Muslim immigrants are being assimilated," the *Monitor* declared, "feeding a growing sense of concern among Americans about immigration, and about Muslim immigrants in particular."

But the *Times* tends to see assimilation as something that steals cultural identity and leaves immigrants floating randomly in the melting pot. An editorial about the surging Latino population says, with apparent satisfaction, that changes in communications and business "guarantee that assimilation won't replace heritage." A review by Michiko Kakutani of a book about assimilation, among other topics, by the late Harvard political scientist Samuel Huntington was condescendingly headlined "An Identity Crisis for Norman Rockwell America."

The rejection of assimilation comes down to earth in reporting on the customs and values, attitudes and practices of various immigrant communities. While celebrating cultural difference, the *Times* does not scrutinize the implications of those differences for immigrants or for Americans generally. David Brooks, one of the paper's two house conservatives, has written about "cultural geography," a term used by sociologists to explain "why some groups' values make them embrace technology and prosper and others don't," which, Brooks adds, is "a line of inquiry" that P.C. piety makes it "impolite to pursue." It is certainly a line of inquiry that has been rigorously ignored by his own paper. If immigrants leave home with problematic cultural baggage, the *Times* believes it is dropped on the tarmac when they land on U.S. soil or left behind when they scoot across the Mexican border. Ironically, the paper tacitly endorses problematic customs and attitudes that Third World progressives are trying to fight in their countries.

Many Indian immigrants to America see no problem with bringing their discriminatory and un-American caste system along with them. Indians may be a model minority for their above-average incomes and levels of education, but their impaired sense of social equality and their ethnocentric exclusivity are problems that they should not import into their new country. You won't hear any concerns about it in the *Times,* however. In a 2004 piece about caste, Joseph Berger wrote that the practice may have "stowed away" to America, but quickly concluded that it survived here mainly as a form of "tribal bonding," with Indians finding kindred spirits among people who grew up with the same foods and cultural signals. "Just as descendants of the Pilgrims use the Mayflower Society as a social outlet to mingle with people of congenial backgrounds, a few castes have formed societies like the Brahmin Samaj of North America."

Yet the article contradicts itself. While Berger contends that caste is "withering," he found plenty of examples where it has a "stubborn resilience": bias in business dealings, discrimination in hiring, obstruction of "love marriages," and disownments. One business owner from the untouchable caste said, "Our friends who came here from India from the upper classes, they're supposed to leave this kind of thing behind, but unfortunately they brought it with them." Yet this man told Berger that he was active in his Dalit (untouchable) group and would prefer that his son marry a Dalit.

While ethnic intermarriage has been the most dynamic engine of social integration that America has known, arranged or assisted marriages lead Indians to have the lowest rate of intermarriage of any group in the United States, perpetuating ethnocentrism and a separatist outlook. The *Times* has reported this phenomenon nonjudgmentally, even positively. The "Vows" column in the Sunday *Times* regularly honors various South Asian or Middle Eastern immigrants or ethnics for finding their soul mate within their same group—Muslim, Sikh, Christian Arab.

Even voodoo gets good ink now. "Americans are hungry for spiritual fulfillment and voodoo offers a direct experience of the sacred that appeals to more and more people," Steven Kinzer wrote in a 2003 piece. Timeswoman Neela Banderjee wrote positively in 2009 about a Christian African congregation, part of the Pentecostal "Spiritual Warfare" movement, that comes together at midnight to fight the devil, literally punching, kicking and slashing at him. "Some situations you need to address at night, because in the ministry of spiritual warfare, demons, the spirits bewitching people, choose this time to work," said Nicole Sangamay, who came from Congo in 1998 to study and is a co-pastor of the ministry. "And we pick this time to pray to nullify what they are doing." It's hard to imagine Banderjee giving a group of white American Pentecostals the same slack if they held similarly wacky beliefs.

Another dimension of the assimilation issue that the *Times* has handled badly is a set of indicators that portend the creation of a permanent Latino underclass. Latinos have the highest dropout rate in America, the lowest rate of college-going and the lowest rate of GED attainment. They have high unemployment, high levels of crime and incarceration, and high levels of obesity. Latinos also have a high reliance on social services, which actually increases over the years, contrary to other immigrants' historical experience. Illegitimacy has soared as well: half of all new babies in the United States are Hispanic, and half of these have unmarried mothers.

In his 1998 book, *Strangers Among Us*, the former *Times* reporter Roberto Suro said it was possible that the "great wave" of Latino immigrants would achieve upward mobility and fully integrate into American society. "It seems equally likely," he continued, "that Latino immigration could become a powerful demographic engine of social fragmentation, discord, and even violence." Yet the *Times* is timid about getting its hands around this story. Jason DeParle only scratched the surface of the problem with his April 2009 report headlined "Struggling to Rise in Suburbs Where Failing Means Fitting In," which examined the culture of Latino low achievement and self-sabotage.

The paper's indifference if not hostility to assimilation shows also in the near-total neglect of the issues raised by dual citizenship. At least ninety-three countries now allow their émigrés to keep their citizenship even as they become American citizens, and the list keeps growing. Dual citizenship has implications for cultural cohesion and for "the basic cultural, psychological, institutional and political organizations that have been the foundation of the country's republican democracy for the last 200 years," argues Stanley Renshon of the City University of New York. Might too much diversity lead to "a fragmented, and thus dysfunctional, national identity?" he asks.

This is a question that the *Times* has never seriously examined. Reporting on the Dominican immigrants in America who are now allowed to vote in their native country's elections, it describes them as being "closer to home than ever," whatever that means. The *Times* has reported on how African immigrants might say they will stay two years but "Africa will always be home," and how Mexicans living in the United States want to be buried in their "homeland." A story in June 2010 by Kirk Semple described a Mexican immigrant as "Running for Mayor, Back Home in Mexico" after almost two decades of living in the United States without naturalizing; he had slipped over the border illegally in 1992. And the *Times* has featured statements like this one from a former official of the Mexican American Legal Defense Fund: "California is going to be a Mexican state. Anyone who doesn't like it should leave."

Furthering the deconstruction of American citizenship, the *Times* has reported favorably on noncitizen suffrage. In August 2004, Rachel Swarns wrote a piece called "Immigrants Raise Call for Right to Be Voters," examining efforts nationwide to expand the franchise to people who are residents but not citizens. Although Swarns did quote one critic, Congressman Tom Tancredo, the story was mostly a platform for supporters of noncitizen voting. One New York academic was quoted as saying, "A lot of communities are not represented by [political] representatives who reflect the diversity in their communities and are responsive to their needs."

·

Compared with other immigrant groups, Muslims in America have a disproportionately high rate of advanced education and high per capita income, along with lower-than-average rates of divorce and illegitimacy. One thing they do share with less-well-off Mexican immigrants is the solicitude with which the *Times* reports and comments on their struggles to find their place within American society. Particularly after 9/11, the paper has treated American Muslims, both immigrants and converts, as a protected class and as potential victims of "Islamophobia." Through writers like Mark Lilla, the *Times* encourages its readers to have high sympathies but low expectations for Muslim immigrants: "So long as a sizable population believes in the truth of a comprehensive political theology, its full reconciliation with modern liberal democracy cannot be expected," wrote Lilla in the Sunday magazine.

On the issue of divided loyalties among Muslim immigrants, the *Times* has been particularly dishonest. As John Leo has noted, in place of a serious discussion about how well immigrants are assimilating to modern America, the *Times* has dispensed a "massive cloud of hands-off nonjudgmentalism." There have also been calculated omissions, along with the mistake of reading the subject through rose-colored glasses. A picture and a caption for a November 2003 story capture some of the dishonesty. Beneath a large picture of a Muslim man with a boy perched on his shoulders holding an American flag was a caption that read: "Arab Americans Pray for Victims Soon after the Attacks." The two were from Patterson, New Jersey, a place where it has been reported that a number of Arab Americans cheered in the streets upon hearing news of the World Trade Center catastrophe. The latter image may not be as reassuring as the lone act of patriotic witness, but it is certainly part of the larger picture that we have a right to see.

In May 2007, the Pew Research Center released a study on Muslim immigrant attitudes and experiences that was cause for alarm. According to the survey, which had 60,000 respondents, nearly half of Muslims in the United States (47 percent) say they think of themselves as Muslim first, rather than American. Additionally, Muslim Americans under age thirty are both much more religiously observant and more accepting of Islamic extremism than are older Muslim Americans. Those under age thirty are more than twice as likely to believe that suicide bombings can often or sometimes be justified in the defense of Islam (15 percent vs. 6 percent). As the Muslim writer Tawfik Hamid put it, if the Pew study's estimate that there are 2.35 million American Muslims is right, "that means there are a substantial number of people in the U.S. who think suicide bombing is sometimes justified. Similarly, if 5% of American Muslims support al Qaeda, that's more than 100,000 people."

Among other disturbing findings, relatively few Muslim Americans believe the U.S.-led war on terror is a sincere effort to reduce terrorism, and there is widespread doubt that Arabs were responsible for the 9/11 attacks. By roughly six to one (75 percent to 12 percent), Muslim Americans say the United States did the wrong thing in going to war in Iraq, while the general public is more evenly divided. Only 35 percent of Muslim Americans have a positive view of the decision to go to war in Afghanistan, compared with 61 percent among the public at large.

These findings were covered extensively in almost every media outlet in America—except the *Times*, which did not report on the Pew study at all.

The *Times* has also rigorously ignored evidence of Muslim disloyalty in government service. Right after 9/11, the FBI hired dozens of translators with knowledge of Middle Eastern languages to process tape recordings from jihadists. One of those translators was a Turkish immigrant named Sibel Edmonds, who worked with a fellow Turkish immigrant, Jan Dickerson, whom Edmonds came to suspect of spying for Turkey. Dickerson would often preview a certain tape and tell Edmonds that it was not important and she would translate it herself. Curious about what was going on, Edmonds went through the tapes that Dickerson processed and found she had omitted crucial information from the final transcript.

It turned out that Dickerson had worked for a Turkish organization being investigated by the FBI—something that had not been caught in the rush to complete background checks after 9/11. Dickerson also had a relationship with a Turkish intelligence officer stationed in Washington D.C. who was a target of that government investigation. Dickerson had tried to recruit Edmonds into her conspiracy, promising an early and well-paid retirement back in Turkey if she cooperated and warning of trouble for her family back home if she didn't. Edmonds went to FBI officials about her well-founded suspicions of espionage; but like many whistleblowers, she was the one eventually terminated.

The *Washington Post* gave a full account of the case, emphasizing the espionage. So did *60 Minutes* and *Vanity Fair,* of all places. But the *Times* not only got into the story late, it also arrived with considerable ambivalence, focusing on malfeasance in the FBI rather than the spying itself.

There was also the story of Gamal Abdel Hafiz, an immigrant Muslim FBI agent who twice refused on principle to secretly tape-record his coreligionists, thus hampering ongoing investigations. One of the cases to which he was assigned involved a bank that may have played a role in financing the bombings of two U.S. embassies in East Africa in 1998. He would not tape-record the bank president because he claimed it was against his religion to record a fellow Muslim. Hafiz also refused to record Sami al-Arian, the notorious University of Florida professor who was eventually convicted and ordered deported for helping to finance Palestinian Islamic Jihad. Other media outlets hopped on this story, but not the *Times.*

Stories involving Muslim disloyalty in the armed forces are another *Times* taboo. In early 2003, just before the invasion of Iraq, Sergeant Hasan Akbar of the 101st Airborne Division "fragged" members of his unit, killing two officers and injuring fourteen noncoms. Other news organizations such as Reuters and NBC News reported that Akbar objected to the war on religious grounds, saying that the Army was going to kill "my people." But the *Times* didn't mention this until months later, after it had done many stories. One front-page story casually referred to Akbar as a "Muslim convert." The only link I could find in the *Times* to the religious motivation for Akbar's crime was in a story of late June 2003, which described an Army major testifying by video hookup that "They asked why he had done it and Akbar said he had deliberately targeted the leadership of the brigade because they were going after Muslims."

In 2009 and 2010 there were news pegs galore to justify examining the issue of dual loyalty on the part of Muslim immigrants and even the native-born. One was the September 2009 attempt by Najibullah Zazi, a naturalized Afghani immigrant, to blow up the New York subway system. In 2010, a New Jersey man named Sharif Mobley was arrested among jihadists in Yemen, joining a long list of Americans, many of them ex-convicts, who have traveled there to fight. Shortly before this, an American convert from the Philadelphia suburbs, Colleen LaRose, who called herself "Jihad Jane," was arrested for plotting to kill the Swedish cartoonist who had parodied the Prophet Muhammad. There was the Fort Hood attacker, Major Nidal Hasan, who openly proclaimed that his loyalties lay with the Koran over the U.S. Constitution. Hasan had been inspired by the charismatic Internet preacher Anwar al-Awlaki, an American-born cleric of Yemeni descent who was put on a government hit list in 2010, and who asserts that "jihad is becoming as American as apple pie." In May 2010, Faisal Shahzad, a naturalized Pakistani immigrant who was married to a U.S. citizen, tried unsuccessfully to set off a car bomb in Times Square, and was apprehended while trying to board a plane at JFK International Airport two days later. At a court hearing where he pleaded guilty, Shahzad called himself a "Muslim soldier" and said, "I don't care for the laws of the United States." He declared that he would plead guilty "100 times over" until the United States stopped killing Muslims abroad and reporting Muslims here to the government.

It's not that the *Times* has avoided the issue of radicalization, but in some cases it has tended to give jihadists the benefit of the doubt. In the case of the five American citizens of Pakistani descent who were captured in Pakistan trying to volunteer for jihad, the *Times* downplayed the "farewell video" that one of them made, and did not carry the statements quoted by the Press Trust of India that they were intent on killing "American imperialists" and wanted to be hanged as martyrs. What is almost never brought out in the discussion of radicalization is the elephant in the living room: the failure of the assimilative process and the lack of loyalty to America. It's as if the idea were so archaic that people might not understand it, or might think it chauvinistic. What's usually cited instead is the putative discrimination against Muslims in America, the length of the wars in Afghanistan and Iraq, and the view among many American Muslims that the U.S. government is waging a "war against Islam."

·⌣

Right after the 9/11 attacks, some news organizations went into Islamic schools and found disturbing evidence of a separatist mentality, with virtually no emotional connections to the American commonweal. The *Washington Post*'s Marc Fisher, for example, visited an Islamic school just outside the District of Columbia and reported that one South Asian eighth grader said, "Being an American means nothing to me. I'm not even proud of telling my cousins in Pakistan that I'm American."

The *New York Times*, however, treads carefully on the subject of Islamic education, avoiding the issue of divided loyalties. When Susan Sachs did a piece on attitudes of Muslim teenagers in a private Islamic academy in Brooklyn, some of the Pakistani, Egyptian, Yemeni and Palestinian immigrants she interviewed exhibited the same ill will toward their new nation. They made no separation between religion and state, and thought the ideal society would follow Islamic law. One 17-year-old boy said he would support any observant Muslim leader who is fighting for an Islamic cause, even if that meant abandoning the United States or going to jail to avoid U.S. military service. Other students expressed "empathy for the young Muslims around the world who profess hatred for America and Americans." Instead of seeing such sentiments as worrying examples of dual (or no) loyalty, Sachs tepidly described them as a sign of "the strain" that immigrants can feel "between their adopted and native culture."

In a similar vein, Michael Luo wrote in August 2006 about a madrassa-like school in Queens where students, all boys, spend their entire educational day memorizing the Koran. "The carpeted room is full of children in skullcaps crouched on prayer mats, reciting verses from a holy text. Some mumble the words under their breath; others sing them out. They rock back and forth as they chant, their disparate voices blending into an ethereal melody," Luo wrote, obviously transported. "But they are not studying math, science or English. Instead, they are memorizing all 6,200 verses in the Koran, a task that usually takes two to three years."

Luo did acknowledge that "By not offering instruction in other subjects, the school may be inadvertently running afoul of state law, according to city and state education officials." Private religious schools are required to provide instruction "substantially equivalent" to what is offered in public schools. "But tracking every school-age child who leaves the public school system can be difficult," Luo pointed out. Nevertheless, the parents he talked to felt confident that their boys were "smart enough to make up the academic work" like math and science so they could become lawyers, doctors and other kinds of professionals. The parents liked the school because their children were "free to have it both ways," to be Islamic and American. Luo never explained how memorizing the Koran would serve that end.

A TimesWatch editor asked dubiously whether Christian homeschoolers who taught the Bible and nothing else would be allowed to make the thin excuse that their kids (all boys, no girls) are "smart enough to make up the academic work"? In such a case, the *Times* would probably have called for an investigation, amid lamentations about violations of church-state separation.

The *Times'* worst reporting on Islamic education involved the establishment of the Khalil Gibran International Academy in 2007 and 2008. The academy was to be a public charter school built around the theme of Arabic language and culture, using a "full immersion" method of teaching. Its students would become "ambassadors of peace," according to the proposed principal, Debbie Almontaser. The announcement of the school, however, set off a huge culture battle.

Having immigrated from Yemen at the age of three, Almontaser was depicted as a moderate Muslim by the *Times* reporters Andrea Elliott and Dan Wakin. In fact, she was a radical activist whose record of anti-American remarks was widely distributed by a coalition of New Yorkers that formed to protest the school. In one interview she said, "I have realized that our foreign policy is racist; in the 'war against terror' people of color are the target. . . . [T]he terrorist attacks have been triggered by the way the USA breaks its promises with countries across the world, especially in the Middle East." Almontaser also refused to reply when asked whether she considered Hamas and Hezbollah to be terrorist organizations and who she thought was behind the 9/11 attacks.

The campaign for Almontaser's principalship was not helped by the fact that all the members of her board were clerics, three of them radical Islamists. Also working against Almontaser were her unwillingness to indicate what books would be used in the curriculum, and her links to the often-militant Council on American-Islamic Relations (CAIR), which had given her an award. What finally did her in, though, was her seeming support for an organization for young women in the arts and media who had printed up T-shirts with the words "Intifada NY." Almontaser tried to shrug the matter off by saying that it merely meant "throwing off oppression" and had nothing to do with support for terrorism. In short order she was forced to resign, as announced by Mayor Michael Bloomberg on his radio show.

Through all this, the *Times* defended Almontaser. It ignored her anti-American statements, made the opposition to her candidacy seem like an exercise in McCarthyism, and implied that Islamophobia was at the root of her travail. In his education column, Sam Freedman angrily accused Almontaser's critics of having run a "smear campaign" and asserted that her resignation represented "the triumph of a concerted exercise in character assassination."

In reporting the story, the *Times* did not touch on the question of whether separatist schools like the Khalil Gibran Academy should exist at all. On the contrary, six months after Almontaser's resignation, Andrea Elliott wrote about the "Dream School" brought down by "the work of a growing and organized movement to stop Muslim citizens who are seeking an expanded role in American public life. . . . As the authorities have stepped up the war on terror, those critics have shifted their gaze to a new frontier, what they describe as law-abiding Muslim-Americans who are imposing their religious values in the public domain."

·—

The double standard that the *Times* displays on Islamic education is echoed in its deferential attitude toward Muslim sexual apartheid and the oppression of women. Consider Neil MacFarquhar's ode to arranged marriage, American style, facilitated by Muslim-only "speed dating" with parents in attendance to arrange meetings. Many participants at these events prefer "not to be assimilated," MacFarquhar reported, adding that parents still equate "anything related to dating with hellfire" and many don't even let their kids meet in public at all. Buying into the premise, MacFarquhar noted that one imam says having families involved in picking mates reduces the divorce rate. (The fact that Muslim culture stigmatizes divorce to such an extent that it can lead to ostracism and even "honor killing" goes unmentioned.)

MacFarquhar and others at the *Times* have expressed enthusiasm for another manifestation of gender apartheid: the practice of veiling. In September 2006, MacFarquhar wrote a profile of Dena al-Atassi, a 21-year-old Syrian American girl, for "Echoes of 9-11 Define Life Five Years Later," an anniversary collection of reported reflections on the terrorist attack. Al-Atassi claimed to have lost a job opportunity at the Jenny Craig weight loss chain because she chose to wear a Muslim head scarf, or hijab. She had begun wearing it, along with a floor-length trench coat, during a three-year stay in Syria as a teenager, MacFarquhar reported.

About a year later, in July 2002, al-Atassi was passing through the airport in Amsterdam on her first trip outside the Arab world after the September 11 attack, she said, when the security screeners singled her out, questioned her and made her remove her coat. Feeling violated, she went into a bathroom, where she tore off her scarf and wept. "I had gained such a strong relationship with God that I didn't want to do anything to distance myself from him, and I felt like I was doing just that," she told MacFarquhar, who closed the piece with his subject heroically declaring: "I made the decision when I put it back on that I will never take it off again."

The Style section weighed in on the subject of veiling in June 2010 with "Behind the Veil," by Lorraine Ali. It featured two Muslim sisters in Albuquerque who since 2001 had worn Islamic attire that entirely covered their heads and faces—which many Muslims say has no Koranic justification and isolates the wearer from society. One of the women told Ali that she wanted to offer a positive example of her faith after the 9/11 attack. Ali quoted her as saying that the garb was "liberating," since men "have to deal with my brain because I don't give them any other choice." The other sister said, "The more clothes you wear, the closer you are to God." When the strain of wearing the conspicuous attire in American society gets to them, she said, "We think of paradise at that point. Heaven is where we're supposed to rest. That's what gets us through."

Veiling is the least of the Muslim customs that seem to oppress women. On other misogynistic practices embedded in Islamic culture—such as forced domestic servitude, female circumcision and honor killings—the *Times* has shown an obtrusive nonjudgmentalism or inattention. For example, it did not report on a 2005 case that ended in the conviction of a married, 37-year-old graduate student from Saudi Arabia. According to prosecutors, Homaidan Ali al-Turki brought an Indonesian nanny to Colorado, paying her two dollars a day and making her sleep in the kitchen or the basement. Soon al-Turki made the woman his sex slave. During the trial, al-Turki's attorney said the charges arose from the state's failure to understand "cultural differences" and from "cynical Islamophobia."

After his conviction on twelve felony counts, al-Turki received a sentence of twenty years to life. At the sentencing he shouted, "The state has criminalized these basic Muslim behaviors."

Because al-Turki was connected to the Saudi royal family, his conviction caused the U.S. Department of State to urge Colorado's attorney general to fly to Saudi Arabia and brief King Abdullah on the case. Meanwhile, al-Turki's supporters began a campaign on his behalf, calling on Saudi students in America to arrange peaceful demonstrations, to leave the country as soon as possible, and to publicize the case any way they could.

That the *Times* didn't report on a domestic servitude case in Colorado is not the issue. What *is* the issue, and the news peg, is that the perpetrator invoked Islam as justification, and that Saudi students in the United States saw injustice in the prosecution and conviction.

The subject of female genital mutilation (FGM) among Muslim immigrants is another that has caused the *Times* visible discomfort. The least invasive form of the procedure—mostly practiced by natives of African countries—involves cutting of the clitoral hood or clitoris; the most radical involves total excision of the genitalia, followed by the sewing up of the vagina with thread or twine. There is no Koranic justification for the practice, but it does mesh well with Islam's notion of female submission to men. In the United States, the incidence of FGM has been rising along with Muslim immigration. Estimates are that 150,000 to 225,000 girls in the United States are at risk for the practice, and perhaps hundreds of daughters of African parents are circumcised in the United States every year. The *Times* has commendably reported on FGM in the developing world, and denounced it in editorials and op-ed columns (particularly Abe Rosenthal's column), but has been timid and nonjudgmental when it comes to FGM among U.S. immigrants.

Strangely enough, one relativist voice on this issue has been that of John Tierney, who used to represent a conservative-libertarian view on the *Times* op-ed page. In November 2007, Tierney used his online column for a "New Debate on Female Circumcision," as it was headlined. "Should African women be allowed to engage in the practice sometimes called female circumcision?" he asked. "Are critics of this practice, who call it female genital mutilation, justified in trying to outlaw it, or are they guilty of ignorance and cultural imperialism?"

Tierney allotted space to two "circumcised African women scholars," Wairimu Njambi, a Kenyan, and Fuambai Ahmadu, from Sierra Leone. Dr. Ahmadu, a postdoctoral fellow at the University of Chicago, was raised in America and went back to Sierra Leone as an adult to undergo the procedure along with fellow members of the Kono ethnic group. She claimed that critics exaggerate the medical dangers, misunderstand the effect on sexual pleasure, and mistakenly view the removal of parts of the clitoris as being oppressive. She lamented that her Westernized "feminist sisters insist on denying us this critical aspect of becoming a woman in accordance with our unique and powerful cultural heritage." She also argued that most of the Kono women she has met uphold the rituals because they relish the supernatural powers of their ritual leaders over men in society, and they embrace the legitimacy of female authority, particularly that of their mothers and grandmothers.

Tierney also gave space to Richard Shweder, a University of Chicago anthropologist who said that many Westerners trying to impose a "zero tolerance" policy don't realize that these initiation rites are generally controlled by women, who regard it as a cosmetic procedure with aesthetic benefits. He criticized Americans and Europeans for outlawing it at the same time they endorse their own forms of genital modification, like the circumcision of boys or the cosmetic surgery for women called "vaginal rejuvenation." In Dr. Shweder's view, "feminist issues and political correctness and activism have triumphed over the critical assessment of evidence." Although Tierney himself admitted that he wouldn't choose circumcision for his own daughter, he cited the work of anthropologists in asking, "Should outsiders be telling African women what initiation practices are acceptable?"

The *Times* has brought a light-handed approach to the topic of polygamy in America, too. In March 2007, the immigration correspondent Nina Bernstein reported on the custom as practiced in New York, one of the American cities where immigration "has soared from places where polygamy is lawful and widespread, especially from West African countries like Mali." Bernstein found evidence of "a clandestine practice that probably involves thousands of New Yorkers." She had been on the immigration beat for years before writing about this, and did so only in response to a tragic fire in the Bronx, when it was revealed that "the Mali-born American citizen who owned the house and was the father of five children who perished, had two wives in the home, on different floors."

Bernstein emphasized that the custom was usually kept secret because it was grounds for exclusion from the United States, and could be punished with up to four years in prison. "No agency is known to collect data on polygamous unions, which typically take shape over time and under the radar, often with religious ceremonies overseas and a visitor's visa for the wife, arranged by other relatives," Bernstein wrote. She explained that "Don't-ask-don't-know policies prevail in many agencies that deal with immigrant families in New York, perhaps because there is no framework for addressing polygamy in a city that prides itself on tolerance of religious, cultural and sexual differences—and on support for human rights and equality."

These claims were all probably true. Still, one wonders how such an experienced reporter as Bernstein could not know about the prevalence of such a practice, especially when one woman likened it to being "in effect the slave of the man." It was as if Bernstein had gone out of her way not to be curious about the practice. But she became a quick enough study to assure readers that while "Islam is often cited as the authority that allows polygamy" in Africa, "the practice is a cultural tradition that crosses religious lines, while some Muslim lands elsewhere sharply restrict it."

By any measure, however, the *Times'* reporting has been worst on the subject of Islamic honor killings. True, the *Times* has done a commendable job reporting on the practice in countries like Pakistan, Egypt, Syria, Jordan, Turkey, Iraq, Iran and the Palestinian Territories, and explaining the anthropological and cultural subtleties behind it. But when it comes to honor killings among immigrant Muslims on American soil, the *Times* has turned its head. Most American Muslim honor killings are not reported at all in the *Times,* or else they are reported as "domestic abuse." The more specific cultural attributes—especially the psychotically violent overkill of beheadings, strangulations, immolations and electrocutions—are purged from the reports, as are other common "signatures" (in police terminology), such as participation by a number of family members, including mothers, fathers, brothers, cousins and uncles, and the lengths they often go to hunt the victim down. And reports on honor killings are accompanied by outraged, defensive statements from Muslim advocacy organizations denying that Islam has any role—although such killings are *popularly* defended in Koranic terms in the Middle East.

In July 2008, a Pakistani immigrant allegedly strangled his 25-year-old daughter with a bungee cord in the Atlanta suburb of Jonesboro because she was determined to end her arranged marriage and had gotten involved with a new man. According to the *Atlanta Journal-Constitution,* Sandeela Kanwal's father, Chaudhry Rashid, "told police he is Muslim and that extramarital affairs and divorce are against his religion [and] that's why he killed her." In one court session, the paper reported, a detective testified that Rashid had said: "God will protect me. God is watching me. I strangled my daughter." The *New York Times* was missing in action.

A few weeks before that, Waheed Allah Mohammad, an immigrant from Afghanistan who lived in upstate New York, was charged with attempted murder after repeatedly stabbing his 19-year-old sister. The *Rochester Democrat* reported that Mohammad was "infuriated because his younger sister was going to clubs, wearing immodest clothing, and planning to leave her family for a new life in New York City." His sister was a "bad Muslim girl," he told sheriff's investigators. The *Times* ignored this story too.

On New Year's Day 2008 in Irving, Texas, the bullet-riddled bodies of the Said sisters—Sarah, 17, and Amina, 18—were found in an abandoned taxi in an empty parking lot. Police issued an arrest warrant for their father, an Egyptian immigrant named Yaser Abdel Said, who had reportedly threatened to kill them upon learning that they had boyfriends. According to authorities, one of the girls died instantly, but the other one lived long enough to make a cell phone call to police, pleading for help and saying that she was dying. Yaser Said fled and was put on the FBI's Most Wanted list. The girls' brother, who authorities believe knew of the father's plans, took flight too. He eventually wound up in Egypt, from where he wrote taunting notes to reporters covering the case, as well as to extended family members in America who spoke out critically about the murders. Despite the horrific details of the case, and the extensive coverage it got from other news organizations, the *Times* remained silent.

One Muslim wife-killing that the *Times* did report involved the television network executive who killed his wife after she had filed for divorce and received an order of protection against him in February 2009. Muzzammil Hassan attacked his wife in the network studios, stabbed her with hunting knives, then decapitated her. Afterward he went to the local police station, announced that his wife was dead, and then led the police to the scene and gave them the weapons he had used. He was charged with second-degree murder.

The *Times* took a week to report the story, and then refused to use the words "beheading" or "decapitation," instead delicately noting that police found the woman's head "separated" from her body. Although the case, in tandem with the honor killings of the previous year, cried out for a follow-up or a trend story, there was none. Instead, the *Times* showed its ideological aversion to saying what really occurred by echoing Islamic advocacy groups who insisted that such violence had no place in their religion and that the murder had to be understood merely as a form of "domestic abuse," as Liz Robbins' account put it.

Readers commenting on the *Times* Web edition didn't buy it. One noted that what seemed particularly Islamic (and therefore germane) was the beheading: "Why would you kill someone in *that* particular way?" Another wrote: "Many Muslim-American organizations insist that honor killing is 'Un-Islamic.' Yet, many scholars of Islam equally assert that the Qur'an as well as custom permits grave punishment for disobedient women. The argument that Islam is a 'religion of peace' has grown so tiresome in the face of so much evidence to the contrary."

The killing triggered a major denunciation from Marcia Pappas, president of the New York State chapter of the National Organization of Women. "This is apparently a terroristic version of an honor killing, a murder rooted in cultural notions about women's subordination to men," Pappas said. "Why is this horrendous story not all over the news? Is a Muslim woman's life not worth a five-minute report?" Pappas' statement itself was newsworthy in that it represented a major breach with the national organization, which refused comment on the matter. The *Times* gave it no coverage.

·~

Since the days right after 9/11, when it predicted an open season on American Muslims, the *Times* has doggedly followed a script built around the claim of Muslim victimization and Islamophobia. This wave of oppression never crested, yet the *Times* has continued to treat Muslims as an endangered species, always on the brink of being caught up in an American pogrom. Every year, the Council on American-Islamic Relations (CAIR) puts out a report claiming increases in bias crimes, and every year, the *Times* laps it up. Not surprisingly, the paper has refused to admit that many "hate crimes" have been hoaxes.

On May 12, 2005, Andrea Elliott filed a story headlined "Muslims Report 50% Increase in Bias Crimes." She wrote: "The report outlined more than 1,500 cases of harassment and anti-Muslim violence around the country in 2004, including 141 hate crimes, compared with 1,019 harassment cases and 93 hate crimes in 2003." But a random sampling of these "hate crimes" by Daniel Pipes of the Middle East Forum discovered "a pattern of sloppiness, exaggeration and distortion." For instance, CAIR had cited the July 9, 2004, case of apparent arson at a Muslim-owned grocery store in Everett, Washington. But according to Pipes, investigators quickly determined that the store's operator, Mirza Akram, staged the fire to avoid meeting his scheduled payments and to collect on an insurance policy. CAIR also stated that "a Muslim-owned market was burned down in Texas" on August 6, 2004. But by the time CAIR released its report, the owner had already been arrested for having set fire to his own business. These were small-fry "cry wolf" cases, but they should have been reported in some kind of omnibus package by the *Times,* especially since the paper has acted as a mouthpiece for so many of CAIR's charges in the first place.

On the flip side of the coin, the *Times* also refuses to acknowledge the jihadi subtext to hate crimes committed by Muslims. A case in point is the Muslim who ran his SUV into a crowd of students in March 2006. According to TimesWatch, "The man charged with nine counts of attempted murder for driving a Jeep through a crowd at the University of North Carolina at Chapel Hill last Friday told the police that he deliberately rented a four-wheel-drive vehicle so he could 'run over things and keep going,' according to court papers released yesterday by investigators." TimesWatch further quoted statements made to the police in which Mohammed Reza Taheri-azar, an Iranian-born graduate of the university, said he felt the United States government had been "'killing his people across the sea' and that his actions reflected 'an eye for an eye.'" According to Chapel Hill news organizations, the suspect told the police that the attack was to "avenge the deaths of Muslims around the world." Nevertheless, the *Times* did not even use the word "Muslim" at any point in its story, which was buried on page 18.

The features of domestic Islamic extremism are further softened with favorable profiles that accent philosophical and social moderation. While an analysis of the relationship between free speech and hate speech by Adam Liptak in January 2004 mentions that "militant Wahhabism and other religious doctrines advocating violence are freely preached in the United States," the *Times* rarely goes into the mosques and tells us what these radical imams are actually preaching. Nor has the paper looked at the phenomenon of "mosque coups," where militants take over the executive committees, sometimes by intimidation or threats, and change the tone of the mosque. In May 2004, a Muslim feminist, Asra Nomani, wrote in the *Wall Street Journal* about the transformation of her hometown mosque in Morgantown, West Virginia, from mild to militant.

The *Times* highlights the gentler face of Islam through positive profiles of clerics who, it says, stand for moderation. An October 2001 piece by Laurie Goodstein mentioned the fact that before 9/11, "incendiary anti-American messages" were long a "staple" at some Muslim events, but said the attack had prompted influential American Muslim clerics to "temper their tone." One cleric quoted in the piece is Anwar al-Awlaki, thirty years old, the spiritual leader of a mega-mosque in northern Virginia. According to Goodstein, al-Awlaki was being "held up as a new generation of Muslim leader capable of merging East and West: born in New Mexico to parents from Yemen, who studied Islam in Yemen and civil engineering at Colorado State University." Al-Awlaki told Goodstein that in the past, there had been "some statements that were inflammatory, and were considered just talk, but now we realize that talk can be taken seriously and acted upon in a violent radical way." He assured her, "What we might have tolerated in the past, we won't tolerate any more."

Goodstein does not mention that two of the 9/11 hijackers worshipped at al-Awlaki's mosque or that law enforcement officials strongly suspected he was involved in the 9/11 plot, though they could not prove it. And by the end of the decade, al-Awlaki had established himself as an Internet jihadist superstar from a base in Yemen, and played a central role in radicalizing Nidal Hasan, the Fort Hood killer, and recruiting Umar Farouk Abdulmutallab, a.k.a. the "Christmas Bomber" of 2009.

Another radical Islamic cleric given a moderate face by the *Times* was Ali al-Timimi, leader of a mosque in northern Virginia. In 2005 he was convicted of inciting his followers to go to Afghanistan to wage war against the United States right after the 9/11 attacks, and was sentenced to life. At the sentencing, according to Timesman Eric Lichtblau, "Mr. Timimi delivered to the court an impassioned and often eloquent speech that lasted nearly 10 minutes touching on Greek and Roman philosophy, religious history and the United States Constitution. Quoting Aaron Burr, Mr. Timimi said the idea that a cancer researcher like himself would incite his followers to violence was the stuff of 'crudities and absurdities.'" Absent from Lichtblau's account, but included in the *Washington Post* story, was al-Timimi's assertion that his religious beliefs do not recognize "secular law."

Fawaz Damra is another imam who got kid-glove treatment in the *Times*, at least for a while. On September 22, 2001, the religion columnist Gustav Niebuhr described how the Cleveland mosque where Damra preached was the target of a hate crime when a man rammed his car into the building, shattering the front doors and damaging a marble fountain inside. Instead of displaying anger, the congregation prayed for the man, Damra told Niebuhr, who obviously was struck by the imam's compassion. What he was angry about, Damra said, were the 9/11 terror attacks, "because I'm an American."

A month later, Damra was forced to apologize to the city of Cleveland after local television stations broadcast a ten-year-old tape in which he called for the death of Jews as the enemies of the Islamic nation. The tape had been released by federal immigration authorities who used it in a Florida deportation case, and Damra said it no longer reflected his views. Then in 2004, Damra was charged with lying about his ties to terrorist organizations, tax evasion, money laundering, mail and wire fraud, and with providing false information in applying for U.S. citizenship. He was finally convicted of concealing his ties to Palestinian Islamic Jihad and deported to his native West Bank in 2007. Even in the news brief in which it relayed this information, the *Times* found space to say that "His lawyer, Michael Birach, called him a healer who made a real contribution to religious understanding in the Cleveland area and said Damra was a victim of federal officials who wanted to look tough after the Sept. 11 attacks."

Then there was a three-part series in April 2007 by Andrea Elliott, exploring the world of Reda Shata, an Egyptian-born imam in Bay Ridge, Brooklyn, as he negotiated the moral contours of a post-9/11 world for his flock. Headlined "An Imam in America," the series was clearly an effort on Elliott's part to overcome the prejudices instilled in American readers by "a vilifying media":

> *Sheik Reda, as he is called, arrived in Brooklyn one year after Sept. 11. Virtually overnight, he became an Islamic judge and nursery school principal, a matchmaker and marriage counselor, a 24-hour hot line on all things Islamic.*
>
> *Day after day, he must find ways to reconcile Muslim tradition with American life. Little in his rural Egyptian upbringing or years of Islamic scholarship prepared him for the challenge of leading a mosque in America.*
>
> *The job has worn him down and opened his mind. It has landed him, exhausted, in the hospital and earned him a following far beyond Brooklyn.*
>
> *"America transformed me from a person of rigidity to flexibility," said Mr. Shata, speaking through an Arabic translator. "I went from a country where a sheik would speak and the people listened to one where the sheik talks and the people talk back."*

As well written and incisive as it was, the series raised a storm in some quarters. While many read the piece as a calculated bid to make Sheik Reda out to be a moderate, there were many discordant notes belying this impression. "Like Arabs around the world," Elliott reported, "Mr. Shata disagrees profoundly with the United States' steadfast support of Israel, and views the militant group Hamas as a powerful symbol of resistance." Elliott noted that "When Sheik Ahmed Yassin, the founder and spiritual leader of the terror group Hamas, was killed by Israelis in March 2004, Mr. Shata told hundreds who gathered at a memorial service in Brooklyn that the 'lion of Palestine has been martyred.'"

The moderate image was also belied by recorded remarks of the imam that appeared as a multimedia sidebar on the *Times'* own website. Asserting that recent U.S. history has been marked by injustice, the imam says, "Anything about the conduct of Muslims can be used as an excuse to make threats or give punishment. . . . They find us inferior so they target us. They find us so inferior they are unjust to us. . . . Injustice, injustice, injustice. If it strikes a nation and misfortune and disaster starts spreading, then beware, beware people of the Lord of Heavens."

In an interview, Elliott maintained that Sheik Reda "didn't fit into facile categories like 'moderate' or 'conservative.' He's a complex person whose views about Islam in America were still being formed and whose ministry was a work in progress."

The series on Sheik Reda won the Pulitzer Prize. Elliott's editor, Joe Sexton, echoing the imam, said it helped to subtract a few bricks from "the wall of hatred."

But "An Imam in America" had a disturbing coda. Almost a year later, Andrea Elliott wrote a piece headlined "A Cleric's Journey Leads to a Suburban Frontier." It described how Reda Shata had been forced to relocate to New Jersey after receiving threats from more rigid Muslims who objected to his "liberal" teachings that married couples could have oral sex and that a Muslim could sell pork and alcohol if no other work could be found. "In Bay Ridge, the Pulitzer-winning articles prompted a fistfight outside a Dunkin' Donuts," Elliott reported. "Fliers warned in Arabic that the imam was 'a devil.' . . . After weeks of defending himself, Mr. Shata felt worn down." He had already been courted by a mosque in Middletown, New Jersey, and the controversy and implied threats influenced his decision to move.

The fact that it took months for this bit of the story to get into the newspaper suggests a reluctance to admit that much of the Islamic community is filled with intolerance and violence. Instead of the innocuous headline it was given, this report could just as easily have been called "Violent Muslims Play Role in Driving Iman out of Bay Ridge," and it could have examined the distance between the American ideal of tolerance and Islamic norms. When I asked Elliott about this at a panel discussion in New York in March 2010, she said the news value of the attacks on the cleric was "debatable," and in an interview I did with her, she said that other factors aside from intimidation were behind his relocation.

With its hypersensitivity toward Islamic immigrants, the *Times* offers consistently soft-edged reporting about the Council on American-Islamic Relations, which presents itself as "an Islamic NAACP." The communications director of CAIR, Ibrahim Hooper, says its official mission is "to enhance understanding of Islam, encourage dialogue, protect civil liberties, empower American Muslims, and build coalitions that promote justice and mutual understanding." CAIR's real aim, however, is Islamic hegemony. In 1998, its cofounder and former board chairman Omar Ahmad told a Muslim audience that "Islam isn't in America to be equal to any other faith, but to become dominant. . . . The Koran, the Muslim book of scripture, should be the highest authority in America, and Islam the only accepted religion on Earth." A Washington representative of CAIR has said that Muslims "can never be full citizens" of the United States "because there is no way we can be fully committed to the institutions and ideologies of this country."

Yet the *New York Times* has consistently produced articles on CAIR that are little more than repurposed CAIR press releases. As criticism of CAIR mounted on Capitol Hill in the spring of 2007, Neil MacFarquhar came to its defense in a piece headlined "Scrutiny Increases for a Group Advocating for Muslims in the US." He criticized "a small band of people who hate Muslims and deal in half-truths," and maintained that "more than one" government official in Washington "described the standards used by critics to link CAIR to terrorism as akin to McCarthyism, essentially guilt by association."

MacFarquhar went to bat for CAIR again when it was listed as an unindicted co-conspirator in the terrorism trial against the Holy Land Foundation for Relief and Development in Dallas, Texas, beginning in 2007. Under the headline "Muslim Groups Oppose List of 'Co-Conspirators,'" MacFarquhar quoted Muslim activists who claimed that naming the organization as a co-conspirator could "ratchet up the discrimination faced by American Muslims since the Sept. 11 attacks." The legal brief he cited says that the list of co-conspirators "furthers a pattern of the 'demonization of all

things Muslim' that has unrolled in the United States since 2001."
MacFarquhar did not mention that an FBI agent testified during
the trial that CAIR was "a front for Hamas," or that conclusive FBI
evidence has its executive director, Nihad Awad, participating in a
planning meeting with Hamas fundraisers in 1993.

Following a mistrial, a second trial against the Holy Land
Foundation ended in November 2008 when five of its officials
were convicted on charges of funneling $12.4 million to Hamas.
Another outcome was that the FBI, after years of including CAIR
in its Islamic outreach efforts, severed its ties to the organization
in late January 2009—which was news by any definition of the
word. But the *Times* did not report this, nor did it take notice when
a federal grand jury subpoenaed CAIR's records in December of
that year.

Coverage of the Muslim Brotherhood in the United States
carries an even softer journalistic edge. The group operates in
secret through such organizations as the Islamic Society of North
America and the Muslim American Society. Its intent is to spread
Islam throughout various American institutions with the goal of
establishing Sharia. An "explanatory memorandum" captured by
the FBI in 1991 read: "The Ikhwan [brotherhood] must understand that their work in America is a kind of grand Jihad in elimi-
nating and destroying the Western civilization from within and
sabotaging their miserable house by their hands and the hands of
the believers so that it is eliminated and God's religion is made
victorious over all other religions." In September 2004, the *Chicago Tribune* published an exposé on the origins and operations
of the Muslim Brotherhood's American branch. But in the forty
years it has existed in the United States, the *New York Times* has
never once taken on the subject.

The two dominant themes of *Times* reporting on Islam in
America—that Islam has a moderate face and that America is
deeply Islamophobic—fused together in coverage of the controversy in 2010 over the plan to build a Muslim cultural center and
mosque near the site of the destroyed World Trade Center. The
Times responded to the debate surrounding the "Ground Zero
Mosque," as it is popularly called, with one of the most demagogic

pile-ons in its history, with glaring examples of reportage echoing opinion, and with the condescending elitism that has alienated so many Americans.

According to Feisal Abdul Rauf, the imam behind the project, the Islamic center would promote cross-cultural bridge building and represent the "common impulse of our great faith traditions." Supporters said it would symbolize American tolerance toward Islam as well as the constitutional right to freedom of religion.

Opponents of the plan, including family members of 9/11 victims, said it was a sacrilege to put a mosque two short blocks away from "hallowed ground." In fact, the roof of the building to be torn down on the site was pierced by wreckage from the airplanes that hit the World Trade Center, and according to some New York firefighters who worked at Ground Zero after the attack, body parts of victims were found as close as a block away. Victims' families were joined by the Jewish Anti-Defamation League and some Republican political figures, including Newt Gingrich and Sarah Palin. Some prominent Democrats, such as Harry Reid and Howard Dean, also objected to having a mosque on that site, as did some journalistic free-speechers such as Nat Hentoff and Christopher Hitchens.

Some opponents of the mosque said it would feed Islamist triumphalism, since militant Muslim forces have a history of building mosques on the holy sites of their conquests. Opponents also took exception to some of Imam Rauf's past statements, including his claim that America bore complicity for the 9/11 attacks, and to evidence that his tone was less moderate when he addressed audiences outside the United States. There was also the project's murky finances. Rauf had little money to develop the site, and what he did have came from a Muslim who had given money to Hamas and had been dunned by the government for fraud. Some critics thought the project might attract Saudi money and Wahhabi extremists.

The *Times* could have stepped back from the fray and parsed the competing claims of supporters and opponents in a neutral way. It might have examined why, according to some polls, between 65 and 70 percent of Americans objected to the mosque, and why elite opinion was so divergent from popular opinion. It might have examined how its own soft reporting on Islam may have contributed to popular distrust.

Instead, the *Times* produced shrill, scolding editorials, as well as reporting skewed in favor of the project. Additionally, almost every *Times* op-ed and Web columnist wrote favorably about the mosque, throwing shallow and unfair charges of bigotry against dissenters. Supporters of the mosque, such as New York's Mayor Michael Bloomberg, were hailed as heroes of conscience, while opponents, such as the New York gubernatorial candidate Rick Lazio, were smeared as craven opportunists. Imam Rauf was the subject of puff pieces that airbrushed the more dubious facets of his ideology and finances. "For Imam in Muslim Center Furor, a Hard Balancing Act" was the headline of a piece by Anne Barnard, who breezily dismissed the opponents' claims about Rauf. "Some charges, the available record suggests, are unsupported. Some are simplifications of his ideas," she wrote. "In any case, calling him a jihadist appears even less credible than calling him a United States agent."

There were numerous reports on the resistance that other mosque plans were encountering around the country, which painted Americans who objected to these mosques as small-minded Archie Bunkers. When Judea Pearl, father of the slain *Wall Street Journal* reporter Daniel Pearl, announced his opposition to the mosque in an interview with an Israeli news service, it was ignored; he had previously thanked Rauf for his words of solidarity at his son's memorial service in 2002. The *Times'* coverage had its share of victimology, too. A report by Laurie Goodstein was headlined "American Muslims Ask, Will We Ever Belong?"

In a column headlined "Mosque Madness," Maureen Dowd slammed the "moral timidity that would ban a mosque from that neighborhood." Wrote Dowd: "Our enemies struck at our heart, but did they also warp our identity? . . . By now you have to be willfully blind not to know that the imam in charge of the project, Feisal Abdul Rauf, is the moderate Muslim we have allegedly been yearning for."

The most overwrought opinion columns were those by Nicholas Kristof, who wrote four times about the nativism and bigotry he perceived behind the opposition to the mosque. "We're seeing extremists, but not the Muslim kind," read the pull quote of one column, headlined "Is This America?" In another, "America's History of Fear," Kristof maintained that the screeds against Catholics in the nineteenth century "sounded just like the invective today against the Not-at-Ground-Zero Mosque," and that historically, "suspicion of outsiders" had led Americans to "burn witches, intern Japanese and turn away Jewish refugees from the Holocaust." In still another column, he apologized to Muslims around the world for American behavior.

In early September, the *Times* op-ed page featured a piece by Imam Rauf in which he made veiled threats of violence and expressed a repugnant moral equivalence. America's national security and "the personal security of Americans worldwide" were at risk if the project was scuttled, Rauf claimed. "This is why Americans must not back away from completion of this project. If we do, we cede the discourse, and essentially our future, to radicals on both sides." At that point, the *Times'* own polling showed that 60 percent of New Yorkers were against the mosque. The size and the diversity of the opposition made Rauf's assertion about "radicals on both sides" particularly tendentious.

In late August, former Democratic National Committee chairman Howard Dean told interviewers from ABC radio and MSNBC that the mosque was "a real affront to people who lost their lives on 9/11" and said it should be moved. Political and media elites, he said, should recognize that "sixty-five percent of the people were not right-wing bigots." Dean's remarks were eminently newsworthy, as was the furor they set off in the left-wing blogosphere. Other news organizations did stand-alone news stories on the comments; the *Times* did not.

·ᴖ

A *New York Times* editorial from 1982, "Immigration and Purity," articulated a realist view of the subject, saying: "Unlimited immigration was a need, and a glory, of the undeveloped American past. Yet no one believes America can still support it. We must choose how many people to admit, and which ones. That can be done only if we can control the borders." By 2004, when a new push began for tough, enforcement-driven immigration reform, the *Times* had changed its perspective markedly.

When the Comprehensive Immigration Reform Act of 2006 was introduced in Congress, the *Times* showed its bias by failing to report the bill's various "hidden bombs," as one critic called them. For example, it would have replaced the entire immigration bench with activists, since it required that lawyers proposed for immigration judgeships have at least five years practicing immigration law and that existing judges give up lifetime spots on the bench after seven years. The bill had an amendment called the "Dream Act," which would have allowed illegals to attend college at in-state tuition rates, while U.S. citizens from out of state have to pay full freight. The bill also called for a massive granting of citizenship, but did not give the Citizenship and Immigration Service the budget or infrastructure to handle its new responsibilities—which many saw as simply implementing "amnesty" for up to twelve million illegal immigrants. The bill was premised on the idea that the documents that illegals would be filing to prove residency would be authentic, an unrealistic expectation given the easy availability of counterfeit Social Security cards, counterfeit visas, bank statements, tax returns and other fraudulent forms of documentation. Supporters of the bill said that no illegal would be allowed to cut in line ahead of someone patiently waiting in another country for approval to immigrate. Yet they did not specify if illegals who applied for what was nebulously called a "path to citizenship" would have to go home first or could remain here while they were being processed, which was virtually the same thing as cutting the line.

While hesitant to discuss these issues, the *Times* charged into the fray against those calling for felony penalties for facilitating illegal immigration. One editorial claimed, falsely and sensationally, that such penalties could lead to jail for church groups running soup kitchens, or neighbors taking an illegal to a hospital or a pharmacy.

Opponents of the bill flooded Capitol Hill with so many telephone calls, faxes and emails that the Senate switchboard had to be shut down. On this, at least, the *Times* headline writers were honest. "The Grassroots Roared and an Immigration Plan Fell," read one headline. But some of the columnists almost choked on sour grapes. Timothy Egan, a former reporter turned website columnist, blamed conservative radio and television talk show hosts like Rush Limbaugh and Bill O'Reilly. "Pragmatism is being drowned out by bullies with electronic bullhorns, who've got their [Republican] party leaders running scared," Egan said.

The bitterness continued in *Times* analyses where opposition to the liberal view was equated with rank nativism. David Leonhardt, a business columnist, wrote that the backlash "had a familiar feel to it." He went on to associate the tidal wave of illegals entering the United States over the previous two decades with other great eras of immigration into the country—in the 1850s, 1880s and early 1900s. He noted that they too caused a hysterical reaction, the most famous being the rise of the Know-Nothing movement. History looked as if it would repeat itself, suggested Leonhardt—ignoring the fact that this latest group of immigrants, unlike the previous generations, did not come legally through Ellis Island.

The editorial rhetoric from the *Times* got increasingly nasty. Although the editorial page called for civil discourse, it hardly practiced what it preached, instead issuing juvenile insults far more frequently than dependable insights. Even as it denounced the "demagoguery" of the opposition, it practiced its own form. Conservatives who were concerned about enforcement first were said to hold a view of immigration reform that was equivalent to "pest control." Editorialists illogically likened opposing amnesty to favoring segregation. Other editorials indulged in victimology that sounded like self-parody: Hispanics are the new gays; Hispanics are the new Willy Horton; sending them home is immoral and a human rights violation. One editorial, "Ain't That America," said:

Think of America's greatest historical shames. Most have involved the singling out of groups of people for abuse. Name a distinguishing feature—skin color, religion, nationality, language—and it's likely that people here have suffered

*unjustly for it, either through the freelance hatred of citizens
or as a matter of official government policy.*

An especially rich target was the Minutemen, a group of armed volunteers patrolling the southern border with the aim of providing information to the Border Patrol on the movements of illegals trying to sneak into the country. The reporter James McKinley called them "self-proclaimed patriots" whose planned "vigilante watch" along the border was "alarming." Sarah Vowell called them "a nutty experiment" that sprang from America's "violent nativity," further maligning them as "grown men playing army on the Mexican border" because they had nothing better to do. One *Times* story characterized the Minutemen as "anti-immigration," which the paper later had to retract, admitting that they are only against *illegal* immigration.

The Minutemen founder Jim Gilchrist was trying to speak at Columbia University in October 2006 when campus radicals stormed the stage. A melee ensued, as security had to whisk Gilchrist off-stage, ending the event. The *Times* reported some of what happened but omitted some incriminating details, such as students shaking their fists and chanting *"Si se pudo, si se pudo,"* Spanish for "Yes we could!" Others unrolled a banner that read "No one is ever illegal," in Arabic as well as English. But these bits of color were left to other news organizations to report.

Triumphalist hurrahs infused the *Times'* coverage of the large-scale protests by illegal immigrants demanding amnesty in the spring of 2006. Few photographs showed the seas of Mexican flags, and the demonstrators'claims that borders are unnecessary because we're all "one big American landmass" didn't find their way into print.

Meanwhile, the *Times* condemned almost any effort at border enforcement or interior immigration control. Raids on overcrowded immigrant housing on Long Island—such as the modest-sized residence where sixty-four men lived—were denounced, and the targets were quoted as declaring that they were being treated worse than dogs. These raids were painted in totally racial terms and likened to the segregation formerly practiced against blacks. "It's like we're going backwards," one activist told the *Times*.

Unsurprisingly, the paper was apoplectic over Arizona's plans to arrest and deport illegal immigrants in April 2010. The new law was passed in response to drug violence spreading across the border from Mexico, compounding the criminality already associated with rampant immigrant smuggling. The most contested provision entailed permitting local police to arrest and hold people for federal immigration authorities if there was "a reasonable suspicion" they were illegal, after encountering them in the course of traffic stops, domestic violence calls and other routine law enforcement actions.

When the Arizona law was signed, Randal Archibold gave plenty of room in his report for opponents to condemn it as "a recipe for racial and ethnic profiling," and as "an open invitation for harassment and discrimination against Hispanics regardless of their citizenship status." Archibold quoted Cardinal Roger Mahoney of Los Angeles saying that demanding residency documents was equivalent to "Nazism." He said the bill's author, state senator Russell Pearce, was regarded as a "politically incorrect embarrassment by more moderate members of his party."

It was in editorial and op-ed commentary that the *Times* really foamed at the mouth, however. An editorial headlined "Arizona Goes Over the Edge" called the bill "harsh and mean-spirited," and predicted, "If you are brown-skinned and leave home without your wallet, you are in trouble." Timothy Egan referred to Arizona as "a lunatic magnet" and said the "crackpot" law was the work of "crackpots who dominate Republican politics, who in turn cannot get elected without the backing of crackpot media." The former Supreme Court reporter Linda Greenhouse, now a Web columnist and a resident scholar at Yale, went over the edge in a post headlined "Breathing While Undocumented." Greenhouse said she was glad she had already seen the Grand Canyon because "I'm not going back to Arizona as long as it remains a police state," and added: "Wasn't the system of internal passports one of the most distasteful features of life in the Soviet Union and apartheid-era South Africa?"

The very idea of border enforcement and requiring a legal process for immigration has been met by journalistic contempt. Many reports in a myopic and maudlin vein have been the work of Nina Bernstein, whom one former *Times* employee called "nothing more than an advocate" for illegal immigrants. A search of her stories on the *Times* website over the last few years reveals an anthology of charges that immigrants are being abused or victimized in some way.

Bernstein's specialty is stories where immigrant families are split apart because one of the parents got caught up in a raid or a fraud, or where immigrants had spent a substantial length of time in the United States and become integrated into their communities, but were deported for various unfair technicalities. One piece tells of a woman separated from her child, whom she can only visit through the border fence. The teary money quote: "It's like visiting in prison. It's heartbreaking. It's sad because there's a fence when we know we are all supposed to be together." A story in February 2010, "A Fatal Ending for a Family Forced Apart by Immigration Law," told of a 32-year-old father of three and husband of an American citizen who was sent back to his native Ecuador, which he had left when he was seventeen. The man was picked up in an immigration raid and took "voluntary departure" instead of being deported, which boosted his chances of getting back in. But the couple's application for a marriage visa was rejected, and the man committed suicide in Ecuador.

Bernstein also filed a story decrying a perfectly legal program that Immigration and Customs Enforcement had set up at the Rikers Island jail complex in New York to identify undocumented foreign criminals. In a city with a "don't ask, don't tell approach to immigration," the program "may come as a surprise to many," she wrote. Using immigration advocates as her predominant sources, Bernstein allowed them to depict the program as a "warning" of what the rest of the country could expect. The process of deporting criminal aliens once their sentences were up, according to immigrant rights groups, was "leaving the deportees' families abandoned in New York and dependent on our city's strained social service system." True, the process of dealing with twelve million people who broke the law to get here is going to involve some pain. But constantly harping on that does not encourage compassion.

One reason why the *Times'* immigration reporting sounds so off is the success of lobbying groups such as the National Association of Hispanic Journalists. There's also anxiety about "feeding a backlash" against poor Third Worlders. But scorn for patriotism—not nationalism or jingoism, but patriotism—is certainly a factor too, along with an agenda to deconstruct the idea of citizenship. At the *Times,* cosmopolitan postnationalism trumps the traditional notion of American community, and "the cult of ethnicity" that Arthur Schlesinger warned about in *The Disuniting of America* has overshadowed the commonweal. The diversity to which the *Times* is so committed has had mixed blessings for the United States, which the paper has not bothered to investigate. As the Harvard social scientist Robert Putnam found, places with the most ethnic and racial diversity are also places with low civic engagement and social trust. Community life withers and people tend to "hunker down" in order to escape the friction that develops in excessively diverse places. Yet the *Times* promotes "diversity" as an aggressive creed, one whose spirit was captured by the columnist Charles Blow in a taunt at the Tea Partiers: "You may want your country back, but you can't have it. . . . Welcome to America: The Remix."

six

Culture Wars

n his NBC News blog in April 2008, Brian Williams, a fairly mainstream newsman, noted with bemusement that the lead story in that week's Sunday Style section was "Through Sickness, Health, Sex Change." In the same section, Williams also found "Was I on a Date or Baby-Sitting?" and "Let's Say You Want to Date a Hog Farmer." The cover story of the Sunday magazine was about "The Newlywed Gays," while the lead story in the Travel section reported on the rise of vacation resorts catering to nudists. Williams wondered "exactly what readers the paper is speaking to, or seeking."

The public editor Daniel Okrent had wondered the same thing in 2004 when he wrote a column asking "Is The New York Times a Liberal Newspaper?" His answer: "Of course it is." Okrent said the word "postmodern" had been used "an average of four times a week" that year, and if this didn't reflect a Manhattan as opposed to a mainstream sensibility, he remarked, "then I'm Noam Chomsky." (In August 2010, the standards editor, Philip Corbett, urged the *Times* newsroom to limit the use of the word "hipster," which he said had appeared 250 times in the last year alone.) Okrent also noted that the culture pages of the *Times* "often feature forms of art, dance or theater that may pass for normal (or at least tolerable) in New York but might be pretty shocking in other places." The *Times Magazine*, he said, featured photo essays of "models who look like they're preparing to murder (or be murdered), and others arrayed in a mode you could call dominatrix chic." In the Sunday Style section, he found "gay wedding announcements, of course, but also downtown sex clubs and T-shirts bearing the slogan, 'I'm afraid of Americans.' . . . The front page of the Metro section has featured a long piece best described by its subheadline, 'Cross-Dressers Gladly Pay to Get in Touch with Their Feminine Side.'"

Okrent acknowledged that a newspaper has the right to decide what's important and what's not, but stipulated that some readers will think, "This does not represent me or my interests. In fact, it represents my enemy." He finished his controversial meditation: "It's one thing to make the paper's pages a congenial home for editorial polemicists, conceptual artists, the fashion-forward or other like-minded souls (European papers, aligned with specific political parties, have been doing it for centuries), and quite another to tell only the side of the story your co-religionists wish to hear." For those with a different worldview from the one that dominates the *Times*, the paper must necessarily seem "like an alien beast."

Arthur Sulzberger Jr., the publisher, responded to a query from Okrent by saying that he preferred to call the paper's viewpoint "urban." The tumultuous, polyglot metropolitan environment that the *Times* occupies meant that "We're less easily shocked,"

Sulzberger said. He maintained that the paper reflected "a value system that recognizes the power of flexibility."

But the cat was out of the bag. An authoritative voice at the *Times* had said, in effect, that the paper's views—especially in matters of culture—were characterized by moral relativism and a celebration of the transgressive over traditional American norms and values.

Indeed, the *New York Times* has been waging its own war against the traditional culture. In its coverage and criticism of media, film, television, books, poetry and music, the *Times* looks through a radical-chic lens, affirming marginal causes and communities at the expense of normative values, and deriding what members of the academic community ridicule as "heteronormativity." The *Times* has embraced postmodernism with a vengeance, along with a deconstructionist cultural agenda that has spread through the paper like a computer virus.

·⁓

The *Times'* biases have come sharply into view in its media criticism, especially regarding "conservative media," and above all, Fox News. Grudging admiration might have been a legitimate approach for the *Times* to use in covering Fox. As Jack Shafer put it in *Slate,* "you might not like what you see on the Fox News Channel, but you've got to admit the variety of voices heard on cable news increased after [Rupert] Murdoch started the channel in 1996." In his *Washington Post* column, Charles Krauthammer explained that "Fox broke the liberal media's monopoly on the news, altered the intellectual and ideological landscape of America, and gave not only voice but also legitimacy to a worldview that had been utterly excluded from the mainstream media." In the process, Fox News shattered "the scriptural authority" of the *New York Times.*

The *Times* of Abe Rosenthal's day might have criticized Fox but also acknowledged that the more points of view, the better in a robust democracy. The *Times* of Sulzberger Jr., however, saw

Fox only as a dangerous development—a medium that "shills for Republicans and panders to the latest American religious manias," as Howell Raines declared on *Charlie Rose* in 2008. Raines called Rupert Murdoch "a flagrant pirate," and he described Roger Ailes, Fox's founder and president, as "an unprincipled thug who has assumed a journalistic disguise." In 2005, the *Times'* executive editor Bill Keller told the *New Yorker* that Fox's slogan of being "fair and balanced" was "the most ingeniously cynical slogan in the history of media marketing." And in April 2010, the television writer Brian Stelter gave the comedian Jon Stewart a wide berth to call Fox a "truly terrible, cynical news organization."

The biggest lightning rod for the *Times* has been Fox's Bill O'Reilly. The self-declared "Culture Warrior," O'Reilly can be feisty and over-the-top, as when he threatened to make a citizen's arrest on San Francisco's Mayor Gavin Newsom for performing gay marriages under dubious legality. But *The O'Reilly Factor* has used its star's old-fashioned moral fervor to break stories that other news organizations have ignored, and to set a news agenda that other organizations have followed. It led on the United Way's post-9/11 misuse of funds, put a spotlight on child molestation and a legal system that goes too easy on it, insisted on the distinction between legal and illegal aliens, and explored the misappropriation of taxpayer dollars to the left-wing organization ACORN. O'Reilly spares no opportunity to go after the *New York Times*, which he has labeled "a brochure for the far left in America." He aggressively questioned the paper for the number of stories on Abu Ghraib that ran on the front page (more than four dozen), declaring it a sign of the *Times'* antimilitary bias and lack of patriotism. He has done segments insinuating that the *Times* may have known about possible illegal ACORN campaign contributions to Barack Obama but spiked the story.

After ignoring him altogether for years, the *Times* started hitting O'Reilly back. It made fun of his concern about the secularization of Christmas, and allowed Frank Rich to accuse him of having been "deployed" by Mel Gibson to defend Gibson's film *The Passion*—a charge that led to an official *Times* correction. In the spring of 2007, the *Times* featured a study on "propaganda techniques" used on *The O'Reilly Factor,* and was happy to report the study's conclusion that O'Reilly beat Father Charles Coughlin "by a mile" in the use of such techniques.

Another lightning rod for the *Times'* antipathy toward Fox is Glenn Beck, who joined the network in 2009 and instantly started earning through-the-roof ratings. The *Times* most often dismisses Beck with a flick of the wrist, but this contempt has been hard to sustain when Beck has broken important stories that the *Times* ignored.

One of these stories centered on Van Jones, a special advisor to the White House Council on Environmental Quality, whose portfolio was "green energy" and environmental jobs. In July 2009, Beck started banging his drum against Jones, who had been caught on video calling Republicans "assholes" in a February speech. Beck also reported that Jones had signed a "truther" petition claiming that "people within the current [Bush] administration may indeed have allowed 9/11 to happen, perhaps as a pretext to war." Calling Jones a "communist-anarchist radical," Beck demanded that he resign, igniting a national firestorm that achieved exactly that end.

When the *Times* finally ran its first Van Jones story, it called him a "charismatic community organizer and 'green jobs' advocate from the San Francisco Bay Area" who had become "fodder for conservative critics and Republican officials." But it did not report, as Beck had done, that Jones had embraced communism in the early 1990s. The managing editor, Jill Abramson, admitted on the *Times* website that the paper was "a beat behind on this story." To which the *New York Post's* Kyle Smith responded: "The Times purposely ignored [the Van Jones story] because it was hoping that the story would go away, because it likes people like Comrade Jones and was hoping he wouldn't be forced out. The Times doesn't like people like Glenn Beck and didn't want him to be able to claim Jones's scalp."

An even more important story that Beck drove and the *Times* ignored was an undercover video sting of ACORN. Two young filmmakers went to the organization's offices in cities around the country asking ACORN workers for advice on establishing brothels, illegally importing underage girls to work in them, and avoiding detection by the police and trouble from the IRS. The 25-year-old male filmmaker was dressed as a caricature of a pimp; his comely 20-year-old female colleague wore skimpy tops with miniskirts and other streetwalker accessories. In Baltimore, an ACORN worker was caught on camera telling the "prostitute" that she could describe herself to tax authorities as an "independent artist" and that the underage illegal-immigrant sex workers could be claimed as "dependants." In Brooklyn, ACORN workers told the pair how to lie on mortgage documents in order to buy a house of ill repute. In San Diego, an ACORN worker suggested that the two seek their "girls" in Tijuana and said he could help smuggle them into the country.

As the videos were released one by one on the Internet and played on Glenn Beck's show, various government bodies with links to ACORN severed their ties. The Senate voted to end all funding for ACORN, and the Census Bureau, which uses ACORN as an unpaid resource, cut its connections. The New York City Council froze all its funding for ACORN, and the Brooklyn district attorney opened a criminal probe. In late March, ACORN announced that it was closing all its offices nationwide. Yet the *Times* ran nothing whatsoever until a week after the first video was posted. And then, as with Van Jones, it claimed that Republicans were mobilizing people to dig up dirt.

The paper's slow reflexes on the ACORN story, following the controversy over Van Jones, "suggested that it has trouble dealing with stories arising from the polemical world of talk radio, cable television and partisan blogs," wrote the public editor, Clark Hoyt. "Some stories, lacking facts, never catch fire. But others do, and a newspaper like The Times needs to be alert to them or wind up looking clueless or, worse, partisan itself." Hoyt said that many readers who wrote him said the *Times* was "protecting the progressive movement."

But the *Times* was definitely not slow off the mark when the filmmaker who produced the ACORN videos, James O'Keefe, was arrested with three others in January 2010 for allegedly trying to tamper with the telephones in the office of Senator Mary Landrieu of Louisiana. "High Jinks to Handcuffs for Landrieu Provocateur," read the front-page headline, with the foursome's mug shots below it. They had plotted a sting to determine whether Landrieu may have been avoiding constituents' complaints during the debate over health care reform. (In May, O'Keefe and his cohorts pleaded guilty to a federal misdemeanor charge.)

Antipathy to Fox News translated into bias in the reporting of Rupert Murdoch's successful bid to buy the *Wall Street Journal* in 2007. During the run-up to the sale, the *Times* did two hostile pieces that were produced to make the Bancroft family, which owned the *Journal,* think twice about selling to Murdoch. One was centered on his business practices, especially in China, where the *Times* suggested he regularly caved in to the Communist Party to protect his financial interests. The other story focused on alleged worry among *Journal* reporters about Murdoch's journalistic ethics and the possibility that he might inject his conservative political ideology into the news. "If Mr. Murdoch does acquire The Journal," fretted Paul Krugman on the op-ed page, "it will be a dark day for America's news media—and American democracy. If there were any justice in the world, Mr. Murdoch, who did more than anyone in the news business to mislead this country into an unjustified, disastrous war, would be a discredited outcast. Instead, he's expanding his empire."

While Fox gets hate mail from the *Times,* liberal media figures and their organizations routinely get valentines. An October 2006 profile of Tavis Smiley, a black former NPR radio host who now has a show on PBS, was headlined "Media Man on a Mission: The Whirl of Tavis Smiley." The piece by Felicia Lee gushed about how he had just left a meeting with Venezuela's president, Hugo Chavez, and likened his media saturation to that of Ann Coulter and Rush Limbaugh (about whom the *Times* rarely has anything nice to say). "Do I cop to trying to motivate people, trying to inspire people, trying to uplift people through my symposiums, my books, my radio, my speeches?" Smiley is quoted as asking. "Yes, I cop to that. But it's all born of love." Lee did not mention some of his less uplifting statements, such as comparing George W. Bush to a serial killer in 2000, or insisting that O. J. Simpson was a sympathetic figure.

Coverage of the now-defunct liberal radio network Air America, always a relatively marginal enterprise, showed the same high regard. A puff piece headlined "They Look Nothing Like Rush Limbaugh" profiled two female personalities on the network, Rachel Maddow, who would go on to have her own cable television show on MSNBC, and Randi Rhodes, who made veiled calls for Bush's assassination on the air, denounced Hillary Clinton and Geraldine Ferraro as "whores" in a YouTube video, and made false allegations of being attacked on the Upper West Side—all of which called her mental balance into question but didn't qualify for mention in the *Times*. Grasping at straws, the piece said that Air America could become a "station brand," even though at that point (November 2005) it was heard in only seventy-two cities nationwide and ranked number 24 in New York City, which is considered a liberal stronghold.

When she moved from the bankrupted Air America to her own show in an MSNBC primetime slot, Rachel Maddow was the focus of a string of positive stories in the *Times*, including a vacuous Q&A with Edward Levine headlined "A Pundit in the Country." In the interview, conducted at her weekend home in Berkshire, Massachusetts, Maddow revealed that she always carried a handkerchief and that her partner, Susan Mikula, "buys me cute ones." Not long afterward, the *Times* declared Maddow a lesbian icon. Daphne Merkin—who once famously wrote in the *New Yorker* about her fetish for being spanked—applauded Maddow in a magazine story headlined "Butch Fatale: Lesbian Glamour Steps Out of the Closet." Until recently, Merkin wrote, "lesbians have been the wallflowers at the homosexual dance, waiting to get their share of recognition." Now, however, "Lesbianism has finally come into a glamour of its own, an appeal that goes beyond butch and femme archetypes into a more universal seduction. Her name is Rachel Maddow, the polished-looking, self-declared gay newscaster who stares out from the MSNBC studio every weekday night and makes love to her audience."

·‑

In its treatment of film, television, theater, music and other arts, the *Times'* politicization is more subtle, involving ideological innuendo, radical-chic attitudinizing and liberal "editorial needles," as Abe Rosenthal called them. But sometimes the subtlety gives way to naked political preaching. According to Peter Bart, a former Timesman and now *Variety* editor, "The Times has vastly stepped up its coverage of popular culture and in doing so, seems to be bending its normal rules of journalistic fairness."

Reviewing George Clooney's *Syriana* (2005), a sinister look at American foreign policy, A. O. Scott wrote:

> *Someone is sure to complain that the world doesn't really work the way it does in "Syriana": that oil companies, law firms and Middle Eastern regimes are not really engaged in semiclandestine collusion, to control the global oil supply and thus influence the destinies of millions of people. O.K., maybe. Call me naïve—or paranoid, or liberal, or whatever the favored epithet is this week—but I'm inclined to give Mr. Gaghan [the screenwriter] the benefit of the doubt.*

The Kingdom of Heaven (2005), Ridley Scott's expensive box office failure, was seen even by some liberal filmgoers as a rabid exercise in anti-Western, anti-Christian, pro-Islamic bias. But it drew a rave from the *Times* critic Manohla Dargis, who called it "an even-handed account of one of the least fair-minded, even-handed chapters in human history, during which European Christians descended on the Middle East for more than 200 years." It spoke to the current world situation, Dargis declared, with parallels to the West "invading Muslim lands." Dargis was in a minority in this judgment. The eminent Cambridge University historian Jonathan Riley-Smith criticized the film's false portrayal of Muslims as sophisticated and the Christian Crusaders as barbaric. In an interview with the *Telegraph* of London, he called it "Osama Bin Laden's version of the Crusades," which would "fuel Islamic fundamentalists." And in the *Times* of London, he wrote, "At a time of interfaith tension, nonsense like this will only reinforce existing myths."

Movies about the wars in Iraq and Afghanistan, and the larger War on Terror, may have failed at the box office, but they have succeeded at the *Times*. Manohla Dargis favorably reviewed *Lions for Lambs* (2007), a triptych involving two soldiers who die in a remote mountain area of Afghanistan, the college professor who influenced them to join the service, and a newswoman being briefed on a (doomed) forward outpost strategy by an unctuous U.S. senator. From this film, Dargis asserted, viewers will learn that "America is no longer only the land of the free, home of the brave, but also the opportunistic and the compromised."

A. O. Scott hailed Brian DePalma's *Redacted* (2007), about the rape of a teenage girl and the murder of her and her family by U.S. troops in Iraq, because it brought us "face to face with what we have been unable to see or acknowledge with a collage of raw feelings and angry arguments." In his review of *Rendition* (2007), which thrust an innocent CIA analyst into the black world of "torture, kidnapping and other abuses," Scott wrote that the film used "the resources of mainstream movie-making to get viewers thinking about a moral crisis that many of us would prefer to ignore." He added, however, that it was "inevitable that someone with a loud voice and a small mind will label *Rendition* anti-American." In *Body of Lies* (2008), Scott saw a likeness between a heedless CIA agent portrayed in the film and President George W. Bush. "It's possible that this resemblance is meant to imply a parallel between the president and Hoffman, who is immune to self-doubt and allergic to second thoughts about the righteousness of his actions." A feature on the film by Robert Mackay cited its themes of "ruthlessness, political expediency and moral bankruptcy."

The Matt Damon vehicle *Green Zone* (2010) has a preposterous plot and flopped at the box office, but that didn't stop *Times* critics and feature writers from praising it. The story involves an Army staff sergeant (Damon) who explores what A. O. Scott calls "the hidden history of manipulation and double dealing" in the quest for Iraqi weapons of mass destruction. Although a noncom,

Damon's character breaks the chain of command to search out the deception behind the WMD issue. He ends up being targeted for assassination by scheming civilian political appointees. Nevertheless, Scott hails *Green Zone* for its ability "to fictionalize without falsifying," and says that while the film "may not be literally accurate in every particular, it has the rough authority of novelistic truth." An arts feature by Robert Mackay gave the director, Paul Greengrass, a platform to explain that he wanted to tell the story of the invasion of Iraq because "This hugely difficult process by which we ended up going to war there, only then to find that the reason that we went to war was not true, left a huge legacy I think—a legacy of fear, paranoia and mistrust."

The ideological messages are just as pronounced, maybe even more so, in the criticism, commentary and feature coverage of documentaries. Stephen Holden said of *Trumbo* (2008), an homage to the blacklisted Communist screenwriter Dalton Trumbo, "If the story of the Hollywood blacklist and the lives it destroyed has been told many times before, it still bears repeating, especially in the post-9/11 climate of fearmongering, of Guantánamo, of flag pins as gauges of patriotism."

One of the more egregious examples of political naiveté came in a David Halbfinger review of *Winter Soldier* (2005), an antiwar documentary on Scott Camill, a major figure in the protest movement of the 1960s. In the review, Halbfinger equates American military abuses in Iraq with the alleged throwing of prisoners out of helicopters in Vietnam, which is a bit of a historical stretch. He refers to Camill as "Jesus-like," neglecting to mention that Camill had fantasized about assassinating political figures on Capitol Hill during congressional hearings.

The *Times'* critics have also been effusive in praising Michael Moore, especially his recent look at the American health care system. When *Sicko* premiered at Cannes in May 2007, Manohla Dargis praised it as Moore's "most fluid provocation to date." A. O. Scott was not concerned that Moore had "no use for neutrality, balance or objectivity," and seemed to revel in the fact that the filmmaker's "polemical, left-wing manner seems calculated to drive guardians of conventional wisdom bananas."

Poetry and pop music can also become ideologically charged at the *Times*. In a review of *Poems from Guantanamo*, a volume containing twenty-two poems from prisoners at that camp, Dan Chiasson said, "You don't read this book for pleasure; you read it for evidence. And if you are an American citizen you read it for evidence of the violence your government is doing to total strangers in a distant place, some of whom (perhaps all of whom, since without due process how are we to tell?) are as innocent of crimes against our nation as you are." According to the Pentagon, one of the poets praised by Chiasson was among the scores of former Guantanamo detainees who re-enlisted in terror activities once they were released and returned to their home countries.

With its taste for the transgressive, the *Times* even celebrates the political and pornographic dimensions of hip-hop and rap, which John McWhorter characterizes as "the most overtly and consistently misogynistic music ever produced in human history." He puts blame on "an academic establishment and intellectual elite that seems unwilling to judge the dynamics of black life by the standards that it applies to others." The *Times,* a paragon of that intellectual elite, has averted its eyes from the harsher aspects of the music and the "gangsta" lifestyle its performers affect as a way of preserving street cred. In a July 2007 website Q&A, the culture editor Sam Sifton stood behind his paper's coverage of hip-hop, "because it's an art form. You may find some of it trite and repetitious, crude and juvenile, but it is," he said to one dubious reader, adding patronizingly, "It may be that you're just not listening hard enough."

The in-your-face style of the *Times'* rap criticism was apparent in an August 2007 piece by Kelefa Sanneh. Headlined "Still Here by Being Stubborn, Not Mellow," the story was about a comeback CD by a pair of Texas rappers calling themselves UGK, one of whom had gone to prison in 2001 for aggravated assault. "What do rappers lose when they get older?" Sanneh asked. "In the case of Bun B and Pimp C, two rappers in their 30s from Port Arthur, Texas, who perform together as UGK, the answer is, not much."

Sanneh reviewed the duo's history, explaining that in 1992 they had made a major-label debut with *Too Hard to Swallow*. Their lyrics chronicle a Texan underworld "full of pimps who talk slick, pushers who talk tough, snitches who talk too much." In a "silky" song called "Gravy," Bun B waxed physiological, as Sanneh quoted him: "When I put one up in your dome / You'll be leakin' out plasma and pus, and your mouth'll fill up with foam." Sanneh continued, "There is plenty of old-fashioned trash talking here too. More than once, Bun B reminds listeners that he and his partner have brash new nicknames: Big Dick Cheney and Tony Snow," the second, apparently, a reference to cocaine. "Throughout these two CDs, kilos are sold, foes are threatened, cars are painted and repainted, and prostitutes are put in their place."

Most normal people would regard these two as psycho-paths, but Sanneh sees them as prophets. "Gangsta rap, broadly speaking—streetwise protagonists, explicit lyrics, hard-boiled stories—turned out to be hip-hop's future, to the consternation of gripers past and present. Southern gangsta rap, in particular. It's now clear that Bun B and Pimp C were ahead of their time." (In some archived versions of Sanneh's review, some of the dumber and more offensive material noted above has been cut.)

·-

Times critics are always alert to possible victories by the left in the culture war. In 2003, as this war was growing fiercer because of the invasion of Iraq, the Sunday Week in Review section ran a piece about a possible literary upswing for progressives. "For the first time in recent memory," Emily Eakin noted, "The Times [best-seller] list, the nation's most influential barometer of book sales, is pitting liberals and conservatives against each other in roughly equal numbers, ending what some publishing execu-tives say is nearly a decade of dominance by right-wing authors." Alongside such conservative best-selling authors as Bill O'Reilly, Ann Coulter and Laura Ingraham were liberal-minded books like *Lies and the Lying Liars Who Tell Them* by Al Franken, *Bushwhacked* by Molly Ivins, *The Great Unraveling* by Paul Krugman, *Big Lies* by Joe Conason, and *Thieves in High Places* by Jim Hightower.

Eakin may have been right in calling the *Times Book Review*'s best-seller list "the nation's most influential barometer of book sales." But its value as an objective measurement of American literary taste is compromised in view of the fact that all the liberal books Eakin noted had gotten reviews in that same publication, while none of the conservative authors did—as dozens of conservative books have been studiously ignored by the *Times* despite their commercial success.

Since late 1970, when John Leonard as editor turned an entire issue over to Neil Sheehan as a forum to protest the Vietnam War, the *Times Book Review* (or TBR as it's called in the trade) has leaned to the left. The bias was especially pronounced from 1989 to 1994, when the TBR was controlled by Rebecca Sinkler and became "ruthlessly partisan," as the literary scholar John Ellis famously remarked. "The Times management has decided to donate the Book Review to the cause of political reeducation," Ellis wrote, turning it into "a lobby for political correctness" as well as "mindless bourgeois bashing and freakish sexual attitudes."

Ellis described how "p.c. books are protected by assigning them to ideological clones of their author, while books that object to any aspect of p.c. ideology are given to the very people the book criticizes, who respond with predictable animosity." Among the liberal books that got sweetheart literary deals at the TBR, as Ellis noted, were Gloria Steinem's *Revolution from Within,* reviewed by *Mother Jones* editor Deirdre English; Susan Faludi's *Backlash,* reviewed by Ellen Goodman; and Michael Harrington's *Socialism: Past and Future,* reviewed by Paul Berman. "With matchmaking skills like these," Ellis observed acidly, "Ms. Sinkler is wasted in journalism. She should run a dating service." Meanwhile, conservative authors such as Dinesh D'Souza, Thomas Sowell and Shelby Steele, all of whom had "established themselves as major contributors to the national debate" on race, were assigned to antagonists and got reviews that were nasty or dismissive, or that purposively ignored their central arguments.

Ellis scored Sinkler for her love of the postmodern jargon of university cultural radicals, and for her obsession with radical feminism and the associated "discourse on gender that sustains it." Sinkler, he charged, had managed to make the TBR "a place where just as in Women's Studies Departments no reality check operates to slow the radical feminist slide into ever greater unreality."

In the Sinkler years, the TBR projected an unremitting hostility to anything resembling normative culture, especially if the book in question came from a high-profile conservative. Rush Limbaugh's *The Way Things Ought to Be* spent 53 weeks on the *Times* best-seller list, 24 of them as number one, but was not reviewed until a year after its first appearance on the list. And then it was derided by Walter Goodman, who said that Limbaugh's writing alternated "between slobberings of sincerity and slaverings of invective." Goodman was appalled that the book was aimed at "a part of middle America—call it the silent majority or The American People or the booboisie—that feels it has been on the receiving end of the droppings of the bicoastals as they wing first class from abortion-rights rallies to AIDS galas to save-the-pornographer parties."

Rebecca Sinkler was followed as editor of the TBR by Charles (Chip) McGrath, who institutionalized her double standards, praising liberals and penalizing conservatives. He ignored Ann Coulter's best-selling *High Crimes and Misdemeanors,* which was scalding in its criticism of President Clinton, while he affirmed such pro-Clinton books as Sidney Blumenthal's *The Clinton Wars* and Joe Klein's *The Natural: The Misunderstood Presidency of Bill Clinton.*

During the McGrath years, Regnery Books, which is based in Washington D.C. and specializes in conservative titles, perfected the marketing art of doing an end run around the TBR. *Dereliction of Duty* by Robert Patterson, *Useful Idiots* by Mona Charen, *The Politically Incorrect Guide to American History* by Thomas E. Woods, and *Bias* by Bernard Goldberg all made it to the *Times* best-seller list, but none got a TBR review. Regnery's ability to promote the steak without getting the sizzle suggested that the TBR had become obsolete as a cultural arbiter because of its decision to participate in the culture wars rather than merely report on them.

McGrath's principle of exclusion went so far as to ignore a series of extremely important books on Soviet espionage in America. Two of these were part of Yale University Press's Annals of Communism series by Harvey Klehr and John Haynes, which used materials from the recently opened Soviet archives. *The Secret World of Soviet Espionage* (1995) and *The Soviet World of American Communism* (1998) were not reviewed, although (or perhaps because) they revealed extensive, hitherto undocumented evidence of broad Soviet manipulation of members of the Communist Party of the USA, and they named names of Americans who were on the KGB payroll.

In the immediate post-9/11 period, McGrath drew the lines on correctness ever more tightly. The TBR refused to review Oriana Fallaci's European blockbuster, published in the United States as *The Rage and the Pride*, which attacked radical Islamic terrorism and much of Islam itself for being antidemocratic, misogynistic and violent. (According to Fallaci, "to believe that a good Islam and a bad Islam exist goes against all reason.") Instead, the TBR reviewed Noam Chomsky's anti-American screed *Hegemony and Survival*, published about the same time as Fallaci's work. Samantha Power, a left-wing human rights scholar from Harvard, complained about Chomsky's "glib and caustic tone," but added respectfully that "his critiques have come to influence and reflect mainstream opinion elsewhere in the world," and closed her review by insisting that Chomsky was "right to demand that officials in Washington devote themselves more zealously to strengthening international institutions, curbing arms flows and advancing human rights."

That the TBR would give so much space to someone whom Arthur Schlesinger Jr. referred to as "an intellectual crook" was striking. But the real scandal of Power's Chomsky review is what she left out. Although she herself was the author of *The Problem from Hell: America and the Age of Genocide* (which won a Pulitzer Prize), she failed to mention Chomsky's support for the French Holocaust denier Robert Faurisson, or his role in denying Pol Pot's systematic slaughter and starvation of between two and three million Cambodians.

In 2004, when the *Times* chose Sam Tanenhaus as McGrath's successor, many conservatives were surprised, and elated, because Tanenhaus was not identified as a leftist. He had written a well-reviewed book about Whittaker Chambers and was working on a biography of William F. Buckley Jr. Not only was he fluent in conservative ideas, he seemed at first to sympathize with some of them. Tanenhaus assigned reviews of some conservative books, including Jonah Goldberg's *Liberal Fascism*, which earned a mixed review from David Oshinsky. Fred Siegel's *Prince of the City: Giuliani, New York and the Genius of American Life* appeared on the front page.

It was not long, however, before the bloom was off the rose. James Piereson's book about the ideological impact of the JFK assassination, *Camelot and the Cultural Revolution*, was savaged in a sneering review by Jacob Heilbrunn. More and more, Tanenhaus simply ignored conservative titles. Like his predecessors, Tanenhaus continued to snub Regnery books, even when they were riding high on the *Times'* own best-seller list, such as *America Alone* by Mark Steyn, *Power to the People* by Laura Ingraham, and *A Slobbering Love Affair* by Bernard Goldberg. Likewise books from the publisher of this book, Encounter, which in June 2008 ran an open letter on its website declaring that it would no longer be sending review copies of its books to the *Times*. Two Encounter books had been on the *Times* extended best-seller list that month and yet no reviews were forthcoming. The TBR redlined books by conservative authors with provocative arguments that would have added much to the national conversation. One of these was Mark Krikorian's *The New Case Against Immigration: Both Legal and Illegal,* which received spectacular advance praise by people ranging from neoconservatives like William Bennett to the neoliberal super-blogger Mickey Kaus. Also ignored were books on Islamism, such as Andrew McCarthy's *Willful Blindness* (2008) and *The Grand Jihad* (2010), both of which made the *Times'* extended best-seller list.

Meanwhile, the TBR ran reviews of such fare as *Hung: A Meditation on the Measure of Black Men in America*, Jenna Jameson's *How to Make Love Like a Porn Star*, and *The Surrender*, a paean to sodomy by a former ballerina.

Bill O'Reilly's *Culture Warrior* got a review, but it was by Jacob Heilbrunn, who dissed O'Reilly as "an expert at making mountains out of molehills" and as a reincarnation of Joe McCarthy and Father Coughlin. After five previous best-sellers, Ann Coulter finally got her first TBR review, for *Godless*. But it was by a self-proclaimed liberal, Liesl Schillinger, who wrote that the book was "loaded with recorded sound bites of conservative vitriol from the venomous vixen herself."

The TBR under Tanenhaus has continued to ignore the work of John Earl Haynes and Harvey Klehr, specifically their blockbuster *Spies: The Rise and Fall of the KGB*, where they indisputably established that I. F. Stone was a paid agent for the KGB, along with numerous other Americans. While icing *Spies*, the TBR instead reviewed a pro-Stone biography, *The Life and Times of I. F. Stone* by David Gutterplan, which weakly challenged the evidence that Stone "worked closely with the KGB in 1936 and 1938," and then went on to paint a mostly positive picture of the journalist.

The *Times*' hostility to the architects of the Bush administration's Iraq policy could be seen in the review of Jacob Heilbrunn's book on neoconservatives, *They Knew They Were Right: The Rise of the Neocons* (2008). Once considered a member of that set, Heilbrunn used the book as a way to distance himself from it. Reviewing the book, Tim Noah of the liberal webzine *Slate* affirmed Heilbrunn's argument that neocons had an "uncompromising temperament" and an "artificial clarity" about the world.

But something unexpected and ultimately embarrassing to the TBR came along during Heilbrunn's effort to reinvent himself. A British critic, Corey Robin, noted in the *Nation* that Heilbrunn had lifted language and ideas in several places from his own work and that of others. The charge of plagiarism was echoed a year later, again in the *Nation*, when the paperback edition of Heilbrunn's book was issued with minimal changes in the area of concern. The plagiarism went unnoted in the pages of the TBR, which often relays gossip about the literary-industrial complex.

The nasty edge that Tanenhaus had allowed to creep into reviews of conservative authors grew nastier. When another former conservative, Damon Linker, reviewed two books about Norman Podhoretz in 2010, he closed by describing "the Brownsville Wunderkind" as an "embittered, paranoid crank, standing by and for himself alone." Surely a man who has a large body of important writing and editing behind him deserves more civility than that.

Meanwhile, over in the section of the daily paper dealing with literary matters, the *Times* has aided and abetted at least two major frauds. One of them involved the literary persona of JT LeRoy, a 25-year-old alleged former transvestite truck-stop prostitute and drug addict who became an underground cult novelist, with celebrity admirers like Madonna, Courtney Love and Bono, and literary luminaries like Michael Chabon, Tobias Wolff and Mary Gaitskill. In 2006 it was disclosed that the cult novelist whose books include *Sarah* and *The Heart Is Deceitful Above All Things* had not been a cross-dressing truck-stop hooker, did not come from West Virginia, had not been rescued in San Francisco by a bohemian couple with connections to a prominent psychiatrist, and had not overcome his past through years of therapy to "shed the Warholian wig and sunglasses" that had become his public mask—all of which were reported as true in a *Times* story by Warren St. John, published in November 2004 and headlined "A Literary Life Born of Brutality." This piece was built around an interview with LeRoy conducted over an expensive sushi lunch in broad daylight, during which St. John apparently thought "she" was a "he," a mistake that people in New York have been known to make but usually after midnight. So it must have been embarrassing, once LeRoy's cover was blown, for St. John to have to write in November 2006 that LeRoy was not a man but a twenty-something woman pretending to be a transgendered man. Her half brother had enlisted her to play the public persona of LeRoy, while his girlfriend, with whom he concocted the scheme, did the writing.

The other literary hoax centered on *Love and Consequences* (2008), a memoir by Margaret B. Jones. The author claimed to be part white and part Native American, and to have been sexually abused and removed from her family at age five, then shuttled through a series of foster homes, eventually coming to live with a black family in South Central Los Angeles headed by a tough but loving grandmother named Big Momma who worked two jobs as her grandchildren dealt and used crack. The author wrote about becoming a member of the Bloods and getting a .38 for her birthday, and once making crack cocaine to help pay the household's water bill. She also described how her older brothers were sent to prison, and how friends and family were brutalized both by gang violence and by the police. Jones managed to pull herself out of this unpromising situation and went to the University of Oregon on scholarship, graduating as an ethnic studies major.

The *Times*' star literary critic Michiko Kakutani offered high praise: "What sets Ms. Jones's humane and deeply affecting memoir apart is not just that it's told from the point of view of a young girl coming of age in this world, but also that it focuses on the bonds of love and loyalty that can bind relatives and gang members together, and the craving after safety and escape that haunts so many lives in the 'hood.'" Although some of the scenes could seem "self-consciously novelistic at times," Jones had an "eye for the psychological detail and an anthropologist's eye for social rituals and routines."

Following soon was an adulatory feature by Mimi Read, describing the author's now-quiet life at home in a 1940s bungalow near the University of Oregon in Eugene, where she was raising her daughter. While sitting for her profile, Jones pointed to a picture she identified as a dead brother "back when he was in juvie," and told Read that she was no longer an "active member" of the Bloods but was in contact with her former homies, including one she called "Uncle Madd Ronald," who was now in prison.

Days later, Margaret B. Jones was unmasked as a fraud. Seeing the *Times* profile with its accompanying photo, the real-life sister of "Jones" called the publisher to say that the memoir was totally untrue. Once again, the *Times* was forced to admit it was had. In a feature story, it reported that "Margaret B. Jones is a pseudonym for Margaret Seltzer, who is all white and grew up in the well-to-do Sherman Oaks section of Los Angeles, in the San Fernando Valley, with her biological family. She graduated from the Campbell Hall School, a private Episcopal day school in the North Hollywood neighborhood. She has never lived with a foster family, nor did she run drugs for any gang members. Nor did she graduate from the University of Oregon, as she had claimed." When confronted by the *Times,* Seltzer began crying and said she had pieced together the "memoir" from the experiences of friends and hoped to do good by humanizing the plight of various people she talked to in L.A. coffee shops.

A postmortem by the public editor, Clark Hoyt, asked how the *Times* could be gulled so easily. The answer, he said, lay in "risky assumptions and warning signs that were not looked for or were ignored." Hoyt claimed that a quick online search would have revealed that Margaret B. Jones did not own a house in Eugene. He also noted that a check with Los Angeles County "would have determined that Jones's description of being taken from school and never seeing her family again was improbable."

The paper's "takeaway" was not reassuring. If the *Times* couldn't find ways "to check key facts, names, graduation claims, etc.," an internal memo advised, "we should hold the story until we can verify them, and if we can't, we should be suspicious." The memo concluded: "Live and learn . . ."

·—

The *Times'* taste for radical chic in arts and letters is matched by its esteem for radically chic countercultural figures, past and present. In part, this penchant stems from sixties-era reporters, or those who identify with them. In part, it's a provocative shot across the bow of the bourgeoisie. There's also an element of curdled idealism in the perception that American society has been ungrateful for such things as the role of journalists in bringing down Nixon, ending the Vietnam War and reining in the CIA.

The classic case in point was a profile of the former Weather Underground terrorist Bill Ayers, which had the misfortune to appear the morning of September 11, 2001. The piece by Dinitia

Smith centered on *Fugitive Days,* a memoir that Ayers had written about his life in the radical organization and his time spent underground as a result of his terrorist activities. Headlined "No Regrets for Love of Explosives," it said that although the long locks on his FBI Wanted poster were now shorn, Ayers still had the rainbow-and-lightning Weather Underground logo tattooed on his neck and still had "the ebullient ingratiating manner" that had made him "a charismatic figure in the radical student movement." According to Smith, Ayers was hardly penitent about his part in bombings of New York Police Department headquarters in 1970, the U.S. Capitol in 1971 and the Pentagon in 1972, as well as nine other bombings that the Weathermen took credit for. Smith blithely reported him as saying, "I don't regret setting bombs. . . . I feel we didn't do enough." Asked if he would do it again, Ayers said he didn't want "to discount the possibility."

Given that day's events, the Ayers profile would go down as certainly one of the most ill-timed articles ever published by the *Times,* and one of the most criticized. But after Barack Obama was elected, the *Times* gave Ayers, who had been linked to him during the campaign, another chance when it printed an op-ed by the former Weatherman, in which he tried to deflect the national loathing that he and his former terrorist comrades had engendered. Ayers admitted that the Weather Underground did in fact "carry out symbolic acts of extreme vandalism" in order to "convey outrage and determination to end the Vietnam War." But he piously insisted that all they did was "plant small bombs in empty offices," and that they tried to "respect human life." Ayers failed to discuss the bomb that blew up a Greenwich Village townhouse, killing three of his Weathermen comrades; it had been intended for a noncommissioned officers' dance at Fort Dix, New Jersey, and would surely have killed dozens had it been successfully planted and exploded.

A year later, in February 2009, the *Times* gave Ayers another chance for self-rehabilitation in a *Times Magazine* Q&A conducted by Deborah Solomon, which ran under the headline "Radical Cheer." The interview was pegged to a new book that Ayers had written with his wife, Bernardine Dohrn, also a former Weatherman, relating their "long struggle against racism and social injustice." Lighthearted, even jokey in her questions, Solomon let Ayers get off a lot of glib one-liners even when the discussion turned to the subject of terrorism. Did he regret his "involvement in setting off explosions in the Pentagon and the U.S. Capitol?" Solomon asked. Ayers replied, "Anyone who thinks what we did is despicable should look at the fact that the U.S. government killed three million people in Indochina between 1965 and 1975. That's really despicable."

Another former radical who got kid-glove treatment was Kathy Boudin, who had escaped the Greenwich Village townhouse when it exploded, then went underground for more than a decade, joining up with members of the Black Liberation Army. In 1981, she and her husband, David Gilbert, and several other comrades committed an armed robbery on a Brinks payroll truck, killing one of the truck's guards and two policemen. After a contentious trial, Boudin pleaded guilty to armed robbery and second-degree murder, and was given a sentence of twenty years to life.

Boudin was denied parole several times, but in 2003 her supporters—led by her father, Leonard Boudin, a civil liberties attorney and former Communist—mounted a campaign to win her freedom. They acted from a subtle script, acknowledging the seriousness of her crimes and the suffering of her victims' families but emphasizing her exemplary behavior in prison. The *Times* kept the story of Boudin's parole hearing in the news, in a manner calculated to help win her release. It accented the fact that she hadn't pulled the trigger in the Brinks holdup, and made her out to be just shy of Mother Teresa in the good works she performed while incarcerated. The paper quoted supporters calling her "the perfect parolee," and the former SDS president Todd Gitlin saying, "She represents the possibility for redemption."

At the end of the parole coverage, there was a cutaway to Boudin's son, Chesa, who at fourteen months had been left in the care of Bill Ayers and Bernardine Dohrn while Boudin was in prison. Now twenty-two years old, he had gotten a phone call from his mother announcing the parole board's decision to free her. "It's quite a birthday present," he told the *Times* reporters Lydia

Polgreen and James McKinley, who noted that he had recently graduated from Yale and been awarded a Rhodes Scholarship. He quickly added that he and his mother were looking forward to beginning "the healing process" with the families of the men killed in 1981, although he did not mention the victims by name. Then he said, with incredible presumption and lack of self-aware-ness, "I also was a victim of that crime. I know how important it was for me to forgive."

Shortly after Kathy Boudin's release, the *Times* ran a front-page profile of Chesa, headlined "From a Radical Background, a Rhodes Scholar Emerges." Chesa was part of the "radical aris-tocracy," explained Jodi Wilgoren, and had overcome "striking challenges, such as epilepsy, dyslexia and temper tantrums." His parents missed his "Phi Beta Kappa award, high school gradua-tion, Little League games" because they were in prison. Even so, he wanted to walk in their footsteps: "My parents were all dedi-cated to fighting U.S. imperialism around the world. I'm dedi-cated to the same thing."

Another *enfant radical* who got doting treatment is Ivy Meeropol, a granddaughter of the Rosenbergs who produced an HBO documentary in 2004 called *Heir to an Execution: A Grand-daughter's Story.* In his profile of Meeropol, Sam Roberts noted that the film "refuses to issue a definitive judgment about the legal guilt or innocence of the accused. Instead, it generally gives the Rosenbergs the benefit of the doubt, by dwelling on their unal-loyed idealism." But Roberts was not so hesitant to whitewash the Rosenbergs. He bashed the U.S. government's case against them, even while acknowledging that Julius Rosenberg, as well as his brother-in-law David Greenglass, were "atom spies." The govern-ment "framed a guilty man," Roberts oddly declared. "It also cyni-cally prosecuted Ethel on flimsy evidence to bludgeon the couple into confessing and implicating other Soviet agents."

Roberts also offered lots of space for Meeropol's emotional defense of her grandparents, rendered with historical dubious-ness. "If he [Julius] was trying to shore up the Soviet Union to ensure the United States wasn't the only superpower who held the potentially devastating secret," Meeropol told Roberts, "then they—and I say they because she was not the naïve housewife and mother, she would have known and believed in it too—they probably believed they were saving humanity from the destructive force of a single American superpower, and their fears have come true. The notion that if you criticize your government you're a traitor is also very similar."

·—

Part of the late 1970s Sectional Revolution, in which the *Times* became a multisection publication bulging with soft news and life-style journalism, was a greater use of market research and polling of target constituencies, especially in the area of cultural coverage. The research explained that the *Times* needed to "reach out to a new generation, people whose attention spans were shorter," as Warren Hoge, the assistant managing editor, told NPR. It needed to replace its older readers with a new generation, one that was educated but "aliterate," meaning they did not read much. "We have to grab young readers by the lapels because they are less interested in reading," Hoge said.

Over time, this transformation crowded out coverage of high culture in favor of an oddball, wink-and-nod popular culture. "The entire social and moral compass of the paper," as the former *Times* art critic Hilton Kramer later said, was altered to conform to a liberal ethos infused with "the emancipatory ideologies of the 1960's" and drawing no distinction between "media-induced notoriety and significant issues of public life." The *Times* took on more and more lightness of being. It became preoccupied with pop-culture trivia and *über* urban trends, reported on with moral relativism and without intellectual rigor.

The change was met by disaffection and derision within the paper's newsroom. Grace Glueck, who ran the culture desk for a while as replacement editor, was one of the disaffected, and famously once asked, "Who do I have to fuck to get out of this job?" Howard Kissel, the theater critic of the *Daily News,* said the new cultural pages reminded him of a middle-aged woman learning how to disco: "She put on a miniskirt and her varicose veins are showing." Gerry Gold, a staff reporter, commented, "We do all these pieces on pop icons as if they are important *artistes*. In fact they are creations of the big record companies. Yet we try to intellectualize them."

When the *Times* launched a new Sunday section called Styles of the Times on May 3, 1992, it was geared to the sensibility of the MTV generation and New York's increasingly visible and vocal gay community. The section carried stories on gay rodeos and on a store catering to skinheads and dominatrices, and odes to talents like Billy Idol and trends like cyberpunk. Styles raised eyebrows throughout the newspaper industry with its first issue, featuring a cover story on "The Arm Fetish," which according to Tifft and Jones presented a muscular bare arm as a recognizable image for a specific form of sexual activity in the gay community. The story was a public embarrassment for Sulzberger Sr., at whose seventieth birthday party Abe Rosenthal, retired from editing the paper but still writing an op-ed column, said, "I knew we were in a new age when I saw the first edition of Styles of the Times. Not only did it give New York the finger, it gave it the whole arm."

Facing complaints about Styles from longstanding readers, Arthur Sulzberger Jr. sometimes responded sympathetically. To one college professor he said, "Styles isn't intended for you. You're too old. It's for different readers, for those between 30 and 40 years old." Then he added, "Maybe I'm getting too old for it too." But at other times he seemed to revel in upsetting the old guard. The real problem with Styles, however, was that it made no money for the *Times*, so after two years it was absorbed back into the Metro section.

Lifestyle journalism and soft news got a big boost under the two-year tenure of Howell Raines (2001–2003), whose obsession with popular culture earned his regime the sobriquet "charge of the lite brigade." When he took over, Raines wrote a piece for the *Atlantic Monthly* (published only after his dismissal over the Jayson Blair scandal) in which he expatiated on the role that popular culture had to play at the *Times*.

If you want to reach members of this quality audience who are between the ages of twenty and forty, you have to pen-

etrate the worlds of style and popular culture. If the Times'
journalism continues to show contempt for the vernacular of
those worlds, the paper will continue to lose subscribers. To
explore every aspect of American and global experience does
not mean pandering. It does mean that the serial ups and
downs of a Britney Spears are a sociological and economic
phenomenon that is, as a reflection of contemporary Amer-
ican culture, worthy of serious reporting. It means being
astute enough about American society to understand that the
deadly rap wars have nothing to do with what Snoop Dogg
said about Suge Knight. The real story behind the rap wars is
one of huge corporations like Sony and EMI trying to save a
multibillion-dollar industry in economic collapse.

The gravitas of the paper has suffered as a result of key appointments in the area of cultural news. One of them was the promotion of Sam Sifton from editor of the Dining section to cultural
news editor in 2005. His intellectual pedigree was not in doubt:
son of Elisabeth Sifton, a major figure in New York's publishing
community; grandson of Reinhold Niebuhr, the great Protes-
tant theologian. But his obsession with pop-culture trivia came
across full force in a 2007 online "Talk to the Newsroom" Q&A
with readers, where he promised more video game reviews—a
promise he certainly kept. In the same forum the previous year,
he defended his paper's coverage of Hollywood celebrities, and
when a reader asked "Do you party? Do you rock and roll?" Sifton
answered in a tone of desperate hipness by quoting Young Jeezy:
"E'rybody know I rep these streets faithfully."

But the problem at the *Times* was greater than the taste of
the editors it hired. As the current editor Bill Keller has said, the
Times puts out a daily newspaper "plus about 15 weekly magazines," meaning the various freestanding sections in the paper.
These fiefdoms are more and more devoted to lifestyle and less
to news per se.

With a revived Style section appearing on both Sunday and
Thursday, plus Home and Arts sections, and magazine sections on
fashion and design, soft news and lifestyle have come to define the
paper as much or more than hard-news coverage. In a somewhat

humorous—and devastating—*New Republic* article of April 2006, about the *Times*' fascination with "lifestyle porn," Michelle Cottle quoted Trip Gabriel, then editor of both Style sections, as saying that most of Thursday Styles "falls under the general category of coverage about appearance and image and what one sees looking in the mirror. . . . We are another department of basically consumerist pursuits—about the kinds of things that give people pleasure." Cottle took it from there: "On any given Thursday, Styles fans are treated to a mélange of articles examining the hottest trends in looking good—everything from virtual personal trainers to ayurvedic massage to butt implants—with a whole lot of couture coverage in between. The front page features two or three longer pieces, including a photo-laden fashion spread and a nonshopping-related 'lifestyle' piece on topics like parenting or online dating."

One feature of Styles that seems particularly pointless is the "Critical Shopper," where a retail experience, usually high-end, is reviewed as if it were a movie, a play or a museum exhibit. In one review, Alex Kuscinski compared the silkiness of a $30,000 mink coat to the silkiness of her pet dachshund, the dog coming up short against a material "so otherworldly I experienced the bizarre sensation of having never touched such material before." Like the paper's arts and media criticism, these shopping reviews can also have a political edge, though often a vapid one. Mike Albo made a foray into a hipster chotchke store in Brooklyn called Fred Flare in 2008, and wrote that the place was full of "happy, cheap, eclectic thingies" and an "absurdly happy staff," who were "like human text messages from Smurfland." Albo focused on a handmade teddy bear that made his "little blackened, coal-size heart grow and become warm and fuzzy." He hadn't realized how starved for light-heartedness he was, but it made sense, he said: "If you feel as if you have been emotionally, professionally and politically run over by a tank for the last, say, eight years, then the well-selected, fun merchandise and carbonated energy of Fred Flare will bring a smile on your cautious, crabby face."

A lot of these lifestyle features deal with sex, often in a way that's purposefully transgressive, even vulgar. In a feature on sex between clients and contractors in places like the Hamptons, "The

Allure of the Toolbelt," Joyce Wadler described one local as saying that the client-contractor affairs are relatively safe: there is no need to worry when the contractor's car is seen in a woman's driveway in the middle of the afternoon. And client-contractor love, from what he's seen, rarely threatens marriages because when the job is over, the affair is over.

A report on an upscale S&M store in Manhattan was headlined "My Other Riding Crop Is for My Horse." The store, explained Alex Kuscinski, offered "leather restraints with lace insets, cupless bras (delicately renamed the 'frame bra' here), embossed leather paddles, braided leather whips, riding crops, silk bondage ropes and, of course, modernity's most significant addition to the bedroom, the Sony DVD camcorder and lightweight tripod." Many products were designed to "stimulate an extremely personal part of the body"; they were made from tempered glass, obsidian glass and titanium, and sold at prices ranging up to $1,750. These could be displayed on a coffee table as sculptural objects, Kuscinksi added helpfully, "but it would be difficult to explain when your mother came over for coffee."

The queen of dubious trend stories on sex and romance is Stephanie Rosenbloom, author of a series of lifestyle features centered on *au courant* female sexuality. One was about "girl crushes," referring to "that fervent infatuation that one heterosexual woman develops for another woman who may seem impossibly sophisticated, gifted, beautiful or accomplished." Rosenbloom also wrote about "The Taming of the Slur," on the increasing mainstream use of the word "slut," a report that had all the gravitas of *Beverly Hills, 90210*. Perhaps her most absurd piece involved the etymology she produced for the word "vajayjay," a slang term for vagina that originated on the television show *Grey's Anatomy* and found its way to *Oprah* and *Jimmy Kimmel*, as well as the Web. According to Rosenbloom, the word's emergence marked a certain feminist moment. She quoted an actress from *Grey's Anatomy* saying, "It's a word I use, a word my female friends use, a word I've heard women in the grocery store use. I don't even think about where it came from anymore. It doesn't belong to me or anyone at the show. It belongs to all women."

For some, the vulgarity and desperate hipness have been too much. As Joseph Epstein put it in the *Weekly Standard* in 2010, the *New York Times'* traditional sobriquet, "the Gray Lady of American newspapers . . . implied a certain stateliness, a sense of responsibility, the possession of high virtue. But the Gray Lady is far from the *grande dame* she once was. For years now she has been going heavy on the rouge, lipstick, and eyeliner, using a push-up bra, and gadding about in stiletto heels. She's become a bit— perhaps more than a bit—of a slut, whoring after youth through pretending to be with-it. I've had it with the old broad; after nearly 50 years together, I've determined to cut her loose."

seven

Gays

If some of the *Times'* life-style reporting seems almost tongue in cheek, its coverage of the gay world is in earnest. Whether it's gay travel, gay entertainment, gay film, gay sex, gay adoption and parenting, or the ultimate *cause célèbre,* gay marriage, the *Times* brings a crusading voice to what it considers the civil rights movement of the day. Gay-themed stories appear in the paper routinely, sometimes three or four in a day. As Andrew Solomon, a gay author whose wedding was written up for the *Times* "Vows" column, put it, "The love that dared not speak its name is now broadcasting."

Historically, the crusade is an outgrowth of what has been called the paper's "Lavender Enlightenment," which was described back in 1992 in a lengthy piece by Michelangelo Signo-rile, a prominent gay columnist. The feature noted that it had been more than five years since the retirement of Abe Rosenthal, an editor "who ran his empire not unlike recent European despots." Signorile charged that Rosenthal's banning of the word "gay," which he had considered overtly political, had held back the social movement. Rosenthal's renowned homophobia also left gay men and women at the *Times* "immensely frightened and frustrated," most of them remaining deep in the closet, barely acknowledging each other much less openly socializing. Those who were sus-pected of being gay often suffered in their careers, sent to unim-portant dead-end bureaus and desks or even recalled from foreign postings if word of their sexual orientation leaked out.

The famous gay riot in 1969 at the Stonewall Inn hardly received the coverage such a now-mythic event should have earned. In fact, when eyewitnesses or rioters called the *Times* newsroom to report developments and police brutality, they were often shrugged off the phone. Neither would the *Times* take ads for *The Homosexual Handbook,* even after it had sold out its second printing of 50,000 copies.

Once Rosenthal retired in 1986, "the walls of repression came tumbling down," staffers told Signorile. Rosenthal's successor, Max Frankel, confessed, "I knew they'd had a hard time, and I knew they weren't comfortable identifying themselves as gay." But, he added, "I never dreamed that so many homosexuals were hiding in newsroom closets, awaiting the trumpet call."

Frankel sent a major signal that things were going to be dif-ferent almost immediately. "Punch, you're going to have to swallow hard on this one," Frankel told Sulzberger Sr., in a peculiar choice of words. "We're going to start using the word 'gay.'" Frankel's efforts were given a boost by symbolic statements and gestures on the part of the publisher-in-waiting, Sulzberger Jr. According to Charles Kaiser, a former Rosenthal news clerk who is gay, "When he came in, gays in the newsroom lived in terror, and Arthur met them and took each of them to lunch and said, 'What is it like to be gay here? When I take over, it will no longer be a problem.'"

In January 1992, two weeks after becoming the new publisher, Sulzberger Jr. held a meeting with the editorial staff in the newsroom, Signorile reported, and told them that "diversity" would be a priority at the paper. Eventually he blurted out the phrase "sexual orientation." Gay staff members later said they almost fell off their chairs, since it was the first time that phrase had ever been used by a top *Times* executive.

According to Kaiser, Sulzberger's efforts and the signals sent by other editors who took his cue translated into remaking the paper "from the most homophobic institution in America to the most gay-friendly institution." No more fag jokes, people were told, and newsroom staff members with partners felt free to put pictures of them on their desks. It was a period of "vaulting consciousness," wrote Frankel.

Another turning point was Frankel's decision to allow Jeffrey Schmaltz to report on AIDS. Schmaltz was an AIDS victim himself, as was first revealed when he suffered an AIDS-related seizure in the *Times* newsroom in January 1990. When Schmaltz returned to work, he asked Frankel to put him on the AIDS beat and allow him to write subjectively about his disease. Frankel had qualms about the built-in conflict of interest and worried that Schmaltz's reporting could lapse "into partisanship and sentimentality." But the green light was flashed and Schmaltz produced first-person stories for the Sunday magazine and for the Week in Review. "His scoops were the rarest kind," Frankel wrote. "He was always as accurate, sharp and honest as we had a right to expect and obviously labored to restrain his emotions." When Schmaltz died in 1993, Frankel told the obituary writer that he had left "a remarkable bequest to American journalism." In his memoir, Frankel heralded Schmaltz as "the agent of our ultimate enlightenment."

Frankel's successor, Joseph Lelyveld, brought in an openly gay editor, Adam Moss, to consult on a variety of issues related to attracting a younger, hipper readership, with an emphasis on homosexuals. Moss took a leading role in creating and editing the first (and ill-fated) Sunday Style section, characterized by a campy, ironic tone and an in-your-face gay candor. The paper also emphasized the hiring and promoting of openly gay reporters and editors. By 2000, the institutional hospitality to gay values had grown so warm that Richard Berke, then a Washington reporter, could tell members of the National Lesbian and Gay Journalists Association that "literally, three-quarters of the people deciding what's on the front page are not-so-closeted homosexuals." In 2002, Moss got up at a media panel discussion in Lower Manhattan and declared that he basically edited "a gay magazine," at least in terms of its dominant sensibility. Some in New York media circles began referring to the *Times* as "The Pink Lady."

·—

The opening up of news space and editorials to previously slighted subjects related to homosexuality in America is to be applauded, as is the basic respect and career advancement afforded to gay journalists, who no longer have to fear being "out" or "outed" at the *Times*. But looking at the last twenty years of the *Times* in terms of integrity in the coverage of gay issues, there is less to be happy about. On almost every gay-related topic you can name, the *Times* has lost all pretense of objectivity, instead assuming a crusading stance and showing an impulse to deconstruct traditional morality and family structure.

As its own former ombudsman Daniel Okrent observed, on many gay issues, especially gay marriage, the *Times'* position amounts to "cheerleading." On a topic that has produced "one of the defining debates of our time," Okrent wrote, "Times editors have failed to provide the three-dimensional perspective balanced journalism requires." An internal report, to which Okrent contributed, expanded on the problem: "By consistently framing the issue as a civil rights matter i.e.—gays fighting for the right to be treated like everyone else—we failed to convey how disturbing the issue is in many corners of American social, cultural and religious life."

Homosexual sex itself has repeatedly been cheered, even when a more sober response would have better served the subject. A profile of Kevin Brentley, the author of *Let's Shut Out the World* (2005), was headlined "For the Fun of It, Remember?" The book, wrote Guy Trebay, explored the "libertinism" of San Francisco during the "innocent time before AIDS." Trebay failed to acknowledge the role of that very libertinism in causing the devastation.

Another somewhat myopic piece reveling in the more outré aspects of gay sex appeared in September 2005 under the headline "A Sex Stop on the Way Home." Filed by Corey Kilgannon, it focused on a narrow parking lot in Cunningham Park in Queens, set between playing fields for adult softball and youth soccer and baseball. "At one end of the lot, retirees arrive to practice their golf and mothers in minivans gather to wait for their Little Leaguers," Kilgannon wrote. "The other end is popular with another set with a much lower profile in this suburban setting: gay men cruising for sex. Their playing field is the parking lot itself and the goal is a sexual encounter, usually quick and anonymous." Kilgannon scrupulously described the mating rituals that are popular here, "like a chess game." He also noted that the parking lot's two very different camps were not spatially far apart. "One recent evening, a half-dozen mothers stood chatting, waiting for their children to finish soccer," Kilgannon wrote. "A stone's throw away, a group of gay men stood narrating the attempt of a man trolling the lot in a tan sedan to woo the cute man parked in the black SUV. . . . 'Woop, there he goes,' the narrator said [as the man in the sedan hopped into the SUV]. 'You go, girl.'"

Heather Mac Donald remarked in her *City Journal* blog that the point of the story was not to shame the vice squad into cleaning up the parking lot, but to report enthusiastically how many married men patronized the cruising grounds. "I can't tell you how many guys I've had here who were wearing wedding bands, with baby seats in the car and all kinds of kids' toys on the floor," one source told Kilgannon. "It's on their way home and they don't have to get involved in a relationship or any gay lifestyle or social circles. They don't even have to buy anyone a drink or be seen in a gay bar. They just tell the wife, 'Honey, I'll be home an hour late tonight.'"

The married man with a gay appetite made the story appealing for the *Times'* "anti-bourgeois staff," Mac Donald wrote, because "it allows them to throw mud for the ten-millionth time on the Leave-it-to-Beaver 'normalcy' . . . of the white-bread suburbs." In a time of terrorism, Mac Donald closed, when New York leaders face the prospect of evacuating millions from Manhattan in an emergency, "the *Times's* preference for the insignificant trivia of the gay lifestyle defies comprehension. Either the *Times* is even more clueless about the narrowness of its worldview than previously thought, or it knows how out of the mainstream it is and hopes to shock the leaden bourgeoisie with its sexual obsessions."

The *Times'* ever-expanding coverage of gay fashion has included congenial reporting on cross-dressing and "transgendering." A news report in 2004 by Sarah Kershaw examined gay homecomings at a number of colleges and high schools across the country. Under the headline "Gay Students Force New Look at Homecoming Traditions," the article had a pull quote saying that this debate is "in many ways a mirror of the national debate over same-sex marriage." Kershaw wrote about a gay male student at Vanderbilt University who ran for homecoming queen and did not win the crown but was elected to the homecoming court. He appeared at the football game "wearing a black dress with an empire waist and elbow-length red gloves, accentuated by the yellow sash draped over each of the 11 homecoming court students." On his *New York Times* website blog, Stephen Dubner lauded a drag queen named Ryan Allen who was chosen as homecoming queen at George Mason University. "I don't care if G.M.U. professors win 50 Nobel Prizes; if its athletes win 50 Gold Medals; if its researchers win 50 cancer patents," Dubner declared, "20 years from now, I will still remember the tale of Ms. Ryan Allen."

The *Times* has also been attentive to a more serious fashion statement: gender reassignment surgery. A news article in 2006 headlined "The Trouble When Jane Becomes Jack," by Paul Vitello, described the increasing number of lesbians who are "choosing to pursue life as a man." This, Vitello claimed, "can provoke a deep resentment and almost existential anxiety, raising questions of gender loyalty and political identity, as well as debates about who is and who isn't, and who never was, a real woman." Vitello added: "The conflict has raged at some women's colleges and has been explored in academic articles, in magazines for lesbians and in alternative publications, with some—oversimplifying the issue for effect—headlined with the question, 'Is Lesbianism Dead?'"

·⤳

Buckets of positive ink are poured on mainstream Hollywood films with gay themes, such as *Brokeback Mountain,* which received a glowing review and had three features pegged to it. In a long Sunday column, Frank Rich called it "all the more subversive for having no overt politics," as well as "a rebuke and antidote to the sordid politics of gay-baiting that went on during the 2004 election." Pronouncing the film "a landmark in the troubled history of America's relationship to homosexuality," Rich said that it "brings something different to the pop culture marketplace at just the pivotal moment to catch a wave."

The *Times* was even more effusive about *Milk* (2008), which explored the life of San Francisco's first openly gay city supervisor, Harvey Milk. In his first review, A. O. Scott wrote that Milk was "an intriguing, inspiring figure" and the film was "a marvel." In his second review, Scott wrote that "though he may have seemed like a radical at the time, *Milk* places its hero squarely in the American grain. He is an optimist, an idealist, a true believer in the possibilities of American democracy." Several pieces in the *Times* tied the film to the looming culture war over homosexual marriage.

Gay characters on television have drawn applause as well. Alessandra Stanley, the paper's TV critic, reviewed a gay wedding episode of *The Simpsons.* "A few years ago," she wrote, "the coming out of a prime-time character would probably not have caused much of a stir. But in the current climate, with the issue of gay rights spiking in the public discourse, the episode stood out." It was "a tonic," Stanley remarked, "at a moment when television seems increasingly humorless and tame—fearful of advertiser

boycotts by the religious right and fines from the Federal Communications Commission."

The *Times* routinely lionizes gay political activists. One example
is Florent Morellet, a restaurant owner and AIDS activist who got
a double bite of the apple: first a fawning "Public Lives" profile in
2006, and then a piece by the restaurant critic Frank Bruni when
his restaurant closed in 2008. "Genre Bending Restaurant Takes
Its Final Bow" amounted to an oral history of Florent's restaurant
and its place in New York's gay community.

Another example is Daniel O'Donnell, a legislator in the
New York State Assembly who received a "Public Lives" profile in
2007 after he got a gay marriage bill passed in the assembly. (The
state senate did not take up the measure.) Robin Finn described
O'Donnell as "a tennis-crazed former Legal Aid Society lawyer"
and a Mets fan who "confesses to a very unrequited crush on
the tennis star Andy Roddick, pals around with a soprano opera
star, Ruth Ann Swenson, who, as he did, grew up on Long Island
in unassuming Commack, and is the chronically embarrassed
older brother of one of the planet's most opinionated celebrities, the entertainer/blogger/provocateur Rosie O'Donnell." A
second adoring feature on Daniel O'Donnell appeared in 2009,
when another effort was made to legalize gay marriage in the
state. Noting that O'Donnell had "emerged as a tenacious, ingratiating, playful and sometimes prickly leader of the effort to pass
the legislation," Jeremy Peters described his tactics as both persistent and humorous. O'Donnell asked the visiting parents of
a Republican assemblyman to urge their son to support the bill,
and he told the lawmaker himself that he was "the best looking
guy in the Assembly, and he owed it to the gays to vote yes."

Meanwhile, conservative political activists or politicians who
are perceived as hypocritically working against gay rights get
entirely different treatment from the *Times*. After Mark Foley,
a Republican congressman, was caught sending racy emails to
young male interns in 2006, Frank Rich said that "a little creative googling will yield a long list of who else is gay, openly or
not in the highest ranks of both the Bush administration and
the Republican hierarchy." He added, "The split between the

Republicans' outward homophobia and inner gayness isn't just hypocrisy; it's pathology." Then he nastily cited a recent book alleging that Karl Rove's "own (and beloved) adoptive father, Louis Rove, was openly gay in the years before his death in 2004. This will be a future case study for psychiatric clinicians as well as historians.'"

·⁓

By contrast to the *outré* edge that defines its coverage of other aspects of the gay "lifestyle," the *Times* strains to produce evidence for the "normalization of gay life" when it comes to the subject of gay parenting. An analysis headlined "A Change of Life in the Gay Hamptons," written by Corey Kilgannon in 2003, described how a formerly wild scene had gone "from beefcakes to cupcakes," as a maturing gay population was turning its energy to "nesting" with their children. In 2004, Ginia Bellafante's "Two Fathers, with One Happy to Stay Home" looked at the stay-at-home gay dad trend. "Sociologists, gender researchers and gay parents themselves say that because gay men are liberated from the cultural expectations and pressures that women face to balance work and family life, they may approach raising children with a greater sense of freedom and choice," Bellafante claimed. She quoted one gay father from Minnesota: "If I were honest, I'd say that I want to do an excellent job at this because I know the world has me under a microscope." Apparently Bellafante could not find any gay stay-at-home father who regretted the decision, although complaints by stay-at-home mothers have been a staple of feminist discourse since Betty Friedan's *Feminine Mystique*.

An extremely long and hard-to-follow Sunday magazine piece by John Bowe, "Gay Donor or Gay Dad," explored what was referred to as the new "gayby boom." Bowe focused on gay men who had become sperm donors so their lesbian friends could have children as a couple. The piece was built around two different scenarios: one where the sperm donor was eventually welcomed as a father figure for the child, the other where he was held at arm's length and disappointed.

Writing about a mixed-race lesbian couple that had broken up, Bowe said, "The current family tree is a crazy circuit board: The black woman has a new female partner. The white woman is now living with a man, and the two have had their own child. So, as R. [one of the sperm donors] said, between the one child that R. has with the black mother, the twins borne by the white mother with a black donor and the newest, fourth, child born to her with her new male partner, all of whom have some sort of sibling relation to one another, things can be a little confusing." R. told Bowe that they are "quite a little petri dish of a family." Bowe explained: "The children go from the white mother, who lives in a SoHo loft, to their black mother, who lives in a nice, middle-class row house in Crown Heights. On weekends, they often visit the white mother's family's country estate." The children were like those in divorced families, R. maintained. "They've got a family that split up; they go back and forth."

Despite all this chaos, Bowe still put in a dig at the "hetero-active" by quoting one of the story's subjects asking somewhat aggressively, "Why is this worth a story? It's not even worth discussing. We're just as American as our next-door neighbors. You see all these families with stepdads and stepmoms and half brothers and half sisters. . . . We want the same things that every other family wants! You know? We shop at Costco; we shop at Wal-Mart; we buy diapers. We're just average. We're downright boring!"

Occasionally, there is an acknowledgment that the question of gay parenting has two sides. While neither of them is conclusively supported by research, the *Times* favors the side of gay parents and their professional advocates, and tends to say that the research is "getting better" for that side, as the psychology reporter Benedict Carey wrote in 2005.

A long Sunday magazine article of 2005, "Growing Up with Mom and Mom" by Susan Dominus, did not increase confidence in claims that kids raised in gay households suffer no ill effects. Dominus focused on Ry, a teenager in the West Village who was the "queerspawn" of "trail-blazing lesbians." Ry spoke of her "sperm donor" instead of "dad" or "father," words that were "loaded for children of lesbian mothers." How do the children of gay parents turn out in comparison with those of straight parents in terms of eventual marital status, income, psychological well-being? Dominus asked. She cited research on both sides, then declared that there might be a third way, "one that argues passionately that there are differences" and embraces "the uniqueness of being raised in a same-sex household."

What Dominus subsequently reported about her teenage subject made one wonder, though. In a diary, Ry had commented: "It took me a lot of struggle to realize that I really was attracted to men, yet now it is really hard for me to deal with men as human beings, let alone sexually." She was intrigued but also "repulsed" by heterosexual relations, fearing the "soul-losing domain of oppression." She couldn't understand or relate to men because she was "so immersed in gay culture and unfamiliar with what it is to have a healthy straight relationship." She considered it "cool" to be critical of the heterosexual world, which she called "sexist and gross." And her parents were happy with what they had wrought. "It's like our whole lives together have been this one, big, messy, incredible experiment," said one of the mothers. Then, Dominus reported, the mother broke out into a broad smile, a look of pride mixed with amazement. "And it worked."

Lesbian parenting got another ratification in A. O. Scott's gushing review of the summer 2010 comedy *The Kids Are All Right,* starring Annette Bening and Julianne Moore. Coming close to declaring it the best American family comedy ever made, Scott, whose review was headlined "Meet the Sperm Donor: Modern Family Ties," praised the film's "unerring" dialogue and Moore's "offbeat comic timing." The film gave Scott "the thrilling, vertiginous sense of never having seen anything quite like it before."

·‿

The subject of gay marriage is what has most galvanized the *Times,* so much so that Daniel Okrent as public editor went hard on the paper for its skewed coverage. In the *Times,* he had learned "where gay couples go to celebrate their marriages; I've met gay couples picking out bridal dresses; I've been introduced to couples who have been together for decades and have now sanctified their vows in Canada, couples who have successfully integrated the world of competitive ballroom dancing, couples whose lives are the platonic model of suburban stability." While every one of these articles was legitimate, Okrent said, it was "disappointing to see The Times present the social and cultural aspects of same-sex marriage in a tone that approaches cheerleading."

For example, Clifford Krauss implicitly drew a parallel to racial integration when he reported in 2003 on the flow of gay couples to Canada to get married, following in the footsteps of escaped slaves. When gay marriage was legalized by court order in Massachusetts in 2004, Pam Belluck and Kate Zezima's report summed up the excitement in the gay community: "With the failure of last-ditch efforts . . . to reverse a court order legalizing same-sex marriage, starting on Monday (as early as 12.01 a.m. in Cambridge), thousands of gay couples will seal their relationships with a stamp of official recognition that many had never dreamed possible."

Other localities that began to permit gay marriage in early 2004 received saturation coverage, and advocates were allowed to use the *Times* as megaphone, unfiltered and with minimal counterbalance. When Mayor Gavin Newsom of San Francisco began issuing gay marriage licenses on February 12, 2004—in defiance of a California law passed by popular initiative in 2000—the ink flowed prodigally at the *Times*. Dean Murphy gave Newsom a spacious platform to explain, with considerable self-flattery, the genesis of his position. "Most politicians don't get away with doing the right thing at a time when society is not necessarily unanimously ready for that," Newsom said. "I did it because I thought it was right." As for conservative critics, Newsom told Murphy that he wore their enmity as "a code of distinction." He continued: "I have been befuddled by conservatives who talk about taking away rights, yet they claim to be conservatives. The hypocrisy to me is extraordinarily grand." (Even some fellow Democrats, however, criticized Newsom for performing "spectacle weddings," as Barney Frank put it.)

When the experiment was ended by order of the California Supreme Court on March 11, Murphy's report dripped with pathos. Several couples waiting at City Hall for appointments to receive licenses were turned away, some of them in tears. "They were heartbroken," said the county clerk, Nancy Alfaro. "It was very sudden."

Around the same time, in late February, gay marriages started being performed officially in New Paltz, New York, hitherto known mainly for its college and for being the weekend home of Arthur Sulzberger Jr. The *Times* gave several glowing profiles to Jason West, the 26-year-old mayor who launched the experiment. In "Mayor Wedding Gay Couples Has History of Activism," Thomas Crampton wrote, "At age 6, his father says, he refused to eat McDonald's food because of environmental concerns about plastic-foam containers. At age 17, he declined all Christmas presents, to protest commercialization of the holiday." After the first set of weddings, which involved twenty-five couples, Mayor West told Crampton, "I am willing to go to jail to hold these marriages," and added, "This is a stand any decent American should take."

Some of the weddings received cloying coverage. "Rushing Out of the Closet and Down the Aisle" described a retired U.S. Army major who was marrying a Dutch-born "sometime designer of haute couture accessories for pets." The two had wanted more time to plan but decided that seizing the opportunity was wise. The Dutchman called his wedding day "the greatest day of his life." He was grateful "to Mayor Jason West for permitting me to make a public declaration of my love for Jeff. Jeff and I sat down in the front of the bus for the first time and began a new phase of our lives together."

A *Times* editorial of March 7 cheered local officials such as Mayor Newsom and Mayor West for pushing the next step in civil rights:

> To the Virginia judge who ruled that Mildred Jeter, a black woman, and Richard Loving, a white man, could not marry, the reason was self-evident. "Almighty God created the races white, black, yellow, malay and red, and he placed them on

separate continents," he [the judge] wrote. "And but for the
interference with his arrangement there would be no cause
for such marriages." Calling marriage one of the "basic
civil rights of man," the Supreme Court ruled in 1967 that
Virginia had to let interracial couples marry. Thirty-seven
years from now, the reasons for opposing gay marriage will
no doubt feel just as archaic, and the right to enter into it will
be just as widely accepted.

The editorial maintained that "Testing the law is a civil rights tradition: Jim Crow laws were undone by blacks who refused to obey
them."

In July 2006, New York State's highest court ruled against gay
marriage, rejecting the comparison with antimiscegenation laws
and declaring that the state had a legitimate interest in protecting
children. "Intuition and experience suggest that a child benefits
from having before his or her eyes, every day, living models of
what both a man and a woman are like," the judges said, which
meant that the state had a legitimate interest in promoting heterosexual marriages over same-sex ones. The *Times* was livid. A gay
reporter, Patrick Healy, wrote in a front-page account:

Yesterday's court ruling against gay marriage was more than
a legal rebuke—it came as a shocking insult to gay rights
groups. Leaders said they were stunned by both the rejection
and the decision's language, which they saw as expressing
more concern for the children of heterosexual couples than for
the children of gay couples. They also took exception to the
ruling's description of homosexuality as a preference rather
than an orientation.

An editorial, "Gay Marriage Setback," took a whip to the court,
accusing it of harming both the constitutional guarantee of equal
protection and its reputation as a guardian of individual liberties.
The argument that "children benefit from being raised by two
natural parents" was, the *Times* claimed, "without hard evidence."
The editorial applauded a dissent by one particularly liberal judge,

Judith Kaye, especially her contention that future generations would "look upon barring gay marriage as akin to the laws that once barred interracial marriage."

The paper's "implicit advocacy," as Daniel Okrent called it, was also underscored by how it characterized the opposition as repressed and unsophisticated homophobes. There was one notable exception: Peter Steinfels, who wrote in his column that the concern about moral values was not "a disguise for ignorance, irrationality and intolerance." Whatever one may think about same-sex marriage, he pointed out, "it takes a real stretch to pretend that it is not a noteworthy departure from existing social and legal norms." But for the most part, the *Times* dismissed all opposition as bigotry and hatred, and assumed that the granting of same-sex marriage privileges was inevitable.

When the California Supreme Court, in May 2008, overturned the law passed in 2000 stating that "only marriage between a man and a woman is valid or recognized in California," the *Times* extolled a new wave of court-sanctioned gay marriage. Patricia Leigh Brown's report in mid June, "California Braces for 'New Summer of Love,'" was illustrated with a picture of two lesbians who had been together for 49 years walking on a beach. Brown noted that California, unlike Massachusetts, did not limit marriage licenses to residents of the state, thus resurrecting old postcard images of California as the "Promised Land." According to this report, California businesses in a wilted economy were welcoming the wanna-be marrieds with open arms. The *Times* used its website powers to solicit stories, photos and video from readers who were heading to California, and then produced a series of multimedia offerings about these California nuptials. A *Times* food writer, Kim Severson, wrote about her own plans to get married in California, as well as the boon to catering businesses.

Meanwhile, California residents quickly gathered signatures to put a new proposition on the ballot, this one to write the language of the earlier measure into the state's constitution. Voters passed Proposition 8 in November 2008, and the *Times* decried the outcome as the "tyranny" of the majority over the minority. An editorial blamed "right-wing forces led by the Mormon Church," which had "poured tens of millions of dollars into the campaign" for "a measure to enshrine bigotry in the state's Constitution." When the California Supreme Court upheld the constitutional amendment in May 2009, a *Times* editorial called the decision "an affront to gay men and lesbians and to fundamental values enshrined in the state Constitution." In addition to denying basic fairness to gay people, the editorial claimed, the court's 6-1 ruling set an unfortunate legal precedent "that could allow the existing rights of any targeted minority to be diminished using the Election Day initiative process."

What distinguished the *Times'* coverage of this round in the California gay marriage saga were the stories omitted as much as the ones reported. Supporters of Proposition 8 had predicted that the legalization of gay marriage might lead to the teaching of gay marriage in the schools. In fact, a group of San Francisco first graders were present at City Hall when their teacher was married, in a ceremony presided over by Gavin Newsom himself—who reportedly was less than pleased to see the kids there. In Hayward, California, five-year-olds were asked to sign pledge cards promising their support to gay, lesbian, bisexual and transgender people. As one Prop 8 organizer noted in the *Wall Street Journal*, not only could these kindergartners barely sign their names to the cards, but many had Spanish-speaking parents who needed to have the cards translated before they realized what their kids had signed. These stories of young children being used in this campaign triggered outrage, but did not appear in the *Times*.

The *Times* did report on how Proposition 8 had stirred up a "new wave of activists," which someone dubbed "Stonewall 2.0." It also reported that some supporters of Prop 8, particularly in the arts, lost their jobs after disclosure laws exposed them to retaliation; that others were intimidated in their homes, courtesy of maps put out on the Web; and that some supporters and donors were sent envelopes containing white powder in the mail. But some of the physical harassment that activists employed against Prop 8 supporters—stomping on signs, attacking elderly people, vandalizing a Catholic Church wrongly assumed to have supported the initiative—apparently wasn't news fit to print. And the editorial page, which might have weighed in for freedom of speech, was silent.

When a federal appeals court judge overturned Proposition 8 on equal protection grounds in August 2010, the *Times* editorialized that this decision was "a stirring and eloquently reasoned denunciation of all forms of irrational discrimination, the latest link in a chain of pathbreaking decisions that permitted interracial marriages and decriminalized gay sex between consenting adults."

·—

On March 29, 2010, the *New York Times Magazine* featured a cover photo of two really cute white bunny rabbits, along with the question "Can Animals Be Gay?" The story inside led with a discussion of the discovery that one-third of Laysan albatrosses, a downy seabird that breeds on the northwestern tip of Oahu, Hawaii, raise their offspring in same-sex pairings. According to the author, Jon Mooallem, "The female-female pairs had been incubating eggs together, rearing chicks and just generally passing under everybody's nose for what you might call 'straight' couples." The piece exhibited a certain self-awareness. Mooallem wrote that when the discovery was first disclosed in a scientific journal, some news stories praised the research while others called it "pure propaganda and selective science at its dumbest" that was intended to "further an agenda."

Animal stories have been a staple of American journalism forever, whether in tabloids, on TV or in the *Times*. I love them, and there's something especially compelling about stories dealing with animal sexuality, don't ask me why. But, rubbing the salt out of my eye, I wondered: did they have to run this particular story on Easter Sunday? As the magazine's cover story?

eight

War on Terror

The November 2009 massacre at an Army deployment center at Fort Hood, Texas, which took thirteen lives and wounded thirty other soldiers and civilian personnel, was the most serious terrorist incident on American soil since 9/11. It also raised deeply disturbing questions about ethnicity and religion in relation to the War on Terror and to the U.S. military. Had the shooter, Major Nidal Malik Hasan, an American-born Palestinian, simply gone berserk, perhaps as a result of treating mentally damaged soldiers upon their return from Iraq and Afghanistan? Or was he following precepts of jihadi extremism, putting his loyalty to the Koran above his oath to the Constitution? Was he a self-radicalized "lone wolf" or part of a wider plot set in motion by an unseen Islamist fifth column in the Army? And whether his actions reflected personal pathology, religious extremism, or both together, how had he come to be commissioned as a highly trained U.S. Army medical officer, and promoted to the rank of major just six months earlier?

The *Washington Post* intensified these questions by reporting that when Hasan was a medical resident in psychiatry at Walter Reed Army Hospital, he gave a PowerPoint presentation not on a medical topic but on "The Koranic World View As It Relates to Muslims in the U.S. Military." He included the comment, "It's getting harder and harder for Muslims in the service to morally justify being in a military that seems constantly engaged against fellow Muslims," and presented some basics of Islamic thought and teaching, such as: "We [Muslims] love death more then [sic] you love life!" The final slide read: "Recommendation: Department of Defense should allow Muslims [sic] Soldiers the option of being released as 'Conscientious objectors' to increase troop morale and decrease adverse events." The *Post* also reported on a presentation that Hasan gave as part of a master's program in public health, this one asking whether the war on terror was "a war against Islam."

According to NPR, such inappropriate actions, along with others, drew the attention of senior Army medical personnel at Walter Reed. The senior psychiatric officer drafted a memo citing Hasan's lack of professionalism and work ethic. NPR also reported that he had been chastised for proselytizing to patients. Colleagues said he was someone with whom they would never want to be "in a foxhole"; others worried that once deployed to Afghanistan he might give secrets to the enemy. One classmate called him a "ticking time bomb."

Many news organizations were upfront about the underlying reasons why Hasan's superiors, especially those at Walter Reed, had dropped the ball so egregiously. As *Time* magazine reported four days after the shooting, the most troubling possibility in the Hasan case was that "the Army looked the other way precisely because he was a Muslim." Some in a position to do or say something were afraid of a discrimination complaint "that could ruin careers."

The *New York Times,* however, was oddly reluctant to explore the facts behind Hasan's religious extremism and the institutional hypersensitivity that may have allowed him to advance in his medical career. The paper took a back seat to other news organizations, citing facts associated with Nidal's apparent jihadist tendencies only well after the *Post* and other media did so, and only in language that downplayed the most disturbing information about Hasan's motives. Instead, the *Times* focused on what had become part of its multicultural creed: anti-Muslim discrimination and second-hand combat stress from an illegitimate, incompetently waged war. In the first ten days after the massacre, beyond reporting that Hasan had gotten up on a desk and screamed *"Allahu Akbar,"* the *Times* saw an isolated psychological event.

A report on day two from a mosque in Fort Hood where Hasan had worshipped carried a statement by another worshipper: "When a white guy shoots up a post office, they call that going postal," said Victor Benjamin II, a former member of the Army. "But when a Muslim does it, they call it jihad." An editorial the same day counseled that it was important "to avoid drawing prejudicial conclusions from the fact that Major Hasan is an American Muslim whose parents came from the Middle East. . . . But until investigations are complete, no one can begin to imagine what could possibly have motivated this latest appalling rampage."

The *Times* expressed concerns about an anti-Muslim backlash in the services and affirmed the much-criticized comments of General George Casey, who said on *Meet the Press* that "Our diversity, not only in our Army but in our country, is a strength. And as horrific as this tragedy was, if our diversity becomes a casualty, I think that's worse." In a report headlined "Complications Grow for Muslims Serving in U.S. Military," Andrea Elliott cited Casey's concern for diversity and stressed the theme of alienation and discrimination. "Whatever his possible motives, the emerging portrait of Major Hasan's life in the military casts light on some of the struggles and frustrations felt by other Muslims in the services,"

Elliott wrote. According to friends and relatives, Hasan was disillusioned with the wars in Afghanistan and Iraq, which he perceived as part of a war on Islam, and had been singled out and taunted by fellow soldiers for being Muslim. Elliott quoted his uncle in Ramallah, Rafik Hamad, saying that Hasan had once been called a "camel jockey."

The other story line that the *Times* used to dodge the idea of religious motivation was "combat stress," which it implied Hasan had developed in treating returning soldiers who themselves had post-traumatic stress disorder. "Every man has his breaking point," wrote Erica Goode, quoting World War II military doctors. For Nidal Hasan, she continued, that breaking point "may have come even before he experienced the reality of war." His own psyche may have been "undone by the kind of stress he treated."

A report on November 15, nearly ten days after the attack, marked the first time the paper reluctantly acknowledged facts that other news organizations had dug up nearly from the beginning. Headlined "Investigators Study Tangle of Clues on Fort Hood Suspect," it disclosed that Hasan had the letters "SOA" (for Soldier of Allah) on the business cards he used when moonlighting as a civilian psychiatrist. The article also noted that some of his supervisors at Walter Reed were wary of "appearing insensitive to Muslim culture," and finally mentioned the PowerPoint presentation about the Koranic worldview and its effects on Muslim soldiers.

Political and moral seriousness was lacking in the *Times'* coverage of the Army's January 2010 report on the Fort Hood case. The *Times* called the report a "sobering look" at "Major Hasan's Smooth Ascension," but never noted—as *Time* did—that the 86-page report "not once mentions Major Nidal Hasan by name or even discusses whether the killings may have had anything to do with the suspect's view of his Muslim faith." (The report referred to him as the "alleged perpetrator.") Although the report, and the *Times*, did acknowledge that there were missteps on the part of Hasan's superiors as he rose through the ranks, both the report and the *Times* failed to identify perhaps the key driving factor in his ascent. As the military analyst Ralph Peters wrote, "Hasan's superiors feared—correctly—that any attempt to call attention to his radicalism or to prevent his promotion would backfire on them, destroying their careers, not his. Hasan was a protected-species minority. Under the p.c. tyranny of today's armed services, no non-minority officer was going to take him on."

⌒

In the immediate aftermath of 9/11, the *Times* reported on the disarray in the country's visa and deportation systems that had allowed Mohammed Atta and his gang to pull off their assault on America, and on the number of Arab men in the United States who fit virtually the same background profile as the nineteen hijackers. The *Times* also reported on problems in communication between our national security, intelligence and law enforcement bureaucracies, most notably "the Wall" erected in the Clinton years that made it illegal for the FBI and the CIA to communicate and cooperate with respect to leads and intelligence reports related to the 9/11 attack. But it was not long before an oppositional stance asserted itself. Within two months of the attack, the paper was casting aspersions on the ability of the government to fight terrorism; expressing grave concerns that the fight against terrorism might lead to the "loss of the country's soul"; and opining that the theoretical loss of civil liberties under the USA Patriot Act would do "lasting damage to our 217-year-old nation of laws," as one editorial put it in 2004.

The paper's antagonistic posture was dictated in part by the sweeping nature of the policy changes required to fight a war on terrorism. A more fundamental reason, however, was a set of *idées fixes* about the nature of the threat represented by militant Islam, and about a supposed overreaction based on "Islamophobia" encoded in the nation's DNA. Instead of seeing the radical Islamic jihad as a fundamental challenge to the West, the *Times* has invoked inappropriate, shallow and alarmist historical analogies— for instance, likening crackdowns on militant Muslims and illegal Islamic immigrants to the infamous Palmer Raids during the Red Scare of the early 1920s or the internment of Japanese American citizens and resident aliens during World War II. Rather than inventory the ways in which the Islamic jihad targets the West's commitment to Enlightenment values of equality between the sexes, religious pluralism and tolerance for dissent, the *Times* has insisted that Islam is "a religion of peace," that the government has overreacted to fringe elements in a cynical grab for power, and that Muslims in this country are victims of Islamophobia just as blacks are victims of racism and Hispanics are victims of nativism. Invoking the anticommunism of the Cold War, the *Times'* regular Web contributor Robert Wright wrote in June 2010, "Once you decide that some group is your implacable enemy, your mind gets a little warped."

One result of this script is that the *Times* has basically put its head in the sand regarding the various terror plots that have been mounted against the United States and its allies. The dangers that these plots represent are typically minimized and the role that jihadism plays in animating them is denied or downplayed, often in a journalistically clumsy way.

The *Times'* treatment of Sami al-Arian was an early example of the paper's prejudices. A Palestinian-born professor of computer science at the University of South Florida who ran an Islamic charity and think tank in Tampa, al-Arian first came under investigation by federal authorities in the mid 1990s, when news reports noted calls for the destruction of Israel and donations to terrorist groups. Later, al-Arian and his organizations came under closer scrutiny when a Palestinian colleague he had brought to the university disappeared abruptly, only to end up in Damascus as the leader of the terrorist group Palestinian Islamic Jihad. The University of South Florida suspended al-Arian at first, then dismissed him. Meanwhile, the government launched a terrorism funding case against al-Arian. According to the government, Palestinian Islamic Jihad, which al-Arian's think tank had helped found, had mounted a number of terrorist bombings that had killed civilians in Israel.

The case polarized the university community and infuriated Muslims throughout the country. Al-Arian's supporters saw him as a free-speech martyr, "the new Alger Hiss." (Al-Arian humbly played the Islamophobia card: "I'm a minority, I'm an Arab, I'm Palestinian. That's not a popular thing to be these days.") But his opponents saw someone who had infiltrated the university to advance a terrorist agenda. As the case against al-Arian grew, many former supporters felt burned, especially fellow faculty who had bought into the argument about free speech and academic freedom.

The *Times* went to bat for al-Arian, seeing him as a victim of a "New McCarthyism." In late January 2002, the editorial board scolded the University of South Florida and the state's Republican governor, Jeb Bush, insisting they dishonored "the ideals of public universities" in trying to fire al-Arian for his "anti-Israel statements."

During his trial in 2005 and 2006, federal prosecutors introduced convincing evidence that al-Arian was not just another tweedy professor with eccentrically heterodox ideas. After a double suicide bombing killed twenty-two people in Israel, al-Arian, the government maintained, had written a letter soliciting "true support of the jihad effort in Palestine so that operations such as these can continue." Al-Arian eventually reached a plea agreement with the government in which he acknowledged that his fundraising efforts were intended to finance terrorist attacks and did, in fact, make terrorist acts possible. Part of the agreement read that "the defendant, knowing the unlawful purpose of the plan, willfully joined it."

Still, the *Times* continued to carry al-Arian's banner. It took his side in a controversy over whether he should be compelled to testify before a federal grand jury in Virginia, which was investigating other branches of Islamic terrorism in America and which, the government claimed, would benefit from his knowledge. In April 2008, Neil MacFarquhar, ignoring all prior court evidence, said that al-Arian was "nothing more sinister than an outspoken Palestinian activist" who was being unjustly punished with threats of being jailed on contempt of court charges.

The *Times* was also solicitous toward Ahmed Omar Abu Ali, a 23-year-old Virginia Muslim who in November 2005 was convicted on charges of plotting to assassinate President George Bush, among other charges. Abu Ali had ties to several men convicted as part of the Virginia Jihad, known derisively to many, including many at the *Times,* as the "Paintball Jihad" because of their military training routines. Abu Ali had traveled to Saudi Arabia and had been arrested there in a government crackdown after terrorist bombings in Riyadh in 2003, thought to be the work of al-Qaeda.

In reporting the indictment in February 2005, the *Times* quoted friends and defense lawyers of Abu Ali who said he was not part of any plot but had given a confession as a result of torture by the Saudis. "Several of the government's major terror prosecutions . . . have suffered significant setbacks in the courtroom or collapsed altogether amid questions of prosecution tactics," said the report. An editorial shortly afterward repeated the claims of torture, and made clear that the *Times* saw the alleged infringement of Abu Ali's civil rights as more serious than his plans to kill the president. "If the Justice Department believed that Mr. Abu Ali was a serious terrorist, he should have been brought back here long ago for trial," the *Times* argued. "Instead, he became part of an unknown number of prisoners who were swept up by American officials or foreign governments working with Americans and questioned in the wake of Sept. 11."

When Abu Ali's jailhouse conversations with family members were put under a gag order, the *Times* sided with the family. James Dao and Eric Lichtblau reported that the case had "outraged members of Northern Virginia's growing Muslim population and escalated a conflict with federal law enforcement authorities over terrorism investigations into religious leaders, mosques, businesses and private Islamic schools in the region." They quoted a spokesman for the Dar al-Hijrah mosque in Falls Church, where Abu Ali and his family worshipped, as saying the whole Muslim community "was under siege."

In the fall of 2005, the government filed additional charges against Abu Ali charging conspiracy to commit aircraft piracy and destroy aircraft, in a broad plan to carry out a major terror attack. An FBI agent told reporters that Abu Ali had discussed killing U.S. congressmen and soldiers and blowing up naval ships in U.S. ports. Later, federal prosecutors alleged that Abu Ali had scouted nuclear plants in the United States at the behest of confederates in al-Qaeda. But the *Times* did not report these additional charges until Abu Ali was actually convicted, and then it stressed the claim that he had been tortured in Saudi Arabia, although no real evidence supported it, and that he had not been read his Miranda rights when first interviewed by the FBI.

Abu Ali was sentenced to thirty years. In 2007, government prosecutors persuaded a federal judge in Virginia that Abu Ali should get a life sentence, partly because he had never renounced his al-Qaeda ties. This was an eminently newsworthy development, yet the *Times* let an AP report carry the news, and buried that AP report inside the paper.

Minimal coverage was given by the *Times* to an episode that may have been a "dry run" for airborne terror attacks. On Northwest flight 327 between Detroit and Los Angeles on June 29, 2004, thirteen Middle Eastern men—twelve Syrians belonging to a band and their Lebanese leader—spent the four-hour flight acting suspiciously. Their seats were scattered all about the plane, but in strategic locations; the men congregated in small groups at the back of the plane and made consecutive trips to the bathroom. During all this, they seemed to be signaling to each other. One of the men stood near the cabin door as the plane prepared to land. At the end of the flight, when the seatbelt sign was flashing, they all stood in unison. At one point, a passenger and her husband had approached a stewardess to express their concern. The stewardess told them that she and her colleagues were also concerned, as were some air marshals secretly on the flight. After landing, the plane was met by law enforcement officials, who whisked the group away for questioning.

The alarmed female passenger, Annie Jacobsen, wrote a website account of the experience, "Terror in the Skies," which the left-wing blogosphere cruelly ridiculed as paranoid and racist. In a piece headlined "What Really Happened on Flight 327?" (in the Business section), *Times* columnist Joe Sharkey asked whether it might have been "an innocent sequence of events that some passengers, overcome by anxiety and perhaps ethnic stereotyping, misinterpreted as a plot to blow up their plane?"

Three years later, inspectors general for several agencies determined that the incident really was a dry run. A Homeland Security report explained that a background check in the FBI's National Crime Information Center database, which was performed as part of a visa-extension application, produced "positive hits" for past criminal records or suspicious behavior for eight of the twelve Syrians. The Department of Homeland Security found a similar incident involving the Lebanese leader of the group five months before the event of June 2004. The report also said that the leader was detained a third time, in September, on a return trip to the United States from Istanbul, and scolded the Transportation Safety Administration for not pursuing the matter further.

Two years after the Northwest flight 327 incident, there was a similar case involving Muslim passengers acting suspiciously, which was dubbed the case of the "Flying Imams." One of the imams involved was the head of the Islamic Center of Tucson, which one terrorism expert called "the first Al Qaeda cell in the U.S.," according to the *Washington Post*. Although the incident was covered extensively in much of the mainstream media, the only coverage of the actual facts of the case in the *Times* appeared in an op-ed piece by former Admiral James Zumwalt—hardly a way to convey important news about a potentially dangerous event.

A conspiracy to blow up airport terminals and fuel tanks at JFK International Airport in June 2007 might have been expected to make the front page (as it did in the *Washington Post* and the *Los Angeles Times*), but instead it was buried on page 30 of the national edition. The four men involved were all Muslim, and authorities tied them to Jamaat al-Muslimeen, an extremist organization in Trinidad. On page one that day, the *Times* chose instead to highlight a story about the youngest detainee at Guantanamo Bay, whose lawyer said he was not a terrorist but a boy who would have been riding horses, playing soccer and reading *Harry Potter* if he hadn't been unjustly imprisoned. It was only deep into the story that readers learned the boy-detainee was the son of "a senior deputy to Osama bin Laden."

Even the public editor, Clark Hoyt, chastised the editors who made the decision to bury news of the JFK plot, hinting that the senior-most editor on duty that day was overly suspicious because of prior cases when he believed the government had hyped a plot for political purposes. The paper should have played the story on page one, Hoyt said. "Newspapers . . . have to be careful not to appear indifferent to plots that, allowed to mature, could pose real threats of death and destruction."

One such plot involved a conspiracy in May 2009 to blow up synagogues in an affluent area of the Bronx and then shoot down military planes at an Air National Guard base in midstate New York. Based on testimony by an informant, four men were arrested in a long-running "sting operation" after planting what they believed to be bombs in cars outside two synagogues in Riverdale.

The *Times'* first-day reporting indicated that three of the four men had converted to Islam in prison and all worshipped at the same mosque in Newburgh, New York. According to the criminal complaint, each said he was willing "to perform jihad." One suspect said that the American military "is killing Muslim brothers and sisters in Muslim countries, so if we kill them here with IEDs and Stingers, it is equal." Even from the paper's own reporting it was abundantly clear that this was a jihadi plot and the criminals were radical Muslims driven by fierce anti-Semitism. Yet the *Times* reported on the second day of coverage that "Law enforcement officials said the four men were Muslims, but their religious backgrounds remained uncertain." The paper also was extremely defensive about the role that incarceration may have played in radicalizing the men. According to Daniel Wakin's "Imams Reject Talk That Islam Radicalizes Inmates," the imam of the mosque who ministered to the four terrorists insisted that his years working with Muslims in prison had turned up little evidence that anyone became radicalized behind bars. "I don't hear any of that wild stuff," he said. "And if I did hear it, I would stomp it out. It is totally un-Islamic." Wakin also wrote that "it is uncertain just how much of a role [the suspects'] faith played in their motivation." Sidebars and follow-ups raised questions about the government's use of a confidential informant—the cornerstone of an "entrapment" defense. The paper also reported that the group had no ties to larger terrorist networks like al-Qaeda, as if this lessened the damage they could have caused.

Just two sentences in the tabloid *New York Post* captured what the handwringing *Times* could not: "They were like a million other petty criminals—until they embraced radical Islam behind bars, launching a terrifying march to a planned mass murder that ended only when authorities sabotaged their sinister plot." The role of prison Islam as a path to radicalization was underscored in 2010 when ABC News reported that there were scores of American ex-convicts now in Yemen who had converted to Islam in prison and might be training for sleeper-cell operations upon returning to the United States.

The *Times* demonstrated its ambivalence again in reporting on the dozens of Somali teens who, the FBI said in 2009, had disappeared in cities across the country, primarily in Minneapolis but also in Seattle, St. Louis and Columbus, Ohio. They were suspected of having been recruited to wage jihad with al-Shabaab, a militant group affiliated with al-Qaeda in Somalia. One of the teenagers was positively identified by DNA as a suicide bomber who drove an explosives-laden vehicle into a compound in a Somali city, leveling a UN building, a presidential palace and an Ethiopian consulate; the FBI called him "the first U.S. citizen suicide bomber." Despite FBI fears that some of these U.S. citizens and/or passport holders could be commissioned to carry out acts of terror on American soil, the *Times* devoted a mere seven paragraphs to the story, restricting its coverage to a stenographic account of the FBI press conference. Meanwhile, NPR and the *Los Angeles Times* did numerous reports, fleshing out details and providing important context.

It was not until July—six months after the other news organizations had reported on the unfolding case—that the *Times* picked up on the story. Andrea Elliott, who had won a Pulitzer Prize for her soft-edged series on "An Imam in America," described the impetus for the young men's travel to Somalia as a "crisis of belonging," born of religious devotion but also discrimination in the United States, where they were "taunted" by African Americans who told them to "Go back to Africa." Months later, in November, Elliott detailed that fourteen people had been charged in the case as either recruits who had returned home or recruiters who had played a key role in convincing them to go and underwriting their travels. Some of them were in federal custody but others were still fugitives. It was, said Elliott, "one of the most extensive domestic terrorism investigations since the September 11 attacks."

Elliott's reporting seemed thorough, even if inexplicably late. But it failed to note that the recruiting had been done in mosques with permission of mosque leaders, that the Council on American-Islamic Relations had advised parents of the missing teens not to cooperate with the FBI, and that the parents had rejected CAIR's counsel, instead mounting protests against the organization—a significant news story in itself. Elliott's piece closed with an odd jibe at the FBI. Although she reported that recruitment seemed to be continuing, she quoted an anonymous friend of a man suspected of recruiting for al-Shabaab as telling her that the FBI's investigation had made an underdog out of the jihadist group, thus aiding recruitment.

While it minimizes the dangers posed by terror plots, the *Times* has been uniformly hostile to the tools used to investigate and prosecute real and potential terrorists. In 2002 alone, the *Times* ran three editorials that condemned sending undercover agents into mosques suspected of supporting terrorism, fingerprinting young male visa holders from countries friendly to terrorism, and temporarily detaining asylum seekers from high-risk countries for additional background screening.

Immediately after the 9/11 attacks, the editorial board demanded to know what was being done to screen airline passengers so that people who fit the threat profile could not board American planes. Yet since then, it has repeatedly editorialized and printed news stories against "racial profiling" of Arabs and Muslims. After the London Tube bombings, for instance, the paper applauded Mayor Michael Bloomberg's new random search policy for subway riders as "a way to treat people fairly and still pursue any real threat." This caused even liberals to roll their eyes. As Kurt Andersen put it in *New York* magazine, it was "deeply disingenuous of Bloomberg to deny the fact that not just 'most' but nearly every jihadi who has attacked a Western European or American target is a young Arab or Pakistani man."

An FBI plan to take a census of mosques in individual communities was characterized in *Times* news accounts as "racial profiling." One report prominently carried a reaction from Ibrahim Hooper, the spokesman of CAIR, who said that the order was obviously a signal to FBI field agents to view every mosque and every Muslim as a terrorist, and that it was "imposing a sense of siege on the Arab-American community." The insertion of undercover police officers and FBI agents into mosques to conduct surveillance was seen by the *Times* as particularly heinous, even though they were not conducting broad surveillance of all worshippers but only of individuals already being watched as part of terrorism investigations.

In June 2006, Andrea Elliott highlighted a survey conducted for the federal government by the left-leaning Vera Institute of Justice, which contended that Muslims were now more afraid of the police than they were of post-9/11 hate crimes. And when the New York Police Department did a study to determine how young Muslim men get radicalized, released in August 2007, Sewell Chan depicted it in the *Times* as opening the door to racial profiling and to "the marginalization of and hostility toward the American Muslim community," as CAIR put it. As the specter of homegrown jihadis began to deepen on the heels of at least ten plots involving American citizens or nationals, Paul Vitello and Kirk Semple of the *Times* filed a report in late 2009 with the headline "Muslims Say FBI Tactics Sow Anger and Fear."

The use of material witness warrants in terrorism cases, an effective tool for sorting out suspicious characters, was condemned by the *Times*. In the spring of 2010, just after the naturalized Pakistani immigrant Faisal Shahzad tried to set off a car bomb in Times Square, the at-large urban critic Ariel Kaminer wrung her hands in worry that the "Big Apple" was becoming the

"Big Eyeball" with all the surveillance cameras popping up in New York—cameras that played a significant role in the investigation of the case. There was a piece laced with victimology about the federal no-fly list, which had been strengthened after the Christmas Bomber nearly blew up an airliner heading to Detroit. An editorial denounced as an infringement of free speech the 2010 Supreme Court decision that upheld the "material support" statute barring humanitarian efforts that wind up helping terror groups abroad.

The *Times* also unfairly dramatized botched government prosecutions. One such misstep involved Brandon Mayfield, the Oregon lawyer caught up in the 2004 Madrid rail bombings. Another involved the Muslim student in Idaho charged in 2003 with terrorism-related offenses for running a website service that inadvertently had jihadi content posted on it. There was also a terrorism case against three Moroccan men in Detroit that fell apart in 2004 when the Justice Department determined that there had been prosecutorial misconduct. Yet these cases hardly added up to a pattern.

Meanwhile, the government was breaking up plots to bomb New York City subway stations and to destroy the Brooklyn Bridge. It broke up a plot in New York's garment district, where al-Qaeda was trying to set up a Kashmiri-owned import-export company as a front to obtain Stinger missiles for use against aircraft at the Newark airport. It successfully prosecuted the Virginia Jihad case and that of the Portland Seven, who were surveilling Jewish schools and synagogues for attack. It got the Lackawanna Six, and also the Yemeni sheik Mohammed Ali Hasan al-Moayad, who was convicted of conspiring to funnel millions of dollars to al-Qaeda and Hamas through his Brooklyn mosque. There was also the "Landmarks Case" of 2004, in which the government stopped a plot to blow up the International Monetary Fund and World Bank headquarters in Washington, the New York Stock Exchange and the Citigroup Center, and the Prudential building in Newark.

But these successes made little impact on the *Times,* which concentrated its fire on the government's three most important antiterror tools: the National Security Agency's wiretapping of telephone calls and email traffic between the United States and terrorist suspects abroad; the Treasury Department and CIA's covert surveillance of the Belgium-based SWIFT banking consortium; and the USA Patriot Act, which the paper has insistently portrayed as ineffective and unconstitutional.

In December 2005, the *Times* broke the NSA wiretapping story in a front-page account by James Risen and Eric Lichtblau. "Months after the Sept. 11 attacks," they wrote, "President Bush secretly authorized the National Security Agency to eavesdrop on certain phone calls and email traffic to search for evidence of terrorist activity without the court-approved warrants ordinarily required for domestic spying, according to government officials." The sources for the story were "nearly a dozen current and former officials, who were granted anonymity because of the classified nature of the program." They had talked to the *Times* "because of their concerns about the operation's legality and oversight." The report clearly sided with critics of the program, who saw the specter of illegal "domestic spying" or "domestic eavesdropping" on U.S. citizens.

Reaction against the report in the *Times* was swift and harsh. The president called its publication a "shameful act" that amounted to "helping the enemy." The *New York Post* asked, "Has The New York Times declared itself to be on the front line in the war against the War on Terror?" The Department of Justice opened a criminal inquiry, hinting that it might subpoena the reporters to determine the source of this highly classified leak.

Self-righteously responding to the furor, Bill Keller, the executive editor, told Murray Waas of the *National Journal,* "Some officials in this administration, and their more vociferous cheerleaders, seem to have a special animus towards reporters doing their jobs. . . . I don't know how far action will follow rhetoric, but some days it sounds like the administration is declaring war at home on the values they profess to be promoting abroad."

The White House had asked the *Times* not to publish the article, arguing that it could jeopardize continuing investigations and alert would-be terrorists that they might be under scrutiny. Risen and Lichtblau reported this, but not the fact that President Bush had summoned Keller and Sulzberger to a meeting in the

Oval Office earlier that month to deliver the request and tell them, according to Keller, "You'll have blood on your hands" if there was another terror attack. Risen and Lichtblau wrote that after meeting with senior administration officials to hear their concerns, "the newspaper delayed publication for a year to conduct additional reporting. Some information that administration officials argued could be useful to terrorists has been omitted." The paper offered no information about what had changed to warrant publication. Nor did it note that one of its reporters, James Risen, would soon be publishing a book containing most of the information that appeared in the *Times* report.

In August 2006, Judge Anna Diggs Taylor ruled against the NSA program, declaring it an unconstitutional expansion of executive power. "There are no hereditary kings in America and no powers not created by the Constitution," she wrote in her ruling. The *Times* editorial board was ecstatic, claiming that the ruling "eviscerated the absurd notion on which the administration's arguments have been based: that Congress authorized Mr. Bush to do whatever he thinks is necessary when it authorized the invasion of Afghanistan." The judge, the editorial said, did what 535 members of Congress could not do: "reassert the rule of law over a lawless administration."

Yet this editorial was itself eviscerated the next day—by the paper's own legal reporter and analyst, Adam Liptak. Under the headline "Experts Fault Reasoning in Surveillance Decision," he explained that "Even legal experts who agreed with a federal judge's conclusion on Thursday that a National Security Agency surveillance program is unlawful were distancing themselves from the decision's reasoning and rhetoric." According to Liptak's legal sources, the opinion "overlooked important precedents, failed to engage the government's major arguments, used circular reasoning, substituted passion for analysis and did not even offer the best reasons for its own conclusions."

A footnote to the NSA story, showing more dishonesty and partisanship from the *Times,* came in 2009 when the paper reported on a classified report from the inspectors general of five different federal agencies who reviewed the effectiveness of the

NSA surveillance program in terms of the quality of the intelligence it yielded. According to James Risen and Eric Lichtblau— who might have declared a conflict of interest in reporting this follow-up to their own NSA exposé—the wiretapping program had limited value. But the five IG reports had actually declared explicitly that the NSA program was a useful tool, providing information that was previously unavailable, as the senior CIA officials maintained, and serving as a very valuable "early warning system."

Six months after their NSA wiretapping story, in June 2006, Risen and Lichtblau sparked controversy again with another highly classified intelligence exposé. This one described top-secret details of the covert SWIFT banking surveillance program to monitor terrorism-related bank transfers. "Under a secret Bush administration program initiated weeks after the Sept. 11 attacks," wrote Risen and Lichtblau, "counter-terrorism officials have gained access to financial records from a vast international database and examined banking transactions involving thousands of Americans and others in the United States, according to government and industry officials."

There was nothing illegal about the program, and it was highly effective. It assisted in the capture of Riduan Isamuddin, an Indonesian who goes by the name Hambali and was considered "the Osama bin Laden of Asia," and who masterminded the Bali bombings of 2002. The SWIFT program was also instrumental in identifying and convicting Uzair Paracha, who was found guilty of conspiring to launder $200,000 to help al-Qaeda.

President Bush, along with the Homeland Security chief John Negroponte and the Treasury secretary John Snow, beseeched the *Times* not to run the story, as Risen and Lichtblau admitted. The government argued that it would undermine one of the most effective instruments of counterterrorism and close down a vital window on the murky doings of international terror. But the *Times* was undeterred. "We have listened closely to the administration's arguments for withholding this information, and given them the most serious and respectful consideration," said Bill Keller. "We remain convinced that the administration's extraordinary access to this vast repository of international financial data, however carefully targeted use of it may be, is a matter of public interest."

The president called the story "disgraceful," saying there was "no excuse" for a newspaper to publish the nation's security secrets in time of war. Vice President Cheney called the story "damaging" to national interests. Secretary Snow said the *Times* had shown "breathtaking arrogance" and had given itself "license to expose any covert activity it learns of."

Equally scalding were the *Wall Street Journal*'s editors, who commented that "Not everything is fit to print." Millions of Americans, said the *Journal,* no longer believe that *Times* editors will make calculations of secrecy versus disclosure "in anything close to good faith. . . . On issue after issue, it has become clear that the Times believes the U.S. is not really at war, and in any case the Bush Administration lacks the legitimacy to wage it." Citing Sulzberger's speech at New Paltz, where he apologized on behalf of his generation for leading the country into a dubious war, the *Journal* closed, "Forgive us if we conclude that a newspaper led by someone who speaks this way to college seniors has as a major goal not winning the war on terror but obstructing it."

Stung by accusations of bad judgment and even of offering aid and comfort to the enemy, the *Times* issued defenses and explanations through a special "letter to readers," an editorial, an ombudsman's report, a string of efforts by the columnists Frank Rich, Paul Krugman and Nicholas Kristof, and an unusual op-ed co-authored by Bill Keller and the *Los Angeles Times* editor Dean Baquet. Keller also took the unusual step of making carefully managed appearances on *Charlie Rose, Face the Nation* and *PBS NewsHour.* As one watchdog website said, it was "all hands on deck" to help a listing ship.

On *PBS NewsHour,* Keller tried to produce a high-minded summary of the paper's justification for giving away government secrets, by summoning the Founding Fathers' vision of "a system whereby ordinary citizens and editors, amateurs, were entitled, under the basic law of the country, to second-guess the leadership of the country." In his open letter to readers, Keller delivered another little lecture on constitutional history: "The people who invented this country saw an aggressive, independent press as a protective measure against the abuse of power in a democracy, and an essential ingredient for self-government. They rejected the idea that it is wise, or patriotic, to always take the President at his word, or to surrender to the government important decisions about what to publish."

As public pressure mounted, however, these grand pronouncements were accompanied by a considerable amount of backing and filling. Although the original story used the word "secret" eight times, including in the headline, Keller now said the program was not a secret. He was echoing Eric Lichtblau, who on CNN tried to justify the paper by citing a *USA Today* front-page story that ran four days before the *Times* exposé and said that "terrorists know their money is being traced." At some points, Keller was reduced to playground logic. If drawing attention to the SWIFT program was "dangerous and unpatriotic," he mused, why were conservative bloggers and pundits "drawing so much attention to the story themselves by yelling about it on the airwaves and the Internet?"

The *Times'* most egregious attack on the tools used to fight terrorism came in its reporting on the USA Patriot Act, especially its campaign against renewal of the act in 2004. Signed into law in October 2001, the Patriot Act's most important provision was to bring down "the Wall" that had prevented domestic law enforcement and intelligence agencies from communicating with each other. The act also enhanced the Treasury Department's ability to disrupt terrorist financing networks, and modestly increased the attorney general's power to detain and deport suspected terrorist aliens. The Patriot Act was important in cases such as the Lackawanna Six, the Virginia Jihad and the Brooklyn Bridge plot; and it helped in apprehending the murderers of Daniel Pearl. (Since then, it's been important in almost all other terror investigations and prosecutions.) According to some counterterrorism specialists, had the Patriot Act been in place prior to 9/11, the attacks might have been prevented. The FBI and CIA could have been in contact about the two hijackers who the CIA believed were in the country; the FBI could have looked at the contents of the "twentieth hijacker" Zacarias Moussaoui's incriminating laptop; and investigators might have discovered that seven of the nineteen hijackers had used public access computers to purchase airline tickets.

Yet the *Times* was almost violently opposed to the Patriot Act, preferring to see terror as a law enforcement issue rather than an act of war requiring wartime powers for the government. The editorial board ran almost a dozen attacks on the legislation, including "The War at Home" in April 2003, which claimed that "the Bush administration has slashed away at core constitutional protections in the name of fighting terrorism." An editorial in August, "An Unpatriotic Act," declared that "many people, both liberals and conservatives alike, consider [the Patriot Act] a dangerous assault on civil liberties."

As the fight for renewal of the Patriot Act was beginning in late 2003, the *Washington Post* reported that many senators, including Democrats such as Dianne Feinstein, agreed with Attorney General John Ashcroft that it did not assault civil liberties. (Feinstein said she had never seen a single abuse of the act.) The *Post* quoted Senator Joe Biden as saying that criticism of the act was "ill-informed and overblown." But the *Times,* downplaying or ignoring such assessments, published several feature stories giving the impression that gumshoes were lurking in community libraries waiting to uncover what seditious books or websites innocent individuals were reading. In a *Times Book Review* roundup of eight books connected to how 9/11 affected civil liberties, Ethan Bronner, the *Times* deputy foreign editor, said, "The message from all these books can be summed up in five simple words: Be worried. Be very worried."

The fiercest editorial attack by the *Times* came right on the eve of the renewal vote in October 2004. Headlined "A Very Bad Deal," it acknowledged that most Americans would willingly trade minor infringements of civil liberties for well-planned and well-executed operations that would make us safer, but claimed that "instead we got a mounting pile of bungled operations, ranging from the merely inept to the scandalously abusive, and military prisons filled with Afghans, Iraqis and other Muslims who have committed no real offenses." The editorial asserted that terror investigators had come back "with a motley crew of hapless innocents, and people who had said and done stupid things but were hardly a threat to the nation's security," that investigators had acted more like Keystone Kops than intelligence operatives, and that cases like the Lackawanna Six were "thin." But that case, in fact, had put away a potentially dangerous sleeper cell and led to the assassination of the group's al-Qaeda-connected recruiter/guide. In July 2004, the Department of Justice issued a report outlining dozens of successful investigations where the Patriot Act played a critical role; the DOJ claimed that it had charged 310 defendants with terrorism-related crimes and that 179 of them had already been convicted. This report had been available to the *Times* editorial board for three months before it ran "A Very Bad Deal."

The *Times* attacked the Patriot Act partly through ad hominem broadsides at its symbolic figurehead, John Ashcroft. In a column headlined "A Travesty of Justice," Paul Krugman called Ashcroft "the worst Attorney General ever." His fellow columnist Frank Rich made a similar gratuitous swipe, calling Ashcroft "The Best Goebbels of Them All." Wrote Rich, "While FDR once told Americans that we have nothing to fear but fear itself, Mr. Ashcroft is delighted to play the part of fear itself, an assignment in which he lets his imagination run riot."

The *Times*' ideological and partisan opposition to the Patriot Act drove it into solidarity with the likes of Lynne Stewart, the radical lawyer who passed notes from her client Omar Abdel Rahman, a.k.a. the "Blind Sheik," to his followers in al-Gamaa al-Islamiyya, the Egyptian terrorist organization that massacred dozens of tourists at Luxor in 1997. When Stewart was convicted of providing support for terrorism, Sabrina Tavernise wrote what amounted to a valentine to her, praising her "legendary compassion." Tavernise recounted how Larry Davis, who shot six New York police officers in 1986, was acquitted after Stewart painted the entire NYPD as racist. Not reported was Stewart's legendary belief in revolutionary violence, or the fact that the *Washington Post* once quoted her as saying, "There is death in history, and it's not all rosebuds and memorial services. Mao, Fidel, Ho Chi Minh understood this."

After receiving a wrist slap of a sentence, Stewart was glib outside the courthouse, claiming to have won a "great victory against an overarching government." She believed that an appeal might return her to the bar, and declared that she would do the same "all over again." As for the twenty-eight-month sentence? She could do that time "standing on her head." The *Times* report of her sentencing closed with an image of Stewart greeting well-wishers "as if she were Gandhi—touching them in the crowd."

Stewart's arrogance backfired, however, as perhaps did the *Times'* glorification of her. In July 2010, a federal judge said the comments she made outside the courthouse showed "a lack of remorse" and extended her sentence to 120 months.

The trust that the *New York Times* put in Judith Miller as its main reporter on the vexing issue of Saddam Hussein's development and possession of weapons of mass destruction in the run-up to the 2003 invasion of Iraq was not at all surprising. Boasting an impressive resumé, Miller had the credentials and, more important, the connections to beat back competition from the *Washington Post* and the *Wall Street Journal* in the fierce struggle to break big news leading up to the war.

A longtime foreign correspondent for the *Times,* Miller had won the national security beat by doing time in the Middle East. She had written a book about Saddam Hussein and another on biological weapons. No other journalist had comparable authority on the subject of the possibility of Iraq possessing WMDs. Miller had also written about the threat of Islamic terrorism in depth; in January 2001 she produced several articles about al-Qaeda as part of a series that won her the 2002 Pulitzer Prize. Flashing her legendary chutzpah, she had traveled to Taliban-dominated Afghanistan and demanded to visit a jihadi camp, before being turned away and eventually expelled from the country.

Miller was known as a deeply networked member of the New York–Washington media elite, whose sources were often personal friends, and in some cases romantic interests. Her work on al-Qaeda and on unconventional weapons of mass destruction had earned her contacts deep inside the Bush administration's national security wing, particularly among the "neoconservatives" who had come to the forefront of post-9/11 strategy and led the way in crafting the case, and the strategy, for war in Iraq. According to reports originating in the *Times* newsroom, Howell Raines reportedly told her to go off and win "another Pulitzer."

Just before the war began and just after, Miller produced a series of ominous scoops relying heavily on anonymous sources. In one piece, she described a defector who alleged that Saddam had recently renovated storage facilities for nuclear, chemical and biological weapons. In another, she told of Saddam's bid to gain a lethal strain of smallpox, as well as antidotes to VX gas and sarin that could facilitate ongoing experimentation with those substances.

Miller's most important story was headlined "U.S. Says Hussein Intensifies Quest for A-Bomb Parts." Written along with Michael Gordon, a military correspondent, it described the interception of thousands of high-strength aluminum tubes, which U.S. experts had determined could have only one purpose: as casings for rotors to be used in enriching weapons-grade uranium toward the production of an atomic bomb. The bid to procure such tubes, Miller and Gordon said, showed that a decade after Saddam claimed to have given up the quest for nuclear weapons, he had resumed it, "embarking on a worldwide hunt" for nuclear materials. And administration "hard-liners" were justly worried that "the first sign of a 'smoking gun' . . . may be a mushroom cloud."

The piece was immediately used by administration officials to lobby for military action. Vice President Dick Cheney recycled Miller and Gordon's assertions about the aluminum tubes on *Meet the Press,* while Condoleezza Rice warned on CNN, "We don't want the smoking gun to be a mushroom cloud." The symmetry between Miller's rhetoric and the administration's was striking.

Although the baying of the dogs of war temporarily drowned out the complaints of *Times* reporters angry that the Gray Lady appeared to have volunteered for combat, the critique of the paper's star reporter continued to build in the early days of military action. Some reporters and editors thought Miller had uncritically bought the policy line of her sources in the upper reaches of the administration, and that her reporting was turning the *Times* into a conduit for the administration's "propaganda." Why had the paper not paid heed to knowledgeable colleagues who had reservations about Miller's reporting, especially those in the Washington bureau, as well as experts who had begun to doubt the existence of WMDs? According to an account in the *Los Angeles Times,* editors who delayed the publication of one Miller report claiming that there were a thousand WMD sites in Iraq were lectured by the managing editor, Gerald Boyd, who reminded them that Miller had a Pulitzer Prize, "and your job is to get her stories into the paper." According to an account in *New York* magazine, Howell Raines told a close friend that he wanted to prove he could do straight coverage of the Iraqi WMD story, and a former *Times* editor said that after Bill Kristol characterized the paper as part of an "axis of appeasement," Raines wanted to "demonstrate that he was fair-minded about the Bush administration."

During the late spring of 2003, various news organizations such as *Time* and the *Washington Post* began to write critically of the government's claims about WMDs. The *Wall Street Journal* wrote about the pressure mounting in Washington for an investigation into how prewar intelligence had run so far off the rails. In the *New Yorker,* Seymour Hersh, relying on mostly anonymous government sources, described how a special unit set up in the

Pentagon had disposed of intelligence that didn't live up to their ideological expectations.

At first, the *Times* ignored these second-guessings. But a lengthy *New York Review of Books* piece in February 2004 by Michael Massing criticized the performance of the *Times* in the run-up to the war as "especially deficient." Massing continued, "While occasionally running articles that questioned administration claims, it more often deferred to them. Compared to other major papers, the *Times* placed more credence in defectors, expressed less confidence in inspectors, and paid less attention to dissenters." The overreliance on the defector Ahmad Chalabi was particularly problematic. Before the war, Massing reported, there had been a loud debate about Chalabi within intelligence circles. But it took the *Times* months to examine the matter. Massing was told by a "senior editor" at the *Times* that this was because "some reporters at the paper had relied heavily on Chalabi as a source and so were not going to write too critically about him."

Massing's piece opened the floodgates to frustration with the *Times* and fed into a growing leftist campaign to accuse the media of "selling a war to the American public based on lies," as Arianna Huffington would later write. Some went so far as to accuse the *Times* of having disinterred the yellow journalism of the Hearst press during the run-up to the Spanish-American War. And most fingers pointed directly at Judy Miller. In *New York* magazine, Kurt Andersen explained that "because her vivid, terrifying pieces appeared in the liberal *Times,* she arguably bears more responsibility than any other American outside government for nudging public opinion in favor of war."

Bill Keller said that, in hindsight, he wished he had dealt with the controversy over WMD reporting as soon as he took over in June 2003. But he feared that retracing the paper's steps in an internal investigation would become "a crippling distraction" if he moved too fast. Instead, he ordered Miller off the national security beat—although, as he later said, she kept "drifting" back, continuing to bigfoot editors to publish her reports on this subject. And he assigned some top reporters to do a postmortem, to find where Miller's reporting had gone off-track. The *Times* published its findings on May 27, 2004, in a formal editor's note on page A10. "We have studied the allegations of official gullibility and hype. It is past time we turned the same light on ourselves," the note said. And in closing: "It is still possible that chemical or biological weapons will be unearthed in Iraq, but in this case it looks as if we, along with the administration, were taken in."

An editorial in July baldly accused the Bush administration of "misleading the American people about Saddam Hussein's weapons of mass destruction and links with Al Qaeda." But it added, with uncharacteristic humility, that if the country wanted Bush to be candid about his mistakes, "we should be equally open about our own." The *Times* had not listened carefully enough to people with dissident points of view, the editorial continued. "Our certainty flowed from the fact that such an overwhelming majority of government officials, past and present, top intelligence officials and other experts were sure that the weapons were there. . . . We had a groupthink of our own."

These *mea culpas* were careful to insist that the faulty WMD reporting was "institutional," sidestepping Miller's personal responsibility. This line was shredded mercilessly by Maureen Dowd in a now-notorious October 2005 column headlined "Woman of Mass Destruction," written in the shadow of Miller's involvement in Plamegate, which had prompted some at the *Times* to accuse Miller of protecting her White House sources. Dowd said that Miller's stories about WMD "fit too perfectly with the White House's case for war. She was close to Ahmad Chalabi, the con man who was conning the neocons to knock out Saddam so he could get his hands on Iraq." In closing, Dowd reported that if Judith Miller returned to the newsroom as planned to cover "threats to our country . . . the institution most in danger would be the newspaper in your hands."

The *Times'* apologies for Miller's credulous WMD reporting initiated a change in the paper's reporting on the Iraq War: from now on, it embraced a simple-minded antagonism. After 2004, its coverage displayed a hostile readiness to read negativity into military events and developments where the actual facts did not warrant it. Much of the paper's war reporting since Keller's dark night of the soul seems animated by the need for penance, to regain "our moral compass" as Paul Krugman wrote. Indeed, the paper has seen the specter of rising fascism on the home front along with imperial overreach abroad—fruit from the same rotten tree. One 2005 editorial asserted that "one of the greatest harms from the Iraq conflict has been the administration's willingness to define democracy down on the pretext of wartime emergency."

A reflexive opposition to the broader War on Terror grew so steadily in the years after 9/11 that in the early summer of 2009 the *Times* actually condemned a "secret" CIA plot to kill Osama bin Laden, because it had not been reported to Congress. Never mind that most of the public would have been shocked if such a program had *not* existed and would have demanded that one be instituted. The *Times* had decided long since that it wasn't marching anymore.

Besides caustically criticizing the administration's many policy miscalculations, diplomatic stumbles and military failures, the *Times* threw a negative light on stories that did not merit such a baby-with-the-bathwater approach. This added up to a body of skewed reportage and commentary on developments in the war zone—all calculated to undercut the war's legitimacy, to make the United States seem incompetent and morally corrupt, to insist that Iraq was a quagmire similar to Vietnam, and to cast "the surge" of 2007 as a failure long after it was an acknowledged success. The *Times* has given short shrift to the heroism of our forces in Iraq and Afghanistan, and defamed their character by painting them mostly as killers of civilians and abusers of prisoners.

·⤳

A preview of what would become the paper's impulse to exaggerate almost any military misstep or setback and preemptively declare a "quagmire" was provided in Afghanistan soon after 9/11 by the paper's legendary R. W. "Johnny" Apple. In a news analysis under the headline "A Military Quagmire Remembered: Afghanistan as Vietnam," Apple lead with: "Like an unwelcome specter from an unhappy past, the ominous word 'quagmire' has begun to haunt conversations among government officials and students of foreign policy, both here and abroad." After a negative assessment of the effects of American bombing on the Taliban, Apple complained about the inability of U.S. Army Special Forces to capture the pivotal town of Mazar-i-Sharif. Yet just after his complaint, Northern Alliance troops with their U.S. advisors overran Mazar-i-Sharif, beginning a swift, almost apocalyptic rout of the Taliban. Apple, finger to the wind, changed his tune—almost comically so. "What a difference a week makes," his lede said, as he blamed "armchair Clauswitzes" and other "pessimistic prophets" of doom, failing to note that he himself had been one of them.

In the Iraq War's earliest days, as U.S. forces rolled toward Baghdad, the *Times* continued to be vigilant for failure. In the estimation of TimesWatch's Clay Waters, it seemed like the paper's headlines were being "edited by the Saddam Hussein propaganda machine." Week one featured headlines such as "The Goal Is Baghdad, but at What Cost?" and "Bush Administration Frustrated by War Doubts." An editorial that week headlined "Diminished Expectations in Iraq" cited a small-arms attack on fifteen U.S. Apache helicopters and said, "It was the latest evidence that some of the initial hopes—even assumptions—that Iraqi resistance would quickly crumble seemed not to be panning out." Of course, that initial resistance in Baghdad did quickly crumble, although it would later be reconstructed as the "insurgency."

The readiness to present the news in Iraq negatively and to look for symbols of disaster showed in how the *Times* covered the looting of the Baghdad Museum. Ian Fisher filed a story quoting an Iraqi archeologist: "A country's identity, its value and civilization resides in its history. If a country's culture is looted, as ours has been, our history ends. Please tell this to President Bush. Please remind him that he promised to liberate the Iraqi people, but that this is not a liberation, this is a humiliation." According to Frank Rich, the alleged ransacking of the museum constituted "the naked revelation of our worst instincts at the very dawn of our grandiose project to bring democratic values to the Middle East."

In truth, the museum was not ransacked; and much of its most priceless collections had simply been secreted away. Pejorative information about America allowing the looting came from former Baath officials, who had a self-interest in representing the U.S. military as the culprit in the cultural "crime of the century." In the *Washington Post,* Howard Kurtz wrote, "We're used to journalists being misled in the famous fog of war, but this is ridiculous." According to Kurtz's sources, the actual number of stolen items was thirty-three. But the *Times* was addicted to the narrative of a looted heritage. When the museum reopened in late February 2009, Steven Lee Myers reported that "thousands of works from its collection of antiquities and art—some of civilization's earliest objects—remain lost." Myers failed to mention the controversy over how much was looted in the first place.

On occasion, the *Times'* defeatist impulse could be risible. The day before Saddam was captured in December 2003, the paper ran an editorial headlined "The Story Gets Worse." It began, "Isn't this about where we did not want to be at this point? The news from the American-led occupation is looking like a catalog of easily predictable, and widely predicted, pitfalls."

It's often said that generals are always fighting the last war. But in Iraq it was journalists, especially from the *Times,* who seemed to be re-enacting the past, forcing the conflict into the mold of Vietnam. In a news analysis headlined "Flashback to the 60's: A Sinking Sensation of Parallels Between Iraq and Vietnam," Todd Purdham wrote that "a range of military experts, historians and politicians" agreed that parallels between Vietnam and Iraq were entirely valid. "Nearly two years after the American invasion of Iraq, such comparisons are no longer dismissed in mainstream political discourse as facile and flawed, but are instead bubbling to the top."

It was the columnists, principally Bob Herbert and Frank Rich, who most often hit the Vietnam replay button. In a 2004 column headlined "Powell, Then and Now," Herbert wrote, "in yet another echo of Vietnam, American commanders are begging for more troops. It was ever thus. Commanders thrust into these un-winnable wars against foreign insurgencies always believe that just a few thousand more troops will turn the tide. Americans were told again and again that there was light at the end of the tunnel in Vietnam. The troops sent into that nightmare would dryly remark that the light was coming from an onrushing train." Also in 2004, Frank Rich dilated on "The War's Lost Weekend," writing:

> *Just when you've persuaded yourself yet again that this isn't Vietnam, you are hit by another acid flashback. Last weekend that flashback was to 1969. It was in June 1969 that Life magazine ran its cover story "The Faces of the American Dead in Vietnam: One Week's Toll," the acknowledged prototype for Ted Koppel's photographic roll-call of the American dead in Iraq on "Nightline." It was in November 1969 that a little-known reporter, Seymour Hersh, broke the story of the 1968 massacre at My Lai, the horrific scoop that has now found its match 35 years later in Mr. Hersh's New Yorker revelation of a 53-page Army report detailing "numerous instances of 'sadistic, blatant and wanton criminal abuses' at Abu Ghraib."*

Vietnam was the prism through which the *Times* saw the Iraqi elections in January 2005, noting that the elections that had taken place in South Vietnam in 1967—which it implied were similar—had been an empty sham. John Burns' analysis on the eve of the vote cited an Iraqi exile: "I would like to believe that we could still somehow reclaim the Iraq we lost in the 1950's, but holding elections in these conditions will be a calamity. They will set a course on which we can easily drift into civil war."

The Vietnam lens was also held up to the so-called "Haditha Massacre" of 2005. As Bob Herbert described it in one column, "Marines are suspected of slaughtering 24 Iraqis, including women and children, in the western town of Haditha last November" after the detonation of an IED killed a lance corporal. The case, wrote Herbert, "in its horror, if not its scale, recalls the My Lai massacre of Vietnam." Paul von Zeilbauer filed at least three dozen stories on the alleged slaughter of innocents in Haditha after the incident first came to light in July 2006. As TimesWatch noted, when the case for calling it a "massacre" was eroding in late 2007, von Zeilbauer sounded rueful, writing: "Last year, when accounts of the killing of 24 Iraqis in Haditha by a group of Marines came to light, it seemed that the Iraq war had produced its defining atrocity, just as the conflict in Vietnam had spawned the My Lai massacre a generation ago."

The *Times'* massive investment in the My Lai analogy came to naught when the whole case fell apart. The one Marine who did go to trial was acquitted in June 2008. News of the trial's outcome was carried in four short paragraphs deep inside the paper, just as earlier instances of dropped or reduced charges had been truncated and buried.

If von Zeilbauer and his editors hadn't been so anxious to uncover a new My Lai in Iraq, they might have seen details about the Haditha incident that would have raised caution flags. As the blogger Bruce Kessler pointed out, the Iraqis killed were hardly innocent, having known about the IED; there were contradictory stories from Iraqis about what really happened, and "forensics that did not support a massacre." Yet even after the prosecutions were abandoned or downgraded, the reality that there was no war crime had difficulty penetrating the *Times'* institutional skull. Reviewing a British film about Haditha in May 2008, Manohla Dargis called it a "massacre" committed by "quick-triggered Marines." In its March 2010 cover story, the *Times Book Review* referred to Haditha as a crime in line with Abu Ghraib.

The battle for Fallujah, which some military analysts believe will join Belleau Woods and Iwo Jima in the Marine Corps epic, was subjected to the same sullen scrutiny. During the first and second battles for that insurgent stronghold, in April and in November 2004, some reporters and columnists accurately conveyed the barbarity of the insurgents and the bravery of the U.S. Marines. Thomas Friedman saluted the scores of wounded Marines who insisted on returning to duty. Dexter Filkins, embedded with a Marine unit, wrote of "the Marines' near-mystical commandment against leaving a comrade behind." But other reporters and commentators fell back on old stereotypes.

In "The War's Lost Weekend," Frank Rich wrote gleefully about images of Marines "retreating" from Fallujah—a term as inaccurate as it was pejorative. Edward Wong, probably the most antimilitary reporter the *Times* sent to Iraq, filed one dispatch headlined "Breaking a City in Order to Save It," a play on the old Vietnam cliché of "destroying the village in order to save it." Wong wrote that "Shelled buildings, bullet-riddled cars and rotting corpses proved one thing: that the Americans are great at taking things apart. What comes after the battlefield victory has always been the real problem for them during their 19 months in Iraq." Wong saw Fallujah as the war's defining slog, akin to what the battle for Hue represented in Vietnam.

By 2005, pressure was building among largely Democratic opponents of the war. The *Times* gave them a boost by lionizing John Murtha, a Democratic congressman and ex-Marine who had initially voted for the war in Iraq but changed his position. As Eric Schmidt reported in November 2005, Murtha believed that "after more than two years of combat, American forces had united a disparate array of insurgents in a seemingly endless cycle of violence that was impeding Iraq's progress toward stability and self-governance. He said the 153,000 American troops in Iraq should be pulled out within six months." Allowing Murtha, and himself, the gratuitous "editorial needle" that Abe Rosenthal was always watching out for, Schmidt quoted Murtha's derisive response to Vice President Cheney's call to stay the course: "I like guys who got five deferments and never been there and send people to war and then don't like to hear suggestions about what needs to be done." For those who didn't get the reference, Schmidt added: "In the Vietnam era, Mr. Cheney had five deferments and did not serve in the military."

Ironically, the talk of withdrawal, so enthusiastically supported by the *Times*, resulted in the surge of 2007, sending an additional 30,000 troops into insurgent areas of Baghdad and other violent cities to establish order and public safety. The plan for the surge enraged the *Times*, and those who supported it were chastised publicly. When the military correspondent Michael Gordon maintained on *Charlie Rose* that the troop increase was a chance worth taking, the comment set off a firestorm in the newsroom. The public editor Byron Calame wrote that "Times editors have carefully made clear their disapproval of the expression of a personal opinion about Iraq on national television by the paper's chief military correspondent, Michael Gordon." In a kind of weird, secondhand Maoist self-criticism, Gordon's editor, Philip Taubman, told Calame, "I would agree with you that he stepped over the line on the 'Charlie Rose' show. I have discussed the appearance with Michael and I am satisfied that the comments on the Rose show were an aberration. . . . He agrees his comments on the show went too far.'"

This was nothing compared with the anti-surge rhetoric from columnists and editorial writers. In early February, Frank Rich opined, "What anyone in Congress with half a brain knows is that the surge was sabotaged before it began." Doubling down on his mistake, Rich wrote another column a month later declaring, in a burst of wishful thinking, that while Moktada al-Sadr's militia appeared to be melting away, it was actually preparing a Tet-like surprise comeback. Nicholas Kristof argued that "Keeping troops in Iraq has steadily increased the risk of a bloodbath. The best way to reduce that risk is, I think, to announce a timetable for withdrawal and to begin a different kind of surge: of diplomacy." Maureen Dowd invoked Vietnam: "So many died because of ego and deceit—because L.B.J. and Robert McNamara wanted to save face or because Henry Kissinger wanted to protect Nixon's re-election chances. Now the Bush administration finds itself at that same hour of shame. It knows the surge is not working. Iraq is in a civil war, with a gruesome bonus of terrorists mixed in." In another column, Dowd called Iraq a "giant Doom Magnet." Finally, there was Paul Krugman, writing in mid September, when the troop increase was beginning to bear fruit: "The smart money, then, knows that the surge has failed, that the war is lost, and that Iraq is going the way of Yugoslavia."

Times editorials were equally gloomy. One in March 2007 maintained that "Victory is no longer an option in Iraq, if it ever was. The only rational objective left is to responsibly organize America's inevitable exit." In April, the editorial page concluded,

"There is no possible triumph in Iraq and very little hope left." The most egregiously defeatist editorial about the surge—about the whole Iraq War, for that matter—came in early July 2007. Head-lined "The Road Home," it said that "additional military forces poured into the Baghdad region have failed to change anything" and that "it is time for the United States to leave Iraq, without any more delay than the Pentagon needs to organize an orderly exit." The editorial board did acknowledge that Iraq might be consumed by political chaos, maybe even genocide, and could become a ter-rorist platform in the future. "Yes, withdrawal might lead to Bos-nian-style partition," the *Times* admitted, but "that would be better than the slow-motion ethnic and religious cleansing that has con-tributed to driving one in seven Iraqis from their homes."

When General David Petraeus testified before Congress in September 2007, Paul Krugman shaped the battlefield by asserting that the general "has a history of making wildly overoptimistic assessments of progress in Iraq that happen to be convenient for his political masters." The editorial page took up the standard by indicting General Petraeus's testimony as filled with "empty calo-ries," and hoped that Congress was not fooled by "the silver stars, charts and rhetoric of yesterday's hearing. Even if the so-called surge has created breathing room, Iraq's sectarian leaders show neither the ability nor the intent to take advantage of it."

What was most disrespectful toward the general, however, was a full-page ad that the paper allowed the antiwar group MoveOn. org to run on the day of his testimony. Under a bold headline, "General Petraeus or General Betray Us?" with the subhead "Cooking the Books for the White House," the ad claimed that "every independent report on the ground situation in Iraq shows that the surge strategy has failed," and that "Iraq is mired in an un-winnable religious civil war."

For this, the *Times* was denounced by politicians on both sides of the aisle and deluged with more than four thousand emails calling the ad despicable, disgraceful and treasonous. When it was rumored that MoveOn.org may have received a dis-count for the ad, the *Times* media reporter Katherine Seelye duly reported a company spokeswoman's denial. But in a postmortem on the controversy, the public editor Clark Hoyt determined that MoveOn.org did indeed get a price break to which it was not entitled. He also argued that the ad violated the paper's own written standards barring "attacks of a personal nature." It was clear from Hoyt's comments that the ad certainly didn't bother Sulzberger, who told him, "Perhaps we did err in this case. If we did, we erred with the intent of giving greater voice to people."

The surge certainly did not solve all of Iraq's problems, but it did provide security and psychological reassurance, and, most importantly, it kept the United States from suffering a humiliating defeat at a time when opponents across the world were watching for a sign of weakness or diminished resolve. Yet it took the *Times* quite a while to acknowledge the success of this audacious political and military move. Finally, on November 20, 2007, it ran a piece headlined "Baghdad's Weary Start to Exhale as Security Improves," where Damien Cave and Alissa Rubin wrote: "Even though the depth and sustainability of the changes remain open to question, Iraqis are clearly surprised and relieved to see commerce and movement finally increase, five months after an extra 30,000 American troops arrived in the country. The security improvements in most neighborhoods are real."

·⁓

Although the *Times* editorial page did express relief that those who served in the military in Iraq and Afghanistan were not demonized as Vietnam veterans had been, the paper has nevertheless routinely disparaged the U.S. military, representing it as mainly lower-class, uneducated and institutionally misogynistic, as well as disproportionately minority—in effect, a mercenary force of false consciousness.

In 2005, Bob Herbert wrote that there was something very, very wrong with a situation in which "College kids in the U.S. are playing video games and looking forward to frat parties while their less fortunate peers are rattling around like moving targets in Baghdad and Mosul, trying to dodge improvised explosive devices and rocket-propelled grenades. . . . If the war in Iraq is worth fighting—if it's a noble venture, as the hawks insist it is—then it's worth fighting with the children of the privileged classes. They should be added to the combat mix. If it's not worth their blood, then we should bring the other troops home."

In a February 2006 piece on efforts to recruit Latinos, Lizette Alvarez wrote that "Critics also say that Latinos often wind up as cannon fodder on the casualty-prone front lines," and that "Hispanics make up only 4.7 percent of the military's officer corps." Sewell Chan did essentially the same piece in 2008, quoting an anti-Bush activist who claimed that "Latinos have been disproportionately represented among service members who have fought and died in Iraq."

There were plenty of experts contradicting the Times' view of the voluntary forces as minority, ill educated and poor, but their views had trouble penetrating the paper's news pages. A Heritage Foundation report, for instance, found that "The average American enlistee is more educated—not less—than the average young civilian. The civilian graduation rate is seventeen percentage points lower than that of military recruits. Wartime recruits also come from wealthier neighborhoods than their civilian counterparts, on average. And the force has been trending towards wealthier troops and smarter troops since the war in Iraq began in 2003." The report added that the one hundred Zip Codes with the highest proportions of African Americans were actually underrepresented among military enlistees in 2005. In fact, Pentagon enlistee data "show that the only group that is lowering its participation in the military is the poor. The percentage of recruits from the poorest American neighborhoods (one-fifth of the U.S. population) declined from 18 percent in 1999 to 13.7 percent in 2005."

According to the Times, the face of the military is also pockmarked with alcoholism, post-traumatic stress disorder, domestic violence and criminal pathology. In "War Torn," a series that ran from January to July of 2008, Deborah Sontag and Lizette Alvarez reported on what they claimed were unacknowledged cases of violence committed by veterans after they returned from wars in Iraq and Afghanistan. The stories all seemed calculated to delegitimize the war, while also demonizing veterans.

The most controversial piece in the series was the first, which ran on January 13. Headlined "Across America, Deadly Echoes of Foreign Wars," it was about veterans who either had been killed or had killed others after coming home. The article ran to almost 7,000 words, and the Sunday front page was almost entirely given over to a montage of twenty-four veterans, all male, some in military uniform and some in prison stripes. Relying on local news reports and court records, along with interviews of veterans and their families, victims' families and law enforcement officials, the reporters said they had found 121 such cases of violence. Many appeared to involve "combat trauma and the stress of deployment—along with alcohol abuse, family discord and other attendant problems." Speculating that their research "most likely uncovered only the minimum number of such cases," Sontag and Alvarez said they had found "a cross-country trail of death and heartbreak."

The editor, Bill Keller, called the series "an important public service that explores in riveting detail the emotional stresses war places on this important community and the problems the military faces in coping with those stresses." But critics quickly dubbed the first piece the "Killer Vets" story and pounced on its methodology. According to Ralph Peters, a military analyst, "to match the homicide rate of their [nonmilitary] peers, our troops would've had to come home and commit about 150 murders a year, for a total of 700 to 750 murders between 2003 and the end of 2007," which was six times the 121 cited in the *Times*. Peters said the paper was trying to cast veterans as "freaks from a slasher flick." Professor John D'Lulio of the University of Pennsylvania examined U.S. Bureau of Justice statistics and found that the homicide rate among vets is far lower than in the general population—a detail the *Times* missed. Others pointed out that many of the cases showed no connection between the stresses of combat and the nature of the crimes, which included car accidents and handgun accidents, as well as legitimate self-defense.

One of the harshest spankings came from the *Wall Street Journal* editorial page, which denounced what it called "The 'Wacko Vet Myth.'" The *Times* didn't try to establish a causal relationship between war service and homicide, the *Journal* maintained. It didn't even try to establish a correlation. Rather, the *Times* was "purporting to test a media stereotype by measuring its prevalence in the media," through heavy use of anecdotes in local news reports. More bluntly, the *Journal* concluded that "the Times hasn't necessarily proved that the stereotype is true—only that it is a stereotype." The *Times* public editor, Clark Hoyt, described the report as "analytically shaky." Hoyt also revealed that the head of the computer assistance unit might have flagged the report's dubious statistics, but had not read the story before it ran.

The paper's effort to color the services as misogynistic came in the form of reports alleging widespread sexual harassment and abuse, especially in theater. One of these was a March 2007 Sunday magazine cover story about post-traumatic stress among women who had served in Iraq, but it backfired. At the time, more than 160,000 female soldiers had been deployed to Iraq and Afghanistan, the article explained, a huge increase compared with Vietnam and even the Gulf War of 1991. "One of every 10 U.S. soldiers in Iraq is female," the article said, and claimed that female veterans returning from Iraq have much higher levels of post-traumatic stress than males, some of it from greater susceptibility to combat exposure, but some a result of sexual trauma. "A 2003 report financed by the Department of Defense revealed that nearly one-third of a nationwide sample of female veterans seeking health care through the V.A. said they experienced rape or attempted rape during their service," the article said. "Of that group, 37 percent said they were raped multiple times, and 14 percent reported they were gang-raped."

A theme of the piece was the indifference of a "male-dominated military culture" to women's concerns. One of the main subjects was Amorita Randall, a Navy construction worker or "Seabee" who said she had been raped once while stateside, and again in Guam while awaiting deployment to Iraq in 2004. "You just don't expect anything to be done about it anyway, so why even try?" Randall said. Compounding her trauma, Randall said her Humvee in Iraq was hit by an IED, killing the soldier who was driving and leaving her with a brain injury.

Three days after the article had gone to press, the Navy called the *Times* to say that Amorita Randall had never been in Iraq. Only part of her unit was sent there; Randall served with another part of it in Guam. The Navy claimed that *Times* fact-checkers had not given it the time to verify Randall's account. But even by deadline, there was information available "to seriously question whether she'd been in Iraq." Within a week, the *Times* issued another embarrassing correction: "Based on the information that came to light after the article was printed, it is now clear that Ms. Randall did not serve in Iraq, but may have become convinced she did."

·⤳

While it seized on any evidence of malfeasance on the part of U.S. servicemen and women, the *Times* also disparaged or ignored instances of heroism. For example, when the former NFL football star Pat Tillman died after his unit of Army Rangers in Afghanistan came under friendly fire, it was a tragedy, and the Army commanders who tried to obscure the details in order to create a heroic narrative were deeply wrong. But could the whole, sad tale be reduced, as one *Times* editorial said, to a "bogus" story of heroism "used to bolster support for the wars in Iraq and Afghanistan"? Was it so awful that his memorial service was "patriotism-drenched," as Frank Rich put it? And just when did "friendly fire" become synonymous with "fratricide," a much darker word that the *Times* used liberally in almost all of its Tillman stories?

While the *Times* was quick to cover such unfortunate incidents and do scores of stories involving abuse at Abu Ghraib and elsewhere, TimesWatch noted that by the end of October 2007, the paper had reported on only two of the twenty men who had been awarded the Air Force Cross, the Distinguished Service Cross, the Navy Cross or the Congressional Medal of Honor. Nevertheless, the *Times* complained about a dearth of Medals of Honor awarded in Iraq and Afghanistan, in a May 2010 Sunday magazine story titled "What Happened to Valor?" It went into bitter detail describing how the Pentagon had denied the nation's highest military decoration to Marine Sergeant Rafael Peralta, who had come from Mexico with his family as a teenager. It did bestow the Navy Cross, the second-highest honor, which his mother refused to accept.

Thus it was all the more egregious when the *Times* did not acknowledge the military heroism of Lieutenant Michael Murphy, a Navy Seal from Patchogue, Long Island. Ambushed in Afghanistan in June 2005, Murphy crawled into the open to radio for help, further exposing himself to enemy fire. He was killed, but his self-sacrifice led to the rescue of one of his men. Murphy became the first Medal of Honor winner in the Afghan conflict. (The story is retold vividly in Marcus Luttrell's *Lone Survivor*.) The *Washington Post* and the *Los Angeles Times* ran reports on Murphy's posthumous Medal of Honor commendation in October 2007, as did the *Daily News*, the *New York Post* and *Newsday*. But the *Times* ran nothing, even though the story had an obvious "local hero" rationale. An editorial in the *New York Post* noted that on the same day the *Times* failed to report on Murphy, "No fewer than three stories reported on how Americans had killed innocent Iraqi civilians."

The *Times'* alienation from military culture comes across in more subtle ways as well. In November 2005, a profile marking the two-thousandth military death in Iraq featured Marine Corporal Jeffrey Starr of Washington State, who was killed in Ramadi on his third tour of duty. As James Dao reported, "Sifting through Corporal Starr's laptop computer after his death, his father found a letter to be delivered to the marine's girlfriend. 'I kind of predicted this,' Corporal Starr wrote of his own death. 'A third time just seemed like I'm pushing my chances.'" This short passage from Starr's letter was presented in a way to make him seem like a prescient and pessimistic victim of an overextended military. But Dao left out an important part of the letter, showing how Starr wanted his death to be perceived in the event he didn't return:

> *I don't regret going, everybody dies but few get to do it for something as important as freedom. It may seem confusing why we are in Iraq, it's not to me. I'm here trying to help these people, so that they can live the way we live. Not have to worry about tyrants or vicious dictators. To do what they*

*want with their lives. To me that is why I died. Others have
died for my freedom, now this is my mark.*

In an interview, James Dao defended his handling of the extract
from Starr's letter, claiming he had captured its essence. In
response, the *New York Post* wrote, "There is saintliness in a soldier's prospective acceptance of an honorable death in combat. To
diminish such a deed, especially in service of a political agenda,
approaches sacrilege."

ᜳ

The war in Iraq is winding down, our combat troops now with-
drawn. What will happen in Afghanistan is still not clear. What
is certain, though, is that "the war over the war" will remain a
contentious aspect of our national politics. It is playing out in the
most polarized way through continuing debates over what some
call "torture," others call "detainee abuse," and still others see as
the necessary evils of a fight against a barbaric enemy from an
alien moral universe. In large measure, the fight over "torture"
has also been a way to fight about how the United States will
defend itself when the threat is from individual actors more than
massed troops. The *Times'* opposition to the War on Terror and to
the Iraq conflict lives on through this unending argument about
the "tortures" inflicted on terror suspects and the alleged corruption to the national soul resulting from the use of dehumanizing
methods of detention and interrogation at Guantanamo Bay and
Abu Ghraib, as well as the CIA's various "black sites."

The first round in the torture debate centered on Abu Ghraib.
The abuses there were serious, representing a corrosion of military discipline and a propaganda coup for America's enemies,
who saw pictures of Iraqi detainees on leashes, with women's
underwear on their heads, stacked naked on top of each other, or
standing on a box while "wired" to simulate imminent electrocu-
tion. Frank Rich characterized Abu Ghraib as the equivalent of
My Lai—even though Seymour Hersh, who broke both stories,
said it didn't come close. The main problem with the *Times'* cov-

erage was overkill, making Abu Ghraib a metaphor for the whole of a complex enterprise. After the photographs were discovered and Hersh's exposé was published in the *New Yorker,* at least fifty-three reports on Abu Ghraib appeared on the front page of the *Times.* Some press critics saw it as an orgy rather than news coverage. As Daniel Henninger of the *Wall Street Journal* wrote, Abu Ghraib was "a real story that got blown into a month-long bonfire that obviously was intended to burn down the legitimacy of the war in Iraq."

The most extreme moment in the *Times'* coverage and commentary on Abu Ghraib was a long Sunday magazine essay by Susan Sontag, which seemed to fulfill Bernard Goldberg's insight that "To the anti-war crowd, what happened at Abu Ghraib was not a tragedy but more an opportunity—one more chance to reveal America as depraved and dishonorable." Sontag wrote, "The issue is not whether a majority or a minority of Americans performs such acts, but whether the nature of the policies prosecuted by this administration and the hierarchies deployed to carry them out makes such acts likely. Considered in this light, the photographs [of the abused prisoners] are us. That is, they are representative of the fundamental corruptions of any foreign occupation together with the Bush administration's distinctive policies." Sontag went on to charge that "The torture of prisoners is not an aberration. It is a direct consequence of the with-us-or-against-us doctrines of world struggle" promoted by the Bush administration. Lynching photographs from the American South were "souvenirs of a collective action whose participants felt perfectly justified in what they had done," Sontag declared. "So are the pictures from Abu Ghraib."

In its eagerness to ladle out bad ink about Abu Ghraib, the *Times* fell for a hoax. On March 11, 2006, in a long front-page article accompanied by several pictures, Hassan M. Fattah reported from Baghdad on the human rights activism of one Ali Shalal Qaissi. Under the headline "Symbol of Abu Ghraib Seeks to Spare Others His Nightmare," Fattah wrote that Qaissi had been the prisoner at Abu Ghraib who was photographed in a hood, standing on a box, with wires dangling from his body. Fattah called this picture

"the indelible symbol of torture at Abu Ghraib." He reported that
Qaissi was now an activist who had joined a lawsuit against U.S.
military contractors, was lobbying on behalf of those still in custody, and was barnstorming the major Arab capitals to publicize
U.S. mistreatment of Iraqis with the infamous photo on his business card.

Within days, *Salon* magazine posted a challenge to the report's
veracity, based on more than 250 images of Abu Ghraib prisoner
abuse it had obtained and related documents. Qaissi was not the
man in the hood, *Salon* claimed. On March 23, the *Times* published an editor's note confessing to having been suckered, and
admitting that a more thorough examination of previous articles
in the *Times* and other newspapers would have shown that military investigators in 2004 had named another man as the one on
the box.

Round two of the torture debate was the crusade to close
down the Guantanamo Bay detention facility. According to the
Times editorial page, most of the detainees there were "hapless
foot soldiers," either caught up in the chaos in Afghanistan or
sold out by unscrupulous countrymen who wanted to settle a
score. The *Times* claimed that the enhanced interrogations of the
detainees yielded no real information of any exigent value that
saved lives or illuminated al-Qaeda's plans. In one report, Lizette
Alvarez quoted Amnesty International saying that Guantanamo
represented "the gulag of our time." (Trying to define the gulag,
she said it was a Stalinist system that killed "thousands," when in
fact it killed millions.)

In early 2009, the *Times* also dismissed the Guantanamo
recidivism rate—the number of released detainees who returned
to terrorism—as "little more than public relations for the Guantanamo Center." A few months later, in May, the Pentagon leaked
a classified report, ironically to the *Times'* Elisabeth Bumiller, esti-
mating that one in seven of the 534 prisoners already released
from Gitmo "are engaged in terrorism or militant activity." The
story led to an editor's note, a critical public editor's column, and
a kind of corrective op-ed. The basic line was that not all the suspected recidivists had been involved in jihad to begin with, and

not all were confirmed to have returned to jihad. According to the public editor, Clark Hoyt, "Had only confirmed cases been considered, one in seven would have changed to one in 20."

Colonel Gordon Cucullu, author of *Inside Gitmo,* maintains that information gleaned from detainees in the program helped break up plots in Lackawanna, Cleveland and Hamburg, and that the Saudi program for rehabilitating former Gitmo detainees—which was examined favorably in a November 2008 *Times Magazine* piece called "Deprogramming Jihadists," by Katherine Zoepf—was little more than "art therapy." One graduate of the Saudi program soon became the deputy leader of al-Qaeda in Yemen and is suspected of involvement in the deadly bombing of the U.S. embassy in Sana, capital of Yemen, in September 2008. Two others were involved in recruiting and training the Nigerian Christmas Bomber who tried to blow up an airliner in 2009. In an interview, Cucullu maintained that many news organizations, such as the *Times,* refuse to look at the pathological hatred and violence among detainees, which have required tough interrogation methods and have resulted in numerous injuries to the facility's personnel. Instead, the *Times* "castigates the soldiers and sailors who work there," Cucullu said. "Everyone Is Lynndie England" (the infamous Abu Ghraib leash-lady).

The *Times* has worked hard to promote the notion that "torture doesn't work." But as the *Atlantic*'s military expert Robert Kaplan and many others have pointed out, it has worked in places like Algeria during the rebellion against the French, in the Philippines in the government's struggle against Muslim separatists, and in Dubai against al-Qaeda. Kaplan noted that a captured al-Qaeda manual advises Muslim prisoners that people in the West don't have the stomach for torture "because they are not warriors."

After the 2008 election, all the *Times'* pent-up hostility to the Bush administration exploded in its coverage of the recriminations over policies on "torture" during the previous six years. The *Times* cheered when President Obama released the so-called "torture memos" detailing previously classified information on CIA interrogation methods; "Memos Spell Out Brutal CIA Mode of Interrogation," its front-page headline screamed. When Obama gave his May 2009 speech on terrorism and detention policy, the editorial board expressed "relief and optimism," saying that for seven years "President George W. Bush tried to frighten the American public—and successfully cowed Congress—with bullying and disinformation." Obama, said the editors, "was exactly right when he said Americans do not have to choose between security and their democratic values. By denying those values, the Bush team fed the furies of anti-Americanism, strengthened our enemies and made the nation more vulnerable."

Obama himself had sent a number of signals that while he would be breaking with certain Bush terror policies, there would be no retribution. But the *Times* wanted blood. When the president announced that he would not be releasing any more pictures similar to those from Abu Ghraib, the *Times* was dismayed; this would nullify the divisive reckoning it had called for. The paper editorialized that Obama risked "missing the chance to make sure the misdeeds and horrors of the Bush years are never repeated."

The news side played its role in the crusade by reporting supportively on the American Civil Liberties Union's "John Adams Project." This was an effort to identify CIA agents who used harsh tactics at "black sites" around the world, so that the ACLU's "clients," i.e. terror suspects, could better defend themselves at military tribunals. ACLU defense teams were very aggressive, at points trailing CIA agents suspected of being part of the "black sites" program and photographing them in front of their homes so terror suspects could identify their "torturers."

The *Times* celebrated another ACLU case involving a massive Freedom of Information Act request for government documents connected to "battles between the FBI and the military over the treatment of detainees at the Guantánamo Bay prison camp; autopsy reports on prisoners who died in custody in Afghanistan and Iraq; the Justice Department's long-secret memorandums justifying harsh interrogation methods and day-by-day descriptions of what happened inside the CIA's overseas prisons." In his report, Scott Shane seemed to be ecstatic that the ACLU had won access to much more information than it ever hoped for. He did quote Michael Hayden, former CIA director, who believed that releasing top-secret documents might undermine cooperation from foreign intelligence services who would no longer believe we "can keep a secret." But the *Times* did not examine at any length—as other news organizations did—what effects the court cases, the release of sensitive information, or the investigations and potential prosecutions were having on the CIA and other agencies fighting terrorism.

Besides having their knives out for the CIA, the *Times* wanted to eviscerate the so-called "torture lawyers" in the Bush administration who had forged the legal reasoning behind the aggressive interrogation techniques. Singled out by the *Times* were John Yoo, Jay S. Bybee and Steven G. Bradbury. A May 2009 editorial said, "They deliberately contorted the law to justify decisions that had already been made, making them complicit in those decisions. Their acts were a grotesque abrogation of duty and breach of faith."

Perhaps the grimmest assessment of the Obama administration's war on the counterterror warriors, which the *Times* cheered at every step, was by Daniel Henninger of the *Wall Street Journal*. Citing a "chilling effect" on government lawyers and investigators, and questioning the decision to limit interrogators to "non-coercive" techniques, he wrote, "The war on terror is being downgraded to not much more than tough talk. Al Qaeda, the Taliban and the Iranians, not yet converts to the West's caricature of its own legal traditions, will take note. In time, they will be back."

On the question of whether "torture" was immoral, many seasoned commentators saw a gray area, but the *Times* had no doubts. A story that underscored the paper's position was a June 2008 profile of Deuce Martinez, the CIA operative who had successfully interrogated the 9/11 mastermind Khalid Sheikh Mohammed (KSM) at a CIA "black site" in Poland. Martinez was not a member of the clandestine services, but a career analyst; he had no Arabic language training and had refused to join the team involved with harsh interrogation tactics. When he joined the CIA he was assigned to the agency's Counter-Narcotics Center, "learning to sift masses of phone numbers, travel records, credit card transactions," as Scott Shane put it. His tool was the computer . . . his expertise was drug cartels and not terrorist networks." Martinez was moved into the agency's counterterrorism program when it expanded after 9/11. He encountered KSM in 2003, as the United States readied for war in Iraq. Intelligence officials feared the invasion would precipitate more al-Qaeda attacks, which KSM either knew about or could provide insight into.

Martinez came in after the rough stuff, "the ultimate good cop with the classic skills: an unimposing presence, inexhaustible patience and a willingness to listen to the gripes and musings of a pitiless killer in rambling, imperfect English," Shane reported. "He achieved a rapport with Mr. Mohammed that astonished his fellow C.I.A. officers. A canny opponent, Mr. Mohammed mixed disinformation and braggadocio with details of plots, past and planned. Eventually, he grew loquacious." They would have long talks about religion, comparing notes on Islam and Catholicism, one CIA officer recalled, adding another detail that no one could have predicted: "He wrote poems to Deuce's wife." The story of Martinez and KSM, suggested Shane and the *Times,* appeared to show that traditional methods alone might have elicited the same information or more from KSM than were obtained by waterboarding.

In running this profile and using Martinez's name, however, the *Times* went against CIA concerns that Martinez would become a target for terrorist retaliation. As in the NSA surveillance case and the SWIFT terror finance story, the *Times* refused official requests for secrecy; though in an analogous situation when the shoe was on the other foot after Robert Novak "outed" the CIA operative Valerie Plame, the *Times* had called for heads to roll. The editors said that Martinez's name was necessary for the credibility and completeness of the article, and that Martinez was not technically an "undercover" CIA agent—just as partisans on the right had said about Plame.

The *Times'* ideological bias was on display once more in how it reported on a private memo sent by Admiral Dennis C. Blair, the director of national intelligence, to his staff in April 2009, affirming that "enhanced techniques" banned by the Obama

White House had in fact yielded important information. "High value information came from interrogations in which those methods were used and provided a deeper understanding of the al Qa'ida organization that was attacking this country," Admiral Blair had written. This disclosure had significant news value, since Blair was not a Bush appointee, and he had sent his memo, according to the *Times* reporter Peter Baker, "on the same day the administration publicly released secret Bush administration legal memos authorizing the use of interrogation methods that the Obama White House has deemed to be illegal torture."

Baker's story on the memo, headlined "Banned Techniques Yielded 'High Value Information,' Memo Says," ran on April 22, but only at 850 words and only on the *Times* website. Two paragraphs of the bombshell online report were shoehorned into a larger story that ran inside the paper with another reporter's byline, under a headline that reflected nothing pertaining to what Baker had reported ("Obama Won't Bar Inquiry of Penalty on Interrogations," by Sheryl Gay Stolberg).

Byron York of the *Washington Examiner* interviewed the *Times'* deputy Washington bureau chief, Richard Stevenson, and asked why Baker's story did not run in the newspaper itself. According to York, Stevenson denied any ideological motivation and blamed deadline pressure and a surfeit of meaty news stories that day.

·⁓

September 11 left an indelible mark on the American psyche and American politics, animating both the War on Terror as an intellectual construct and the military campaigns in Afghanistan and Iraq. Like December 7, it will always, for most Americans, be a day to remember, and to remember in a particular way. Yet it is not obvious that such is also the case at the *New York Times*. Only three years after this national tragedy, the *Times* began nibbling away at its meaning, and since then it has produced a dismissive piece on almost every anniversary of 9/11. Walter Kirn launched the trend on September 12, 2004, in a *Times Magazine* essay titled

"Forget It?" If 9/11 is mostly a way for politicians to manipulate our souls and psyches, Kirn wrote, "Maybe it's time to move on."

In May 2005, Frank Rich wrote "Ground Zero Is So Over." The vacant site, the focus of squabbling over what to rebuild, is a poor memorial for those who died there, Rich charged, "but it's an all too apt symbol for a war on which the country is turning its back." Families of the fallen may not "have turned the page," but other Americans had. As the anniversary neared in August 2006, Rich wrote a column presenting 9/11 as synonymous with a White House effort to "exploit terrorism for political gain."

There was more of the same in a report by N. R. Kleinfield on the anniversary in 2007, headlined "As 9-11 Draws Near, a Debate Rises: How Much Tribute Is Enough?" Kleinfield wrote, "Each year, murmuring about Sept. 11 fatigue arises, a weariness of reliving a day that everyone wishes had never happened. . . . By now, though, many people feel that the collective commemorations, publicly staged, are excessive and vacant, even annoying."

In March 2009, David Dunlap reported on the debate to abandon the name "Freedom Tower" for whatever structure eventually goes up at Ground Zero. "That there is a debate at all," Dunlap wrote in a snappish vein, "suggests how much has changed since the first years after 9/11, when no official pronouncement was complete without an assurance that the attacks, the victims, the rescuers and the survivors would never be forgotten; and when any use of patriotic motifs seemed to be beyond public reproach, no matter how cynical or sentimental."

Most telling about the *Times'* view of our wars, and about its patriotism, was a very small piece published in 2007 the day after that year's 9/11 commemoration, just as the surge was gaining momentum in Iraq. Writing about General David Petraeus's hometown of Cornwall-on-Hudson, Paul Vitello reported that "Some said they were aghast at the dimensions of the problem, some awed by General Petraeus's seeming grasp of the wildly irregular forces in play; but almost none seemed to foresee a happy result for 'our side,' as many in this conservative, Republican-voting place put it."

Our side in quotation marks. This expression of internal exile from America said it all. For the *Times*, "our side" was actually "their side," a foreign place where patriotic Americans lived and which the *Times* had chosen to see as hostile ground.

ten

Conclusion

The ghost of Abe Rosenthal, made unquiet by the contrast between the legacy he left behind and the politicized agenda pursued by Sulzberger Jr., continued to haunt the *Times* in the ensuing years—which even the paper's most ardent defenders had to admit were marked by an aura of decline and fall. Rosenthal had foreseen most of the problems that were in store for the institution to which he had devoted his life. Were he still alive, it is hard to imagine that he would not be feeling a twinge of *Schadenfreude* over the *Times'* current predicament. But being a fierce loyalist, he also would probably feel ashamed that the paper he strove to keep "straight" had embraced so many dubious multicultural nostrums and drifted so far to the left that on some days it read like a broadsheet version of the *Nation*. Rosenthal would also hate the idea of the *Times* airing its institutional problems so publicly. This, after all, was a man who fought to keep the corrections column as unnoticed as possible and resisted the creation of a public editor long after others in the news industry had adopted one. And unlike the kinder, gentler newsroom that Sulzberger has encouraged, where few seem to suffer for their errors, Rosenthal certainly made transgressors feel his wrath. Some walked the plank; others endured internal exile to some obscure career Siberia.

In Rosenthal's era, *Times* editors could say with some confidence, "We're not the story. The story is the story." By 2010 this would no longer be the case. The egregiousness of the Jayson Blair scandal, along with a string of other institutional humiliations that followed, made that old certitude impossible to sustain as the paper's internal chaos itself became news fit to print.

So the *Times* entered a cycle in which error caused by its political commitments was followed by fevered public contrition and promises of amendment delivered publicly through "Notes to Readers," public editor's columns and long editorial *mea culpas,* often on the front page, explaining how and why the paper committed the journalistic sin for which it needed to apologize. This cycle of real and pretended remorse was also marked by the announcement of newsroom reforms and personnel changes designed to rehabilitate the paper's credibility and reputation, and to head off more scandal and embarrassment by encouraging, as one internal report put it, "transparency" and "accountability."

Yet much like the addict who pledges sobriety but can't follow through, the *Times* falls off the wagon regularly. The newsroom reforms either have not been implemented in the way they were designed, or have been ineffectual, undercut by inertia, obduracy, denial, a persisting sense of institutional entitlement and a fundamental failure to get at the root causes of its dysfunction. Also, the paper has been willing to change in every respect except one: the tone of superiority, the leftish partisanship and embrace of countercultural values, all of which have been hallmarks of the Arthur Jr. regime.

⤳

One change that seemed to hold great promise was the appointment of Bill Keller as editor in chief in 2004. Keller came across as more open to outside criticism, especially from conservatives. In an interview with Nick Lemann of the *New Yorker* in 2005, he seemed to validate many of their complaints. "Conservatives feel estranged because they feel excluded," he acknowledged. "They do not always see themselves portrayed in the mainstream press as three-dimensional humans, and they don't see their ideas taken seriously or treated respectfully."

The spasm of institutional introspection, suffused with what appeared to be a genuine willingness to embrace more varied political perspectives, led to the creation of a special "conservative beat" in January 2004, with David Kirkpatrick in the D.C. bureau the first to cover it. The goals of this new beat were to identify the "thinkers" of the conservative movement, describe "the grassroots they organize" and explore "how the conservative movement works to be heard in Washington," as Keller later put it. The plan was not only to cover conservatives and their ideas, but to make these ideas explicable to *Times* editors. Kirkpatrick's beat was discontinued in 2007, however, setting the paper up for the fall it took over its inattentiveness to stories such as the revelations of ACORN corruption in 2009, which seemed to exemplify the paper's political tunnel vision.

The longer Keller stayed at the helm, the more thin-skinned and sarcastic he grew toward the conservative critique. Even in the *New Yorker* interview where he had acknowledged some grounds for conservative complaint, he also condescendingly claimed that the idea of "the liberal press" was a concept manufactured for political gain. And while many thought Keller would lead the paper in a less partisan direction, the reality was a shrill and intractable hostility to the Bush White House. The impetus for the attacks may have come from middle-line editors, but the charge was led by Keller himself. In a *New York* magazine profile headlined "The United States of America vs. Bill Keller," he accused the Bush administration of whipping up "a partisan hate-fest" against the *Times,* which had "really pissed him off." At a *New Yorker* panel discussion in October 2008, Keller was asked about the McCain campaign's attacks on the *Times* regarding the lobbyist/mistress story. He defiantly (and childishly) replied, "my first tendency when they do that is to find the toughest McCain story we've got and put it on the front page just to show that they can't get away with it."

Another reform that seemed to have promise was the creation of a public editor—a readers' advocate or ombudsman, as other news organizations defined the role. The *Times* had historically resisted creating one, Keller said in a note to the staff, worrying that "it would foster nit-picking and navel-gazing, that it might undermine staff morale and, worst of all, that it would absolve other editors of their responsibility to represent the interests of readers." Yet Daniel Okrent, who became the first public editor, defined the job in radically different terms, indicating that there was a crying need to provide "transparency to readers about how and why the Times does what it does."

During his tenure, from December 2003 to May 2005, Okrent issued sage and penetrating critiques of his own paper. People on the right who hated the *Times* were nonetheless "as much a constituency as anyone else," he thought. "Closing one's ears to the complaints of partisans would also entail closing one's mind to the substance of their arguments." To many, Okrent's most important achievement was affirming the criticism that had brought withering scorn from the paper—that it had a bias toward the cultural left. Those who thought the *Times* played it down the middle on controversial social issues, he said, were "reading the paper with [their] eyes closed."

For saying this, Okrent took his lumps from *Times* reporters and editors—confirming I. F. Stone's insight that "persuading others to virtue is an unendearing profession," he remarked. When Okrent left, he wrote of his "18 months of bruised feelings, offended egos, pissed off editors and infuriated writers." Some reporters and editors simply refused to cooperate with him, such as Joe Sexton, editor of the Metro section, who thought the creation of the public editor position was a "profound mistake," says Okrent. Another antagonist was Katherine Roberts, editor of the Week in Review, who thought some of Okrent's questions were doltish and his columns, which appeared in her section, too long.

Okrent's successor, Byron Calame, got his share of guff too. When he corrected Alessandra Stanley's claim that Geraldo Rivera had "nudged" a Hurricane Katrina rescue worker out of the way so he could showboat for the Fox News cameras, Stanley acidly told *Women's Wear Daily* that Calame was like Kenneth Starr, except that "what he was writing about isn't a presidency. It's spelling and ellipses and semicolons." Stanley was a fine one to belittle Calame. In 2005 her correction rate was so bad that editors assigned her a personal fact-checker. Clark Hoyt, the third public editor, had to deal with some attitude as well. In his farewell column in June 2010, he wrote, "On my first day on the job, Arthur Sulzberger Jr., the publisher, sat opposite me in a little room off his office, clapped his hands on his knees and said with a laugh: 'Well, you're here. You must be dumber than you look.'"

Another newsroom reform was the creation in 2006 of a "standards editor" who would coordinate journalistic practices and ethical guidelines involved in all *Times* newsgathering operations. This involved supervising the overhaul of policies governing the use of confidential and anonymous sources—the use and misuse of which had gotten the paper into so much trouble during the Jayson Blair scandal. A confidential source could now be cited in the paper, the new guidelines said, only if at least one editor knew the source's name. These policies were further strengthened after source-related problems surfaced in Judith Miller's reporting on WMDs and in Plamegate. No one at the *Times,* not Sulzberger, not Keller, knew Miller's Plamegate source—a situation that the former Rosenthal acolyte Pranay Gupte told me would never have happened when Abe was in charge. Putting some teeth back into the anonymous-sourcing policy would, executives hoped, get more information "on the record" and provide a fuller sense of the motivation of sources in offering information without identifying themselves—in essence, why they were entitled to speak from the shadows.

Yet these lofty ideals were discarded the moment the *Times* got a chance to publish what it regarded as a killing blow to John McCain's presidential candidacy, with a story about his "mistress" based on a number of unidentified sources. The paper violated its own policy again a few months later when it ran a "blind" story about Caroline Kennedy's nanny and tax problems as she was being considered to fill Hillary Clinton's vacated Senate seat for New York. It was later disclosed that these issues were old and minor, and were part of a smear campaign engineered from the office of New York's governor, David Paterson. During this episode, the paper got hoaxed in a letter to the editor by someone claiming to be Bertrand Delanoe, the mayor of Paris, saying that Caroline Kennedy had "no qualification whatsoever" to be a senator. Her appointment would be wholly "dynastic," representing a "drifting away from a truly democratic model." The "mayor" concluded: "Can we speak of American decline?"

Other hoaxes, also originating in reliance on dubious sources, occurred on April Fool's Day, 2010. David Goodman, a *Times* staff blogger, ran with a claim by a legal blogger named Eric Turkewitz that he had been appointed the official White House legal blogger. Turkewitz later said he was hoping to catch fast-and-loose political bloggers, but instead suckered "the vaunted New York Times." The same day, Andy Newman relied on a source who was an occasional *Times* guest blogger for a story about a theater troupe planning a project involving more than a thousand people riding the subway nude from the waist down. The event turned out to be completely fallacious.

The paper also announced that it was going to be more watchful and more punitive about plagiarism. But when Maureen Dowd cribbed material verbatim from the Talking Points blogger Josh Marshall, in a May 2009 column bashing Dick Cheney's defense of what Dowd called "torture," she didn't even get a wrist-slap.

The admissions of error and resolutions to improve kept rolling in. A 2005 report titled "Preserving Our Readers' Trust," produced by what was called the "Credibility Committee," said that *Times* news coverage needed to "embrace unorthodox views and contrarian opinions and to portray lives both more radical and more conservative than those most of us experience." The paper also needed to "listen carefully to colleagues who are at home in realms that are not familiar to most of us," especially religion. The *Times* should strive to create a climate in which staff members feel free to "propose or criticize coverage from vantage points that lie outside the perceived newsroom consensus." And it should "encourage more reporting from the middle of the country, from exurbs and hinterland, and more coverage of social, demographic, cultural and lifestyle issues."

The committee also recommended an expansion in the diversity of the hires it made, with an accent on more conservative journalists: "Both inside and outside the paper, some people feel that [the *Times* is] missing stories because our staff lacks diversity in viewpoints, intellectual grounding and individual backgrounds. We should look for all manner of diversity. We should seek talented journalists who happen to have military experience, who know rural America first hand, who are at home in different faiths." Likewise, Bill Keller told an interviewer that he wished for "more journalists with military experience, more from rural upbringings, more who grew up in evangelical churches." In a 2005 column headlined "A Slap in the Face," Nick Kristof warned that the *Times,* and American journalism generally, could wind up on the wrong side of history if it didn't correct a failure to hire "red state evangelicals" and people who knew a "12 gauge from an AR-15."

Yet talk was cheap and intended only for the ears of those outside the organization who had loosed a crescendo of criticism on the paper's political and cultural bias. Liberals continued to dominate hiring and to set the tone of the newsroom, encouraging what the 2005 Pew report on media trends called "liberal groupthink." While the *Times* readily hired young journalists from the *Washington Monthly,* the *American Prospect* and other liberal farm teams, as well as the sons and daughters of well-connected members of liberal New York café society, it did not recruit from *National Review* or the *Weekly Standard.*

Those few with conservative opinions or life experience who did get recruited—along with their "nonstandard narrative," as some at the *Times* put it—told Okrent that "they were constantly made aware of their differences, much as black and Hispanic journalists I [Okrent] have known have experienced a persistent feeling of separateness from many of their white colleagues, not because of any racism but simply because of the dissimilarities in their backgrounds, and in the specific perspective they bring to their work because of that background."

The plain truth is that the only kind of diversity the paper really embraces is that of race and ethnicity. Indeed, an official report on the Jayson Blair episode included "A Note on Affirmative Action," an appendix by Roger Wilkins, an activist who had become an urban affairs columnist and a member of the editorial board. Wilkins maintained that staff recruitment occurred within a culture where it was taught that "white men were the only people qualified to carry out the serious business of the world." Thirty-five years of affirmative action had "blunted" but not eradicated "the preferences and prejudices that produced such results," he argued, and therefore, "The countercultural forces of affirmative action and diversity programs are still necessary to assemble the kind of news gathering staff required to produce excellent journalism."

As for ideological diversity, the Credibility Committee report of 2005 admitted that "when numerous articles use the same assumption as a point of departure, [the resulting] monotone can leave the false impression that the paper has chosen sides. As a result, despite the strict divide between editorial pages and news pages, The Times can come across as an advocate." The report said the paper needed to create a procedure to avoid "conveying an impression of one-sidedness."

In April 2008, the public editor Clark Hoyt still saw problems with the news/opinion divide. "The Times, like most newspapers, long ago ventured far from the safe shores of keeping opinions only on the opinion pages," he wrote. "The news pages are laced with columns, news analysis, criticism, reporter's notebooks, memos, journals and appraisals—all forms that depart from the straightforward presentation of facts and carry the risk of blurring the line between news and opinion—a line that I believe is critical to the long-term credibility of any news organization."

Even so, a succession of top editors have gone on the record denying there is bias at the *Times*. At a 2005 advertising convention, Bill Keller extolled the paper for practicing "a journalism of verification" rather than one of "assertion," and for maintaining "agnosticism" about where a story may lead. In a 2007 online Q&A, "Talk to the Newsroom," Keller returned to the subject in observations laced with ambivalence. "It would indeed be preposterous to argue that The Times does not have a liberal editorial page, or that a majority of the columnists (with a couple of outstanding exceptions) do not tend liberal. But it's just plain wrong to say that the newsroom is 'liberal'—in the sense that it toes a certain political or ideological line. Despite what readers might hear from the clamorous partisans of the left and right, reporters have no license to insinuate their politics or ideology into news stories."

It was now possible to hear the boots of the party line clicking in unison. In 2008, the political editor Richard Stevenson maintained that his staff "represents all kinds of backgrounds and beliefs and because we all work so closely and in such a fishbowl we all tend to keep one another on the straight and narrow." And in 2009 the standards editor Craig Whitney demonstrated the paper's institutional denial when he admitted that most of the paper's staff had "blind spots (mostly in the right eye)," but said that if "we live up to our vows of political celibacy in the news columns, you shouldn't be able to say that a news article in The Times has a liberal bent—or a conservative one."

A failure to achieve the promised transparency and accountability was very much on display in the egregious coverage of such incidents as the Duke rape case and the Fort Hood incident. But even if the editorial efforts at an internal cleansing had ever really taken hold, they would still be akin to rearranging deck chairs on a badly listing ship. The real problem at the *Times* comes down to what might be called, for lack of a better term, the armaments of political correctness that crowd its newsroom: the subtle and not-so-subtle anti-Americanism, anti-bourgeois hauteur, hyper-sensitivity toward "victim" groups, double standards, historical shallowness, intellectual dishonesty, cultural relativism, moral righteousness and sanctimony. Journalists are supposed to have an adversarial relationship to the institutions they cover, but when it turns into a reflexive oppositionalism, at odds with the middle register of American society and its values, there's a problem.

·⁓

Unfortunately for the *Times,* a failure to correct its biases has converged with a financial crisis of existential proportions, one that dwarfs the downturn of the 1970s when Abe Rosenthal had his nightmares about waking up one morning and there being no *New York Times.* The fact that it is a time of wrenching change in the newspaper industry as a whole offers no consolation. A series of newsroom embarrassments and a consistent pattern of bias have hurt the *Times* as a brand, and this, along with a dubious business strategy, has made it more vulnerable to the depredations of Wall Street. This could mean that the *Times* and its unique corporate governance, with the Sulzbergers dominating the board and the shareholding structure, may not survive in their current form.

During the flush years of the 1990s and early 2000s, the *Times* made several bad business decisions that now weigh heavily on its balance sheet. It bought the *Boston Globe* in 1993 and then tried to sell it, but stepped back after the bids were deemed too low. It passed up an opportunity to invest in Google, and also passed on a chance to buy part of Amazon.com because the move would have alienated one of its biggest advertisers, Barnes and Noble. In an effort to make itself less likely to be challenged by outside shareholders, the paper's board of directors endorsed a buy-back of *Times* stock just at the point that its share price started to slide sharply, a move which tapped corporate coffers more than expected. Another blunder was to begin the process of capitalizing and constructing its new corporate headquarters on 40th Street in midtown Manhattan, a $600 million skyscraper that many analysts thought was beyond its means, in the middle of its financial malaise. Worse, it raised capital for the new building by selling the old one on 43rd Street in Times Square, which it was then compelled to rent for three years while the new building was under construction. During this time, the value of the old building increased threefold, leaving the new owner a tidy profit of $325 million when he sold it in April 2007—which would have been the *Times'* profit had it structured the deal differently.

The decision not to charge for website access also turned out to be one the *Times* would regret, as would most of the rest of the industry, which took its cues from the *Times*. Although the paper's Web edition is journalistically dynamic, like most other newspaper websites it can charge only one-tenth the advertising rate that the print edition commands. Advertising revenues in the retail and classified categories have tanked, depressing the company's stock price and bond ratings. In 2002, *Times* stock stood at $54; in February 2009 it hit a low of $3.92. (It has rebounded somewhat since then.) In 2008, Standard and Poor's reduced the *Times* bond rating to just above junk status; Deutsche Bank, still believing that *Times* stock was overvalued, advised its clients to take advantage of a "near-term selling opportunity," as did analysts at other financial institutions. In the first quarter of 2008, the New York Times Company lost $335,000; the first-quarter losses for 2009 were *$74.5 million.*

Historically, the *Times* newsroom has been insulated from the corporation's financial condition, with the Sulzbergers' dominance of the board, and their vision of the paper as a quasi-public trust, allowing the family to put quality journalism over profit. But the current financial squeeze has gone beyond renouncing dividends. It has forced cuts, both in the newsroom and in the news product. The paper is now narrower than before; the "news hole" is 5 percent smaller and the magazine has shrunk by 15 percent. (Meanwhile the editorial column has actually been *widened,* which might be emblematic of the increased emphasis on opinion and attitude over reporting.) The *Times* has closed some suburban bureaus, discontinued everyday publication of some freestanding sections like Business, Sports and Metro, and junked altogether its suburban inserts and the City section, although it has retained *both* the Sunday and the Thursday Style section. Such moves have led to legitimate barbs about a continuing loss of seriousness along with the ascendancy of soft news, making the world safe for more stories about Lady Gaga and new columns like "Crib Sheet," which, the *Times* corporate announcement said, "offers a quick primer on the week's hot conversation topics."

In late 2007, the company instituted a corporate hiring freeze, followed in 2009 by offering voluntary buyouts to reporters and editors to meet a goal of trimming the newsroom staff by one hundred. Failing to meet that goal, it laid off twenty-six reporters, editors, graphic artists and Web producers two days before Christmas in 2009. It has instituted a 5 percent pay cut for editors and all employees on the corporate side. In the meantime, even as it has raised its newsstand price to two dollars a day and five dollars on Sundays, it has ceased contributions to the Newspaper Guild's health care fund, suspended its stock dividend, and embraced austerity measures such as advising reporters not to call 411 and canceling magazine and newspaper subscriptions for the Metro staff. Pressure from shareholders and some board members prompted both Arthur Sulzberger Jr. and the company vice chairman, his cousin Michael Golden, to forgo the stock options that went along with their bonus compensation in 2006 and 2007. (Ironically, excessive executive compensation is one of Sulzberger Jr.'s hobbyhorses, getting considerable space in the Business section.) In November 2008, the company cut its dividend from $0.23 a share to $0.06 a share. In February 2009, the board voted to suspend the company's quarterly dividend entirely. According to the *Huffington Post*, the move was "a significant blow" to Sulzberger family members who had gotten used to fat quarterly checks, as well as "a sign of the company's financial struggles."

In 2007, the *Times* faced a challenge from Morgan Stanley, which was trying to get the board opened to more members outside the family. The *Times* beat back this challenge but was unable to deter others, most notably in 2008 from Scott Galloway of

Harbinger Capital and another hedge fund, Firebrand Partners, which engineered the approval of two new outside members to sit on the board. (Harbinger has since sold off some of its stake, and did not stand any candidates for election to the board in 2010.)

In the meantime, mounting debt forced the *Times* to turn to another outsider, the Mexican telecommunications billionaire Carlos "Slim" Helu, for a loan of $250 million so it can make interest payments on that debt. The analyst Henry Blodgett described the transaction with Slim as "the corporate equivalent of borrowing money from a payday loan shop." Whereas the *Times* had once characterized Slim as a "robber baron," now it was calling him a "shrewd investor." When one of Slim's holdings got involved in a Mexican telecommunications scandal in early 2010, the *Times* was accused of dragging its feet in reporting it out of deference to its financial angel. And in May 2010, Slim added to his stake after Harbinger sold off some of its holdings.

Also at the same time, there was increasingly fierce competition from the *Wall Street Journal,* owned by Rupert Murdoch. By all reports, Murdoch is hell-bent on not only beating the *Times* but killing it. So he has been remaking the *Journal* from a "business" newspaper into a general interest publication, an effort described as a "crusade" in an early 2010 *New York* magazine report. The crusade is as much financial as personal and political. Arthur Sulzberger Jr. is, for Murdoch, "a symbol of the *Times'* hypocrisy, its smugness and its shortcomings." Murdoch has pumped money into the *Journal* when almost every other publisher in America is cutting back. He has also, it is said, slashed rates to grab national advertisers from the *Times,* and has launched a "metropolitan section" focused on New York City, traditionally the *Times'* proprietary domain, as well as a stand-alone weekend book review to compete with the TBR. According to *New York* magazine, the new metro section has been conceived as "the ultimate *Times* killer," as it will "directly challenge the paper of record on its home turf."

Given the mounting pressure of the last three years, it is little wonder that the darkening financial picture at the *Times* has brought forth fevered speculation on what the future holds. In one *Vanity Fair* article, "Panic on 43rd Street," the media critic Michael

Wolff pointed to "the dreadful discrepancy between the declining fortunes of business as usual and a more probable upside of dismantling, selling, and letting the market have its certain way." He realized that he had just written a "God is dead" sort of statement, especially for the over-fifty, urban, liberal-minded crowd. "You mean NO New York Times? Nada? Darkness?" Wolff asked rhetorically. "Well, yes, in effect." For a whole social sector that has become accustomed to seeing its political dreams embodied on the *Times'* front page, this is the outcome that dare not speak its name. At the very least, the future of the *paper* paper is in serious doubt. In September 2010, at an international news industry conference in London, Sulzberger Jr. told the audience that his company "will stop printing the New York Times sometime in the future," the date "TBD."

·⁓

If the damage to the *Times'* journalistic reputation and financial footing affected only the Sulzberger clan, it would not be a matter of broad public concern. But the paper has always played a central role in our country's civic life and the public debates that shape our democracy and forge consensus. Even if the *Times* were not suffering from self-inflicted wounds, the proliferation of news sources—cable, the Web, talk radio, Twitter—may have meant that it could no longer be the principal point of contact with the real world for our educated classes, as Dwight Macdonald once described it. And conservatives now would hardly say, as William F. Buckley once did, that going without the *Times* would be "like going without arms and legs." (In late 2004, the idea of "going *Times*less" was endorsed by Jay Nordlinger in Buckley's *National Review*.)

Yet even in its fallen state, this newspaper is important, and any loosening of contact with reality, particularly at this critical moment in our country's history, has significant implications. And so its decline is something that anyone with a gene for public affairs should care about. Even those who are now going *Times*less as a matter of protest and conviction admit that the paper affects "all of America's media, whether individual readers know it or not," as Nordlinger put it. Everyone who supplies the news, "whether in print or over the air, does read the *Times*. And is profoundly influenced by it. The paper is in the bloodstream of this nation's media."

That being so, the *Times* will continue to wield enormous influence over what the average American reads, hears and sees, even if the network newscasts no longer filch the front page of the paper in its entirety on a nightly basis. The *Times* still sets the news agenda. Whether it appears on paper or on a digital screen, it will continue to be the polestar for American journalism.

In this time of increasing social and cultural fragmentation, our civic culture needs a common narrative and a national forum that is free of cant and agnostic toward fact—an honest broker of hard news and detached analysis, where the editorial pages are not spread like invisible ink between the lines of its news reports and cultural reviews. As our political system grows more polarized, and political parties play harder toward their base, it is even more important that we have news organizations whose honest reporting can form a DMZ between opposing forces trapped in their own information cocoons. Some liberals may feel a need to rally around and declare, *le Times, c'est nous,* but this protective impulse is not only intellectually dishonest, it hands a rallying cry to the right-wing forces they castigate.

Although he himself writes for an unapologetically ideological page, the *Wall Street Journal's* Daniel Henninger was right when he wrote awhile back, "We really could use some neutral ground, a space one could enter without having to suspect that 'what we know' about X or Y is being manipulated." While the emergent blogging culture is dynamic, it mostly serves as a check on mainstream news, not a substitute for it. There's energy and loud argument, but hard information and neutral reporting are not this medium's strong suit. An inherent fragmentation and multiplicity, not to mention problems with factual accuracy, make it difficult for the blogosphere to provide the common ground that helps cement a shared sense of civic mission, especially on a national level, or the critical institutional counterweight to the power of corporations, government, vested political interests and self-involved politicians.

The *Times* will not be so easily replaced, which makes its decline—and perhaps even its fall—more worrisome. But if the era we are passing through still demands something like the *Times,* it also cries out for a much better version of the *Times* than is being produced by the current regime.

The new *Times* headquarters, since 2008, is a far cry from the now somewhat seedy Victorian digs of the past. The 52-story tower is made of steel and glass, with a scrim of horizontal ceramic rods encasing it. Designed by the internationally acclaimed architect Renzo Piano, it shimmers and hovers, achieving Piano's goals of "lightness, transparency and immateriality." But if it embodies a certain promise, it also symbolizes what has been left behind in Times Square. As the *Times* veteran David Dunlap wrote in a nostalgic tribute before the move, the old building echoed with "the staccato rapping of manual typewriters" and "the insistent chatter of news-agency teleprinters," with bells and loudspeakers, and the cry of "Copy!" and the printing presses roaring in the basement, setting the whole 15-story building atremble. This was the sound of news being manufactured during the American Century.

Dunlap noted that he and his colleagues were wrestling with the implications of a greater shift than the geographic one: the transition into an unknown future. "Certainly The Times has reinvented itself before," he noted, yet there was nevertheless "some uncertainty as to whether the Times traditions can survive a move from the home in which they were shaped." The new building was therefore less a "factory for news" than a laboratory. "We don't know yet whether the transition will liberate us or leave us unmoored," Dunlap fretted.

And for all of us, whether we read the *Times* or boycott it, something large rides on how this question is ultimately answered.

Acknowledgments

I'd like first to cite the generosity, support and hospitality of my brothers and sisters—Elly, Terrance, Kevin, Bryan, Laureen, Regina and Sean—as well as my enthusiastic nephews and nieces, cousins, aunts and uncles. (A special shout-out to Kyle Salter, IT man extraordinaire.) Thanks also to some of my many friends, who are indeed a blessing—Mary Bemis, Dan and Amy Cotter, Brian and Inger Friedman, Juliet Heeg, Peter Keyes, Alice Malloy, Jack Martin, Dennis and Nancy Meany, Jim Moore, Reg Overlag, Dr. "Crazy" Steve Rayhill, Bob Ripp, David and Libby Seaman, Tom Synan and Steve Voorhees.

Thanks as well to my neighbors, the Charlie Spillane family, especially young Danny Betancourt, future bard of Hell's Kitchen.

Go raibh maith agaibh to the Druid publican Michael Younge, as well as Shane McSorley, Michelle Gallagher and Denny Bess.

My loyal and conscientious agents Glen Hartley and Lynn Chu were key, as were Donna Brodie, executive director of the Writers Room, and Liz Sherman, assistant director.

My thanks as well to Tom Tisch of the Manhattan Institute and to David DesRosiers of Revere Advisors.

Thanks as well to those *New York Times* reporters and editors—current or retired—who, unlike many of their colleagues, broke institutional taboos and consented to interviews.

The editing and production staff of Encounter Books merit special recognition, particularly the copy editor Carol Staswick and the designer Lesley Rock, as well as Nola Tully, Heather Ohle, Emily Pollack, Lauren Miklos and Sam Schneider.

Roger Kimball, the publisher of Encounter Books, deserves a medal for his extraordinary patience and his confidence in me. We made it.

Last, but certainly not least, a thousand thanks to Peter Collier, editor emeritus of Encounter Books and effective taskmaster, whose experience, editing and insight through many manuscript drafts are responsible more than anything else for bringing this vessel to shore. As sailors say of good skippers, he is indeed "finest kind."

Index